Business Grow-How

Bottom-Line Business Guides

Business Grow-How: The Stepping Stones to Successful Growth

Alan Baines
and
Raj Sinhal

BDO Stoy Hayward

Accountancy Books
40 Bernard Street
London
WC1N 1LD
Tel: 0171 920 8991
Fax: 0171 920 8992
E-mail: abgbooks@icaew.co.uk
Website: www.icaew.co.uk/books.htm

© 1999 Institute of Chartered Accountants in England and Wales

ISBN 1 85355 943 1

British Library Cataloguing-in-Publication Data

A catalogue record for this book is available from the British Library.

Typeset by RefineCatch Limited, Bungay, Suffolk
Printed in Great Britain by Bell & Bain, Glasgow

Contents

Contents

Contents

Contents

Preface and acknowledgements

This book is essential reading for any business owner who is serious about growing and overcoming the many hurdles they face during growth and for those who are planning to start their own business.

The book looks at the seven key stages of growth, as depicted by the DIAMOND model, and allows a business to identify its current stage of development. This then enables the business owner and their advisers to recognise potential pitfalls and develop strategies and implementation plans to move on to the next stage of growth.

The UK business community needs to cultivate the conditions that are conducive to helping new and early stage businesses grow, rapidly if possible. But there are clear lessons which entrepreneurs and their advisers should learn too which minimise the risk of failure.

We have written this book based on our extensive first-hand experience of working with growing businesses and providing support to help accelerate their growth. Use has also been made of current management thinking and research of entrepreneurial businesses. The book also includes many practical tips for starting up and running a successful business.

We are indebted to many people for their invaluable contribution in producing this book. A huge debt of gratitude is owed to:

Jon Bostock	Claire Crowder	Margaret Hunt
Andrew Bucklow	Dilip Dattani	Jan King
Paul Castledine	Wendy Dowlman	Robert Matusiewicz
Julian Clough	Patrick Ellward	Peter Moore
Beryl Collins	John Hibbert	Giselle Olivero
Bev Cook	Deborah Hodder	Andy Raynor

Preface and acknowledgements

Stephen Roots   Chris Starnes   James Ward
Penny Ruffell   John Sykes   Michaela Welby
Paul Sharpe   Paul Thompson   Alistair Wesson
Philip Shaw   Michael Thornton

Thanks are also due to the many partners and staff of the South East Firm of BDO Stoy Hayward for their work in developing the DIAMOND model of business growth.

Alan Baines
Raj Sinhal
April 1999

1

Business grow-how

Introduction

The purpose of this book is to guide entrepreneurs and those working with them along the journey from the stage of having an idea for a new business through to its ultimate sale.

We are going to show that a growing business will move through a series of stages which are specific, capable of being defined and always present. It is possible, therefore, to use this phased structure to plan for change, circumvent problems and work through the transitional issues as the growing business moves from one phase into the next.

This collective knowledge of growing business principles we have called Business Grow-How.

To start with, let us agree that it is not every business that wants to grow. Many business owners are content to manage their businesses in such a way that their income remains stable, and there may be a number of reasons why they feel that this is acceptable. They may not wish to develop a business which would become like the companies they have just left. Or they may be happy with a lifestyle business in which they feel comfortable.

Another reason is that they may be running a family-owned business which has been in existence for a number of generations, and the need to preserve the business and hand it on to the next generation may be a more pressing need than ambitious growth. Whatever the reason, this book is not for these businesses or their owners.

The book is dedicated to entrepreneurs and the businesses they form and run.

What is an entrepreneur?

(a) Someone who takes a risk in order to form a business with the specific objective of making profit.

> Dreams are important to have but you mustn't get carried away with the concept. If the numbers don't stack up . . . you can't make it work. It's pure numbers.
>
> David Lloyd, *The Adventure Capitalists.*

(b) Although the overall objective is the making of profit, the risk-taker accepts that some deals will make a premium profit whilst others will result in a loss.

> You will have losses and you will have failures. You can never be an entrepreneur if you are afraid to lose money.
>
> Peter de Savary, *The Adventure Capitalists.*

(c) A business owner and a manager typically in their early thirties.

(d) Someone who has good luck.

> You need a lot of luck. You make a lot of your own but you still have to have it – it's got to break for you.
>
> David Lloyd, *The Adventure Capitalists.*

(e) A business owner who will risk what he can afford but not everything. There is going to be a need to take risk, however.

> The organisational weakness that entrepreneurs confront every day would cause the managers of a mature company to panic.
>
> Amar Bhide, *Harvard Business Review*, 1996.

(f) Only one in two entrepreneurs has a business qualification.

(g) A decision-maker.

> The ability to make mistakes and learn from them is essential. If you take decisions you must make mistakes.
>
> Barry Hearn, *The Adventure Capitalists.*

(h) A flexible operator who is willing to embrace and implement improvement.

> There is never a perfect way – there is only the best way until you find a better way.
>
> Julian Richer, Richer Sounds.

(i) Someone who can build and develop relationships.

So what is entrepreneurship?

The skill in creating something of value from change which involves uncertainty and risk, by using management ability and by being innovative.

> Some observers use the term [entrepreneurship] to refer to all small businesses. Others to all new businesses. In practice, however, a great many well established businesses engage in highly successful entrepreneurship. The term, then, refers not to an enterprise's size or age but to a certain kind of activity. At the heart of that activity is innovation.
>
> Peter Drucker, *Harvard Business Review*, 1998.

How do entrepreneurs behave?

Of course, not everyone who would be considered an entrepreneur has exactly the same set of traits, but they will possess many of the following individual characteristics:

- independent
- need to achieve
- measured risk-takers
- opportunistic
- innovative ideas
- bad delegators (initially)
- proactive
- individualistic
- imaginative
- energetic
- focused

3

- confident
- control freak
- flair
- tough
- observer
- problem solver
- restless
- creative.

What are the differences between entrepreneurs and other business owners?

To grasp clearly why true entrepreneurs are different, it is necessary to compare them with other types of business owner.

> Entrepreneurship is different from small businesses. Most small businesses have limited growth potential and are primarily focused on creating a fair return for the efforts of the small numbers of those who work in the enterprise.
>
> Sue Birley and Daniel Muzyka, *Mastering Enterprise*.

We have already referred to a number of reasons why many business owners deliberately choose not to grow or act in an entrepreneurial way. Furthermore, some business owners fear the inevitable loss of independence which accompanies rapid growth, either through expansion of the top team, delegation or the introduction of other equity providers.

Are you a manager or a leader?

Before you embark on starting an 'entrepreneurial' business, it would first be a wise step to analyse which group you fall into:

(a) there is no matrix or fixed model for a leader and a business may well need different types of leader as it passes through specific stages of growth;

(b) a leader and a manager both have clear skill sets and both

4

personalities will be needed within a successful entrepreneurial business;

(c) a manager's skills encompass familiarity with plans and budgets, the ability to organise, implement, monitor and measure;

(d) a leader's skills include thinking, direction-setting, being visionary, strategy, looking over the horizon, communicating well internally and externally, motivating, being stimulating and instigating change;

(e) leaders need to be heroes.

Beware of under-led and over-managed businesses. They often cannot adapt to or enhance change, yet all growing businesses go through change constantly.

What do we mean by a 'growing' business?

For our purposes we are dividing businesses into three categories, depending upon year-on-year increases in sales, with no reference to profitability:

Category	Growth
Unexceptional	+5%
High	+20%
Hyper	+40%

Hyper growth businesses are highly innovative and often short-lived, as they generally get bought by another business.

High growth businesses do not target high growth markets, but instead focus on niches in markets where high growth is possible.

Entrepreneurs – loners or team players?

In considering whether entrepreneurs are a singular phenomenon or work more effectively in teams, we have drawn on the work of Professor Shailendra Vyakarnam, Dr Robin Jacobs and Jari Handelberg published by the Transitions Consultancy, concerning rapid growth businesses.

Almost 60 per cent of the fastest growing private companies in the USA started with two or more partners.

Thirty per cent of those businesses studied which were formed by individuals achieved sales of $6 million, whereas 70 per cent of team-based firms achieved the same level of growth during the equivalent period.

The reason why teams get formed include likeability, enjoyment of each other's company, and experience and expertise, but often there is insufficient consideration of individuals' relevant capabilities.

To succeed, entrepreneurial teams need to include members who have a balance of expertise and management skills, and compatible decision-making styles, who share trust and a common vision.

Successful management teams probably know one another already.

As the business grows, the founders develop into an inner team, and the integration of newcomers (the outer team) into the vision and values of the inner team is critical.

Entrepreneurial teams should prepare for team changes, as the original team will not usually remain intact. Compared with a successful entrepreneur like Eddie Stobart (who is still very much a hands-on operator and devotes most of his life to his business), teams recognise the importance of a more rounded life.

In conclusion, if teams can summon a common shared purpose, then they will normally be expected to outperform all but the most exceptional individuals.

Hurdles to success

The most common hurdles which an individual or team needs to overcome are:

- a desperately high failure rate in new businesses generally;
- the need to identify a clear gap in the relevant market;
- the need to have a clear understanding about every aspect of running their business;
- getting the calculation of the capital required right;
- having delivered a product or a service, being paid and by the due date;
- having the leadership skills to build an effective and loyal team;

- the need to have a comprehensive awareness of the competition, and the advantages and disadvantages of your business compared with theirs;

- being effective at benchmarking your business against others in your sector;

- the need to be continually focused on 'what next?' to stay ahead of the game;

- as the new business matures and becomes more complex, the need to recognise when systems need designing and implementing to keep you in touch;

- as the business develops, finding that keeping control over every aspect of the venture becomes more difficult, and then impossible, thus making the introduction of delegated responsibility inevitable;

- not spending time and resources developing new technology to aid you in managing the business, but acquiring it from third parties fully developed and tested;

- playing to your strengths within your target niche – do not get involved in taking on the big players;

- when you recognise a key individual, locking them into your long-term team with attractive and potentially valuable reward structures;

- remembering always the importance of leading a happy team – put the sensitive handling of people issues at the top of your priorities;

- finally, making absolutely certain to maintain a fantastic level of service quality at all times.

Managing the process of change

As the new business grows, it will inevitably face change and the need to manage the process effectively on many occasions. Without change businesses stagnate. Standing still is not an option for the entrepreneur, as it leads to shrinkage and perhaps, ultimately, failure.

As a period of change is entered, the business owner needs to design and implement new ways of running the operation more suited to the new changed circumstances.

Change will normally involve the sacrifice of things which are presently familiar and comfortable. Implementing new ideas can be uncomfortable and very different to talking about or planning for change.

It is imperative that the change process is embraced wholeheartedly by all of the top team. Without this acceptance, the process will be doomed to failure. Once the top team have embraced the new circumstances, then acceptance from the rest of the organisation can be called for. Communication downwards concerning the new requirements must be positive in tone, crystal clear and unambiguous.

Almost by definition, the business will reach the stage where further change will eventually require skills that are not present in the existing team. It is important to recognise this and act accordingly. Do not try to create a facilitator from within when you feel it will not work out.

As a leader you need to be able to draw a clear distinction between emotional resistance and rational challenge. The former needs to be overruled immediately, whilst you must use intellectual argument to convert the latter to your cause.

When embarking on what could well be a complicated change programme, you should make sure that you score some easy victories early on, so that your people become more confident when facing up to the bigger and more complicated issues.

You will find that change accompanies a growing need for information, but remain focused and only call for and use information that is at the core of the process.

You will certainly never successfully implement a change programme on your own, and all of your leadership skills will be brought into play in delegating to, and giving real power to, your outer team.

Constantly refer to your projected capital needs, as it is highly likely that change will have an impact on the amount and type of capital you need, and even on the source of capital.

The expansion of your business or the need to diversify may well have long-term consequences for how you use capital, and it could even mean that new equity needs to be raised, which involves diluting your power and control.

Change is a complicated process, made even more complicated by the need for an entrepreneur to be thinking ahead, to maintain competitive advantage, or further product development or diversification.

'Different situations demand different change paths', according to Paul Strebel in FT Mastering Management, but all change involves similar stages, namely identifying the need for change, dealing with resistance, implementing the process and preparing for the next phase.

Finally, involve as many of your team as possible in planning for change as their commitment will be needed if you are to deliver successful implementation.

Pick good advisers

Having developed your dream into a real business, and then built your team, it is important that the business has access to people outside who can really bring a different perspective with their advice. Everyone within the business becomes closely absorbed in the minutiae and can lose the ability to stand back and take a wider view. This is where the key role of adviser comes in. He or she must be able to draw upon their experiences elsewhere to make a clear contribution to problem solving, business development and profitability.

Listed below are some of the skills which you should look for in your professional advisers, in addition to all the usual professional skills:

- real experience of growing businesses;
- personal chemistry with you and your team;
- willingness to make a service investment in your business now, in return for a long-term relationship;
- a good track record of working with successful businesses;
- availability at short notice and outside normal hours;
- the ability to grow with you;
- enthusiasm;
- sharing your vision;
- excellent networks;
- willingness to really challenge your thinking;
- ability to take problems away from you and implement solutions;

- a good decision maker;

- someone who is demonstrably successful in their own business.

In the next chapter we introduce our unique growth model. The model breaks down a corporate life cycle into seven discrete stages, but why did we devise it?

(a) To collect and disseminate a depth of knowledge on growing businesses right throughout BDO Stoy Hayward firms.

(b) To develop our people into 'Expert Advisers to Growing Businesses'.

(c) To enhance the excellence of our service and skills.

(d) To help all our clients plan for growth in a structured manner and anticipate change.

(e) To demonstrate our commitment to all growing businesses and those aspiring to grow, both inside and outside our firm.

(f) Because we knew that we possessed a wealth of growing business experience and problem solving, which we wanted to collect and put to good use for the benefit of all growing businesses.

Conclusion

We have sought in this chapter to define the entrepreneur, to identify their characteristics and explain why they are different from other business owners. We concluded that an entrepreneur was someone who possessed the skill to create something of value from change, involving an element of uncertainty or risk, by using management ability and being innovative.

We also concluded that if teams have a common shared purpose, then they will normally be expected to outperform most individuals in developing a successful business. A further success factor in business performance is the correct mix of management and leadership skills.

There are also many common hurdles to overcome in order to achieve success, one of the key areas being managing the process of change within the business.

In the next chapter we look at our DIAMOND model of business growth.

2

The seven stages of growth

Introduction

At BDO Stoy Hayward we specialise in providing expert advice to growing businesses. Every day we help owners and entrepreneurial managers develop their ideas and their businesses from start-up to maturity.

Daily exposure to the concerns of these people and regular reviews of their businesses have created a huge reservoir of experience.

In 1972, Professor Larry E. Greiner published in the *Harvard Business Review* a model of growth that has been instrumental in stimulating debate ever since.

Greiner's model was quickly taken up by other academics and professional advisers who found it threw useful light on the problems facing businesses and the issues they would need to tackle on the way to the next phase of their development. Notable among Greiner's successors was Ichak Adizes whose model compared the rise and fall of businesses with human landmarks of birth, adolescence, maturity and death.

While the fundamental patterns of growth remain constant, new variations on the themes constantly emerge.

Our own contribution is based upon the practical experience already referred to, plus the result of original academic research. The result of our work is presented here in this book.

The BDO Stoy Hayward DIAMOND model is a tool used every day by our partners, managers and staff in their work for clients. It represents a readily accessible summary of our collective experience of business

11

growth. It helps us frame productive discussions with our clients, and, in turn, it helps them to see their situation more clearly and, by understanding what challenges lie ahead, prepare for them more effectively.

What our model offers

Growth is important to all businesses – these days you have to grow even if in real terms you intend just to stand still.

Our model of business growth provides a universal template against which the progress of any business can be measured. It illustrates the characteristics of growing businesses, regardless of their size or sector.

The purpose of our book is to share our model with the wider business community (see Figure 2.1).

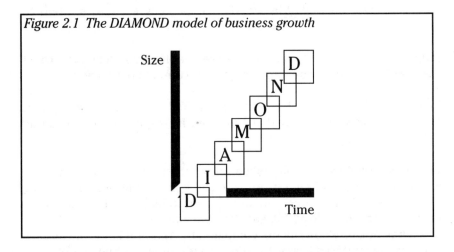

Figure 2.1 The DIAMOND model of business growth

Our model is mapped along size and time axes. Size can obviously be plotted in a number of different ways, e.g., sales, profit, headcount. Time is variable – a business can pass through stages quickly or become locked in a stage for a number of years.

As a business grows it passes through successive stages, marked on the model by a box. The boxes overlap because a business can exhibit characteristics of more than one stage of growth at a time. These overlapping periods represent transitional phases.

The particular issues specific to each transitional phase must be successfully negotiated if the business is to enter the next growth stage intact and competitive.

At BDO Stoy Hayward our core market is the entrepreneurial sector, represented by ambitious businesses with a high propensity for growth. After the all-important planning stage, our experience indicates that entrepreneurial businesses pass through a further six stages, each with clearly identifiable characteristics.

While other models have tended to simplify or contract the process of exponential business growth into only a couple of stages, our model fully addresses this phenomenon, expanding the opportunity for informed debate amongst the many successful entrepreneurs who make up our client base.

Let us now go on to examine each stage of growth in our model.

The seven stages

Each stage in the growth process is easy to diagnose, and once you have read the following stage descriptions, you should have a clearer idea as to which stage your business has reached.

D Dreaming up the idea for a new business

Developing plans

Defining start-up needs

I Initiating the business plan

Inspiring others to establish a presence

Implementation of the dream

A Attacking the first problems of growth. The business has systems to survive and is providing a living for its owners. However, it is not strong enough to sustain a major change in its market, and long-term prospects are limited by its cash flow and customer base

Accelerating pressures of growth can lead to anxiety rather than action

Anticipating the next stage

M Maturing with emphasis on establishing controls

Methodologies and systems

Management is professionalised in order to deal with the size and complexity of the customer base or the organisational structure of the business

O   Overhauling the organisation

Objectives set with a clear focus

Orientation of customers and marketing is strong. Teams and individuals are offered appropriate incentives

N   Networking business. Strategic processes become as important as tactical ones. Maintaining a corporate image is important, and by now earnings are often being managed for a diverse shareholder group

D   Diversifying into new products

Diversifying into new markets

Driving growth via strategic alliances

The culture of organisations in this stage is highly focused. The means by which they operate and the markets in which they operate are highly flexible.

A comprehensive matrix of nine focus issues and their key identifiable characteristics in each DIAMOND stage is included at Appendix 1.

Conclusion

In the following chapters we also describe in greater detail the definition and characteristics of each stage, and the transitional issues, which a business needs to face up to before it is free to move through to the next stage.

3

The early stages of growth

Introduction

Why do people decide to try and set up their own business, and why should they do their homework thoroughly before taking the plunge? Who has what it takes to set up on their own in an environment where thousands of people start businesses each year but, on average, only one in three survives beyond three years?

In this chapter, we will examine the factors that influence individuals to start a business and look in detail at the issues that affect new businesses in the early stages after trading commences.

One of the biggest hurdles facing individuals at the earliest stages of the business cycle is the process of making the transition from conceiving the business idea – the dreaming stage of our DIAMOND model – to the reality of having started a business – the initiating stage.

In addition, once a business has started trading, a key restraint to growth at this early stage is the learning process being undergone by the owner themselves, unless of course they have already been in business before. The owner may try to carry out all major tasks, or to make all of the key decisions. This may not only impact on the development and motivation of the team around him or her, but may eventually restrain the business or force the owner to make poorly thought-out decisions. This is why the early stages of growth need to be carefully planned and monitored.

The dreaming stage

When we visualise the stereotypical entrepreneur, we often have an image of a strong-minded creative thinker with a superior conceptual ability who seizes every opportunity. Alternatively, we consider them to be daring risk-takers.

In reality, these types of entrepreneurs are less common than one might think. Whilst these types of individuals do undoubtedly exist, many ideas for new businesses come from more mundane sources, and the actual start-up situation is far less spectacular than might be envisaged.

Many business start-ups are not simply due to entrepreneurial flair, but more due to individuals' circumstances presenting an alternative to 'normal' paid employment. These budding entrepreneurs often have some or all of the following characteristics:

- a technical background or set of skills;
- the feeling that they can make more money by working for themselves;
- unemployment;
- disillusionment with working for others;
- a desire to have more of a say in their own destiny.

The results from a recent survey of 77 successful start-up businesses started in the last 10 years (the BDO Stoy Hayward Survey of Successful Start-up Businesses) identified a number of factors which motivated individuals to start their own businesses. The top four factors are as shown in Figure 3.1.

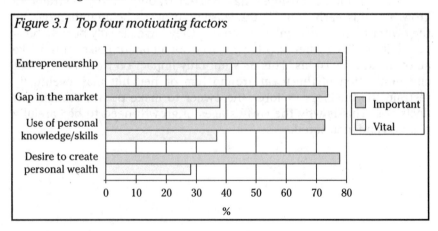

Figure 3.1 Top four motivating factors

Typical everyday situations which may cause someone to consider setting up their own business include:

- opportunity to exploit a new idea/market;

- redundancy;

- compulsory early retirement;

- peer pressure;

- family tradition;

- ambition beyond working for others.

In many cases, individuals believe that setting up a business will give
them greater freedom in both their business and personal lives. However, all too often their business consumes more and more of their time
as they struggle to carry out all of the business functions.

For many individuals, it takes an event such as redundancy to spur
them out of their 'comfort zone' and into the action of starting their own
business. This leads to the conclusion that not all of these individuals
will possess the necessary skills or characteristics to survive in business. It is also likely that there are many potential entrepreneurs who
never take the final plunge and set up their own business.

It is interesting that the list above comprises short-term reasons for
going into business. Very few people go into business with a clear vision
of where they want to end up. Do they want to work for the rest of their
lives, working in the business making the product or delivering the service it was set up for? Or do they want eventually to pull back from the
business and manage its growth, until such time as the business can be
sold for a large capital sum? If there is a clear objective of where the
business is going, it can often help to shape the path taken through the
various stages of the DIAMOND model.

The dreaming stage of the DIAMOND model is the period prior to the
business actually coming into being. This is a time when the business
venture is very much at its conceptual stage (see Figure 3.2).

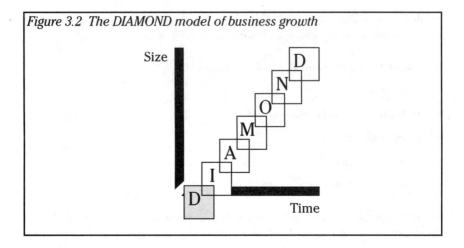

Figure 3.2 The DIAMOND model of business growth

Characteristics

The table below summarises the characteristics of the entrepreneur and his or her business situation at the dreaming stage.

- the individual has strong or emotional vision

- nothing is concrete

- no commitment has been made by others

- contacts are not warmed up to the business

The development of CCW, a successful wine bar business, highlights some of the issues faced by entrepreneurs trying to convert the dream into a reality.

CCW

David and Jonathan first met when they were studying for a degree in Business Management at Leeds University. They had a variety of part-time jobs over their four years there together, including working in a local brasserie and wine bars. Their degree course was a sandwich course and in their year out they had very different jobs. David worked for an airline in their sales and marketing department and Jonathan worked for a local holiday village. David's job gave him an insight into dealing with potential customers and how to promote the airline. Jonathan's job also gave him experience of dealing with customers, but this time face to face working full time in the leisure industry.

The dream

Once they had successfully completed their degree courses, they both looked for work in the leisure industry. Unfortunately, the recession of the early 1990s had begun and jobs were scarce. Jonathan was lucky and managed to re-join the holiday village where he had worked before as an assistant to the general manager. David was less fortunate, taking six months to find a job. He was eventually employed as a trainee manager within a small chain of fun pubs and given the opportunity to develop the catering side of the business on one of the sites. Two years later the business had adopted his ideas throughout the whole chain and he began to dream of running his own wine bar. Jonathan, however, was not moving on as quickly, and was becoming frustrated with not being able to take control to the extent that he wanted to. It was at this point that they both began to think seriously about starting up their own wine bar.

They began to talk to people within their workplaces and were eventually put in touch with a known corporate finance contact who had knowledge of the leisure industry. He advised them that, to put together a successful financial proposal, they would need to develop more than just a wine bar, and across several sites. With his help they pro-duced some projections and concluded that two wine bars with restaurant facilities could provide the required returns. Advantage would also be taken of out-of-town sites within large retail parks and leisure complexes. The success of these first two sites would then finance the set-up of further sites in the chain.

Raising finance

With their new business plan David and Jonathan approached a venture capitalist. The advice that came back from the venture capitalist and their advisers was that David and Jonathan were too passionate about the business and that they needed someone with financial expertise on their team.

However, the venture capitalists were interested, subject to strengthening the management team, and put forward some candidates for a non-executive chairman with finance experience. This position was then filled.

Funding was made available to build the first of the new premises and then, days later, the selected site fell through. This was a particularly traumatic time as both David and Jonathan had now quit their jobs to concentrate on their new project.

Initiating the dream

Three months later a new site was found and six months later the first wine bar was

19

complete. Initially, £800,000 had been allocated to purchase and develop two wine bars with limited catering facilities and finance the first six months of trading. Of this, £470,000 was used on the first wine bar.

Making sacrifices

Three months into trading there was concern that the money would run out and salary sacrifices were made by the directors to demonstrate commitment to the venture capitalists and to aid cash flow. In addition, the venture capitalists agreed to hold over their interest charges until a later date.

Developing the business

It soon became apparent that in order to compete with other businesses in the area the extended restaurant facilities would have to be completed sooner rather than later. The wine bars were doing well and had managed to build up custom as a result of the cinemas, which were also located on the retail parks. However, they were not generating enough income to enable them to self-finance the completion of the restaurant facilities. The company therefore approached its venture capitalists for further funding. The venture capitalists' advisers suggested there were two options:

- the venture capitalists could sell their stake in the business; or

- they could provide the additional finance.

The venture capitalists decided to continue to provide support. As part of this process, the business parted company with the non-executive chairman and new equity arrangements were made with the venture capitalists.

The problems were not over yet. Another restaurant in the area announced plans to expand and started a major advertising campaign which attracted some of the customers away, worsening the financing difficulties. David and Jonathan counteracted by bringing forward their own building plans and offering discounts for new customers and incentives for existing customers to stay. One year later trade was at projected levels and the two wine bars were making the anticipated profits. David and Jonathan now began to dream of opening several more wine bars and restaurants throughout the country.

Learning from mistakes

David reflects that part of the reason that projections were not achieved as quickly as hoped was that they did not carry out sufficient research on the local market before commencing construction. In particular:

- looking at facilities already available, and therefore identifying the marketing action needed to attract the business;

- reviewing the likely sensitivity of the pricing structure;

- understanding the population statistics, e.g., demographics, etc.

Despite significant teething problems the business is now doing well and two further wine bars are due to open within the next year. In addition, other suitable sites for future development have been identified.

To turn the dream into a reality as David and Jonathan did at CCW, the entrepreneur needs to overcome a number of transitional issues and make key decisions in a number of areas. These are considered below.

Transitional issues

The transitional issues confronting the entrepreneur at this stage include:

- the type of entity the business should be

- the need to secure finance

- obtaining premises

- developing knowledge of the market

- developing a business plan

- sourcing stock and suppliers

- dealing with tax and other regulatory issues

The BDO Stoy Hayward Start-up Survey results came up with a number of valuable hints and tips for the would-be entrepreneur. A few of those from the pre-start-up stage were as follows (see Figure 3.3):

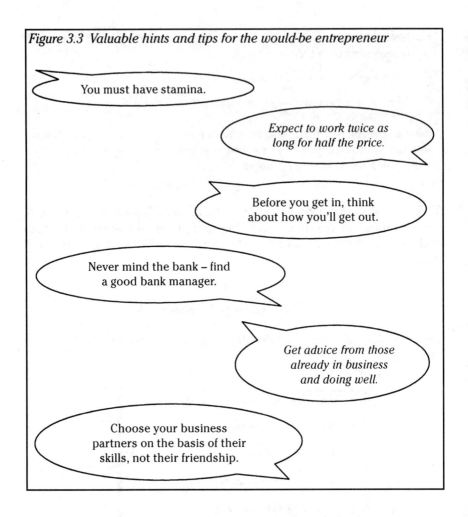

Figure 3.3 Valuable hints and tips for the would-be entrepreneur

What type of vehicle should the business be?

There are essentially three basic types of business entity. The choice that the entrepreneur makes has a number of important impacts on the business from an operational position and from taxation and legislative perspectives.

In Tables 3.1, 3.2 and 3.3 below, we examine each of the three business types together with certain advantages and disadvantages of each structure.

Table 3.1 Sole trader structure

	Advantages	Disadvantages
With a sole trader, the owner and the business are the same.	Few set-up costs.	The owner has unlimited liability and therefore any claims against the business are effectively claims against the owner and may have to be paid from personal funds or assets.
The owner may work on his own, but sole trader status does not preclude him from employing people to work in the business.	Minimum bureaucracy, with the owner only needing to tell the Inland Revenue, Contributions Agency and, potentially, Customs & Excise, depending on the likely nature and size of the business.	Corporate status is often seen as being associated with more substantial and well run businesses. In reality, this may not be true, but the perception remains.
	There can be cash flow advantages as the owner's drawings are not subject to PAYE, as they would be if he were an employee.	
	The financial affairs of the business can be kept completely out of the public domain. These details are therefore not available to competitors or other interested parties.	

Table 3.2 Partnership structure

	Advantages	Disadvantages
This business format is essentially the same as a sole trader, but with the enterprise having two or more owners.	Few set-up costs.	The partners are jointly and severally liable for any and all debts of the business and may therefore have to pay claims made on the business out of personal funds or assets. This liability is regardless of whether the partners had full knowledge of the transactions from which the debt(s) resulted.
The owners do not have to be equal partners in terms of profit-sharing or input into the business.	Minimum bureaucracy, with the owners only needing to tell the Inland Revenue, Contributions Agency and, potentially, Customs & Excise, depending on the likely nature and size the business.	Corporate status is often seen as being associated with more substantial and well run businesses. In reality, this may not be true, but the perception remains.
	There can be cash flow advantages as the owners' drawings are not subject to PAYE, as they would be if they were directors of a limited company.	
	The financial affairs of the business can be kept completely out of the public domain. These details are therefore not available to competitors or other interested parties.	
	A partnership allows high level skills to be pooled to share in responsibility, workload and decision-making.	Partners should choose each other carefully as disagreements over the running of the business, its direction or numerous other business issues can arise.

Table 3.3 Limited company structure

	Advantages	Disadvantages
A limited company is a separate legal entity in its own right. It has owners who are known as shareholders. The directors run the company and can also be the shareholders but do not have to be.	Limited companies give their shareholders limited liability to the extent of the cost of their shares in the company. Therefore, should the company fail and go into liquidation, the shareholders' personal assets are safeguarded.	Statutory legislation affecting a limited company is high compared to sole trader or partnership, which in turn leads to higher set-up costs and time involvement.
As it is a separate legal entity it can sue and be sued in its own name, allowing separation of the shareholders' private assets and liabilities from those of the company.	The company continues to exist regardless of whether a shareholder dies or leaves the business.	Limited liability may not exist if personal guarantees have been given or if the company has been run improperly.
	Operating as a limited company does tend to give the perception of some credibility. But there are a significant number of very reputable and successful businesses which are not limited companies.	Certain information must be filed with the Registrar of Companies, meaning it is available to the general public. This includes company accounts.
		There is greater regulation over the operations of the company. For example, a certain standard of books and records must be kept. Directors, even if they are not shareholders, can become personally liable for debts of the company in certain situations, these being wrongful trading (trading insolvently) and fraudulent trading. Ongoing costs for complying with legislation are likely to be higher than for a sole trader or partnership.

Which type of vehicle is the best?

There is no definitive answer to this question, as it will depend on a number of individual factors, comprising:

- complexity;
- limitation of liability;
- perceived status;
- cash flow;
- desire for confidentiality.

It is necessary to take into account all of the advantages and disadvantages of each type of entity. A single person setting up a small business on his or her own is more likely to opt for setting up as a sole trader, as it is simpler. Once the business takes off and has grown to a level which is better separated from personal assets, it may be appropriate to transfer it to a new limited company.

Two or more people setting up together may also initially opt for the non-corporate start-up. However, the more people that the business involves, the more advantageous, from a personal liability perspective, it is to set up a limited company.

With some types of business, it is better to set them up as a limited company from the start. Those who will be dealing with large corporations, requiring the credibility of company status, will benefit from incorporation. Furthermore, finance is generally easier to raise if the business is a limited company.

Of the businesses surveyed by BDO Stoy Hayward, two-thirds had only been in business for up to three years and the majority were already limited companies. This is illustrated in Figure 3.4.

In considering the choice of trading vehicle, the discussions with the professional advisers would follow this order:

- commercial considerations, e.g.:
    - will customers only deal with companies?
    - is there uninsurable risk?
- ownership:

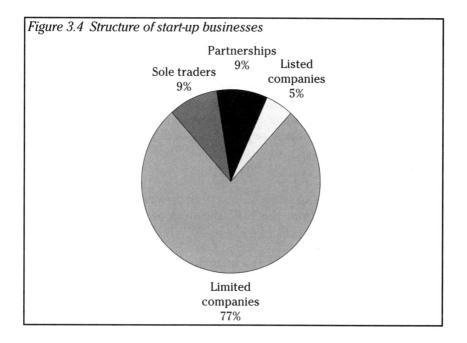

Figure 3.4 Structure of start-up businesses

- – if there are a number of owners, can their different needs best be met through partnership or incorporation?
- – does joint and several liability, which exists in partnerships, pose too much of a threat to some owners?
- financing:
  - – a limited company may be necessary in order to raise sufficient capital.
  - – for businesses making typically more than £30,000 per owner, incorporation offers more flexibility.
  - – those costs, on a small limited company start-up, can make the venture less attractive than an unincorporated start-up.
- taxation:
  - – never let tax be the dominant issue.

How is a business set up?

In the case of a sole trader or partnership, the only formalities required once the business has started are to inform the Inland Revenue and the Contributions Agency that a new business has commenced. One or two simple forms then require completion with basic details about the business.

Starting a limited company is more complex. It is possible to set up a company from scratch or, alternatively, one can buy a shell company 'off the shelf'. Choosing this option is likely to result in the entrepreneur wishing to change the company name. In forming a company, there are a number of documents which require filing with the Registrar of Companies. It is best to use your professional adviser to deal with these formalities.

There are many issues to address in setting up a new business. By way of example, extracts from the BDO Business Start-up Workbook are included as Appendix 2.

Set out below is a checklist of the main areas to consider in starting a business:

- the business plan;
- obtaining finance or financial assistance;
- choosing a banker, accountant, solicitor, insurance broker, etc.;
- company, sole trader or partnership?
- legal matters;
- employing people;
- sourcing suppliers;
- insurances;
- notifying the Inland Revenue and Contributions Agency and tax planning;
- registering for VAT if applicable;
- premises and services;
- accounting systems and management information;
- plant and equipment;
- licences, patents, etc.;
- working capital;
- training needs;
- pricing the product;

- marketing the product;
- business stationery.

Support during the start-up process

Support is available from a number of sources to assist in the starting up of a new business.

The Department of Trade and Industry has nominated accredited Enterprise Agencies throughout the country. These localised agencies work closely with local Training and Enterprise Councils (TECs), District and County Councils and the Chambers of Commerce. See Appendix 3 for the principal contact numbers.

These agencies also work alongside Business Link. Business Link is a national enterprise which operates on a localised basis. It operates as a single point of access to a network of business support. Its role is to help to improve the competitiveness of business by delivering, and providing access to, a range of support and advice.

The range of services offered by Business Link and its associates includes training, counselling, marketing support and assistance with the production of business plans and forecasts.

The prime role of each source of support can be summarised as in Table 3.4.

Table 3.4 Sources of support available				
Agency	Grants	Advice	Information	Training
Business Link		✓	✓	✓
DTI	✓		✓	
TEC			✓	✓
Councils	✓		✓	
Chamber of Commerce	✓		✓	
Enterprise Agencies		✓	✓	✓

The Department of Trade and Industry produces simple guides on the regulations governing a number of areas including:

- health and safety;

- environmental issues;
- premises;
- licences;
- equal opportunities;
- employee rights;
- working hours;
- insurance.

The guides are brief but give detail as to where to obtain more detailed information and are available from the DTI (See Appendix 3 for details).

The Contributions Agency, Inland Revenue and Customs & Excise also produce useful booklets which give information on income tax, National Insurance and VAT for the self-employed.

In addition, most high street banks offer guidance as part of their new business account services.

One of the most important sources of support should come from firms of accountants. They can offer advice as regards the type of vehicle to use and can deal with all of the necessary formalities with the various authorities on behalf of the new business. This then leaves the new entrepreneur free to get on with the running of the business. Accountants often offer incentives, in the form of free initial advice and assistance, in order to be able to introduce the wide range of services that they offer.

The BDO Stoy Hayward Start-up Survey asked who was sought for advice and how valuable that advice was. Accountants were top of the list as the most popular source of advice followed by bankers, lawyers, friends and family, other business owners and former work colleagues.

As far as value of advice was concerned, accountants were still top of the list alongside former work colleagues and friends and family. Lawyers and bankers came next alongside other business owners.

A small percentage mentioned that they had sought the advice of potential customers and felt that their advice was the most valuable of all. The advice of local government agencies and local Business Links was sought by 32 per cent of the respondents.

PAYE, corporation tax and VAT

The framework of taxation in the UK is an integral part of business and is an important factor to come to terms with in the early stages of growth. Whilst it is beyond the scope of this book to give a detailed account of all the rules and the many pitfalls, threats and planning opportunities arising from taxation in the UK, we highlight some of the key aspects in Appendix 4.

Developing a business plan

Planning involves a systematic examination of the company's resources and operations in the light of market conditions. The planning process helps to identify the strengths and weaknesses of the potential business and to develop a realistic and workable way forward.

In the start-up survey, 78 per cent of respondents prepared a business plan and the majority found it important in helping them to develop their business. This can be seen in Figure 3.5.

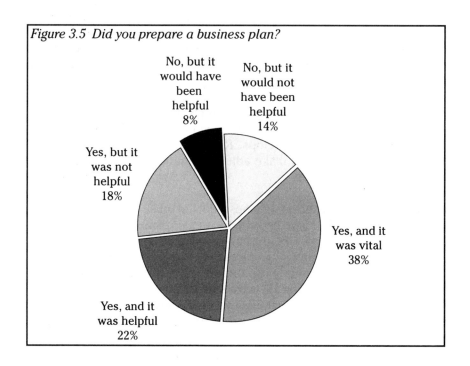

Figure 3.5 Did you prepare a business plan?

What is a business plan?

A business plan is a written statement of what the entrepreneur wishes the business to be and how it is going to achieve its goals. It outlines what the business will do and who will buy the product and/or service. It also includes financial forecasts.

The importance of planning

Good planning is essential for long-term growth and should be at the heart of all business management. This is particularly important in business start-up situations where there is a tendency for the limitation of all resources, particularly time. In order to get the most value from the plan, the process should examine the business concept in detail.

The understanding and knowledge gained through the business planning process will help the entrepreneur to understand the conditions and changes that the new business may have to face. Activities can then be adjusted in good time.

The business planning process also allows the entrepreneur to think through all the alternative options and gives the opportunity to identify any mistakes during the planning stages, rather than in the marketplace. Once completed, the business plan will help entrepreneurs to move towards their goal, by using the plan to monitor the business activities and take appropriate steps to improve performance at every stage.

Having prepared the plan, there is a temptation to regard it as fixed and unchangeable. In fact, it is not a fixed document, but should change as the business grows and develops. Reviewing the plans on a regular basis helps entrepreneurs make adjustments for changes in the business and its marketplace.

Many people starting up in business do not plan. This can be for a variety of reasons. To some people the idea of planning does not enter the equation. They may already have their own source of finance for their new business, so they do not need to convince a lender or investor that he should lend them money, and therefore do not feel the need to formalise their plans. After all, why spend time preparing something that no-one other than the business owner is going to get any use out of? They have a vision and know what they are aiming at and just want to get on with it.

For others, it can often be a case of time. The early days of running a business can be quite chaotic. There are letters to write, telephone calls to make and decisions to make. Day-to-day urgent tasks can push aside the sort of long-term strategic planning that is essential to keep a business on the right track. It is important not to let short-term problems divert from longer-term objectives. It is important to take time to plan.

The purpose of a business plan

In the context of the dreaming stage, the purpose of a business plan is three-fold:

(a) to identify where the entrepreneur wants the business to be and how he intends to get there. If the business cannot realistically achieve the objectives set, it is vital to modify the plan and the objectives before the business starts to trade.

(b) to produce a tool to monitor and progress activities within the company, comparing actual results with planned objectives and making adjustments as necessary.

(c) to raise finance or investment. In this situation, the design of the plan is to 'sell' the business proposal to the potential lender or investor, highlight factors which will make the business a success and give it potential for even greater success.

In summary, business planning should help to:

- identify realistic aims and objectives

- identify a strategy for achieving these aims and objectives

- monitor business activities so that potential problems can be tackled as early as possible

- monitor business activities so that opportunities can be maximised as they arise

- improve decision-making by assessing the effects of available strategies on the business

- attract finance and/or investment to the business

The processes involved in preparing a detailed business plan are set out in Appendix 5.

Once the business plan is complete

By this stage, the entrepreneur should have a good knowledge of the intended marketplace and what the likely financing requirement is.

One of the next key steps in turning the dream into a reality is to secure the necessary finance. This can be a particularly difficult problem for a start-up business as there may be a limit to the security upon which to base the borrowings, making access to finance difficult.

The start-up survey showed that obtaining initial funds and credit facilities was generally considered easy but that maintaining the necessary level of working capital and raising additional working capital once they were underway was not so straightforward. The results are summarised in Figure 3.6.

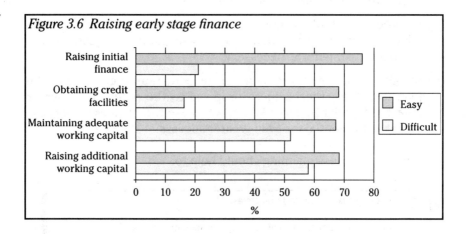

Figure 3.6 Raising early stage finance

At this stage, it is also important for the entrepreneur to get the financing structure of the business correct. For example, it does not make sense to finance the purchase of a property through the use of an overdraft facility which is repayable on demand. A long-term loan is more appropriate. Also, financing day-to-day working capital needs through a fixed term loan is likely to be inappropriate, as the borrowing will not be sufficiently flexible. In this case, an overdraft facility is more appropriate.

If obtaining bank finance, the bank will require some form of security. Security for financing the purchase of assets will be the assets themselves. However, working capital will have to be financed by some other means. For companies, the business's stock and debtors are usually part of that security, but they are not fixed items and the bank may require more than that.

Unincorporated business owners need to be aware that banks do not offer finance against the stock and debtors within the business. This can often force a start-up to be a limited company rather than unincorporated.

Often, the owners of the business may have to put up their personal assets, such as their house, as security for working capital in the early stages of a business. This can add additional risk to the new business venture.

There are, however, other forms of finance available, which do not require security or repayment so long as there is compliance with certain conditions. The creation of employment is usually the basis of these conditions. These include:

- DTI grants;

- EEC grants;

- local government grants;

- TEC grants;

- Princes Youth Business Trust.

Furthermore, there currently exists the small firm's Government Loan Guarantee Scheme – through which the Government will secure up to 85 per cent of the borrowings (70 per cent for new businesses). Loans under this scheme can attract capital repayment holidays of up to two years. The loans are usually repaid over a period of two to seven years. The big attraction here is that bank finance can be raised when the business owner has inadequate security to offer. Unfortunately, there are restrictions on the types of business which are eligible for the loan.

The other source of unsecured finance will be personal funds and loans from friends and family.

A more complex source of finance is through equity investment (introducing cash into the business in return for shares), typically from third parties – individuals or venture capitalists – who are prepared to inject risk capital into a business.

Obtaining equity investment is a complex process and applicable in the start-up phase to companies with a need for high levels of start-up finance and with realistic prospects of achieving high and maintainable levels of turnover, and profits, typically, within the first three years or so.

The start-up survey identified the following sources being used to obtain initial finance (see Figure 3.7).

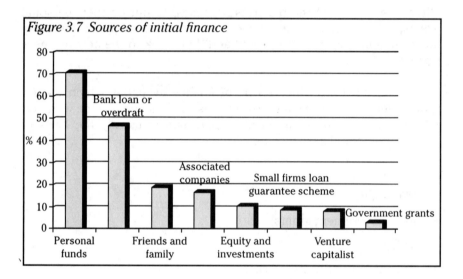

Figure 3.7 Sources of initial finance

Having completed the business plan, the entrepreneur is well placed to take his business through to the initiating stage of growth. There are further details on the contents of business plans in Appendix 5.

The initiating stage

This stage of the DIAMOND model relates to the initiation of the business plan in order to get a foothold in the marketplace. Effectively, the initiating stage is about the implementation of the dream (see Figure 3.8).

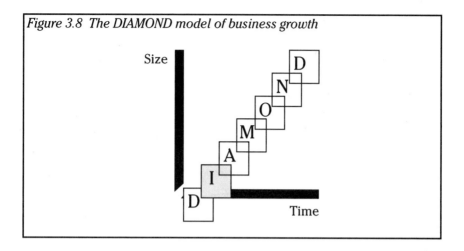

Figure 3.8 The DIAMOND model of business growth

Characteristics

The characteristics of the business during the initiating stage are summarised in the box below.

> • the business has income and expenditure
>
> • winning new customers
>
> • employing resources, e.g., staff
>
> • communications are informal

This stage of the business life cycle is a difficult one. There is the need to build relationships with new customers, to develop internal processes for everything from product manufacture and delivery through to management information systems. Also, there is a need to build the new business team to take the operations forward.

A few valuable lessons for the would-be entrepreneur include those shown in Figure 3.9.

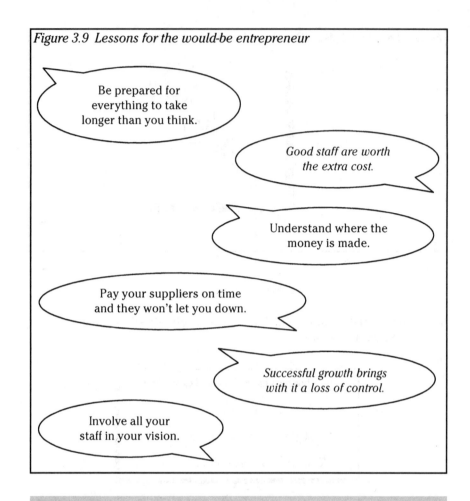

Figure 3.9 Lessons for the would-be entrepreneur

Be prepared for everything to take longer than you think.

Good staff are worth the extra cost.

Understand where the money is made.

Pay your suppliers on time and they won't let you down.

Successful growth brings with it a loss of control.

Involve all your staff in your vision.

PHOENIX NETWORKS LIMITED

Dr Paul Jones and Jenny Adams set up Phoenix Networks Limited in October 1996. They had previously worked for a large private company as technicians, installing and monitoring computer networks in the UK and abroad.

For some time the couple had been astonished at the poor level of service and general customer care that clients seemed prepared to accept as the industry norm. Paul and Jenny found themselves all too often making excuses on behalf of their employer and were sure they could do better.

The break came in September 1996, when Paul was given some time off work to consider a revised remuneration package. Paul still had his company car and had just been offered an installation contract through a contact in the industry.

The first contract for Phoenix itself came directly from Paul's previous employer, as they could not recruit suitable technicians of their own. Paul had the superior technical skills, which were not generally available from the agency workers – it was because of Paul's technical abilities that Phoenix was able to thrive, using less able staff from the agencies for the routine work, with Paul troubleshooting. Paul's previous employer could not match this structure.

A further major development came when Phoenix was asked to provide the networking infrastructure for a group of 26 companies acquired by a team of venture capitalists.

Part of the Phoenix success story is the unique way that installations are carried out. The industry standard is to forward the hardware directly to the client in its raw state, and then to send out a team of installers. Phoenix however, does as much of the configuration and testing as possible at its own premises by technicians under the close guidance of Paul. The advantages of this are three-fold:

- the client has minimum disruption on site;

- the associated costs of working on-site are minimised;

- the technicians employed by Phoenix do not require exceptional skills, as Paul is on hand to oversee each project.

Furthermore, Phoenix has an on-site computer room which has been set up to mirror the set-up of most of its clients. As Phoenix stocks many of the necessary spares to maintain its own equipment, it means that should a client's system fail then spares are readily available. This means that Phoenix can uphold its four-hour fix guarantee – something that most competitors cannot match.

Working capital

Phoenix has chosen to own all of its hardware rather than acquire it on a lease. The industry is generally lease-oriented because of the rapidly changing technology. Paul, however, has the know-how to update each system when necessary, rather than replace it. Phoenix, therefore, makes an initial installation charge which effectively covers the cost of the hardware. The annual lease and maintenance charges help to fund any upgrades that may be necessary.

Marketing

Phoenix was established and has grown purely as a result of recommendations. This has been driven by the unique package offered by Phoenix, and Paul's intimate knowledge of each client's systems. Phoenix are experimenting with fax mailshots, offering consumables for sale at competitive prices.

In summary, Paul puts the success of Phoenix down to several key factors:

- personal determination and enthusiasm to build and maintain a high degree of customer satisfaction and, therefore, loyalty;

- Phoenix does not have a fixed product range as offered by the main competition – instead they are small enough and flexible enough to be able to tailor each product to the customer's needs;

- expert knowledge of the technology available and how this can best be matched with each customer's own needs;

- Jenny's superior administration skills, coupled with her hands-on knowledge of the IT networking industry, make her ideal to complement Paul's technical and practical skills.

Transitional issues

The transitional issues facing the business at this stage include:

- meeting promises made to customers

- getting enough cash to pay the bills

- identifying the need for and recruiting staff

- dealing with the unforeseen – with little experience

- finding the time to do everything

There is a need to stay within the agreed working capital limits, e.g., the overdraft limit agreed with the bank. Therefore, at this stage it is important to get as much work as possible in order to achieve that. There is a need to market the product/service in order to win work.

Getting cash in is critical in the early life of a business. Many business failures occur due to poor working capital management. It may even be necessary at this stage of growth to take on work that is not profitable, but which nevertheless assists in paying the bills. There will be an element of cost which is fixed regardless of the amount of work done.

Any income received is contributing to those costs, and work should not necessarily be turned away at this stage simply because it is not profitable.

Marketing and working capital management are dealt with in more detail in Chapter 4.

At the initiating stage, invariably the owners perform all of the important functions and provide the major source of drive, energy and direction. Inevitably, as the business grows, these tasks will take more and more of the owner's time and will lead to the need to work longer and longer hours just to keep on top of matters.

For example, a new business may start with the owner ordering stock and dealing with the purchasing, going out and getting some new work, coming back to the business and carrying out that new work, delivering the product to the customer, invoicing the customer, writing up the accounting records, and then chasing the debt when it becomes overdue.

Clearly, in a relatively short space of time the owner will have difficulty in carrying out all of these functions. Even in the situation where the owner has an employee or employees from the start, it is often the case that the owner will supervise all the important tasks to a large extent or make all key decisions regarding the day-to-day operations.

One of the typical characteristics of a start-up business is that the owner ends up working 60 to 80 hours a week and cannot find the time to take days off. Family life can suffer if the family is not prepared for this in the first year or two of trading.

Eventually, it will become necessary for the business to take on additional resources to carry out some of these tasks. If this is not done, the business will either self-destruct as the owner succumbs to the day-to-day stresses or will be forced to reduce back to a much smaller operation, where the owner can carry out all the major functions himself.

Delegation of responsibility is a major step for anyone to take. However, if the owner insists on involvement in all decision-making, two things will result:

(a) key employees will become demotivated and their professional development will be stifled. In the long term this is likely to lead to the loss of those key staff; and

41

(b) the owner will make more and more decisions without sufficient thought, which will inevitably lead to poor decisions, having an adverse effect on the business.

Taking on employees

In this chapter, we are not going to dwell on the mechanics of recruiting, interviewing and settling on new staff. These issues are dealt with fully in Appendix 6. The focus in this chapter is on some issues which will arise as a result of taking on these employees.

A common pitfall for new entrepreneurs occurs as a result of the effect of doing all of the business tasks themselves, and then taking on an employee when this is no longer possible. In many cases, the owners will look for an individual to release the pressure on them, by passing off the work that they least like to do.

Due to pressure on the owners, the new employee is often not trained or supervised, and so under-performs. The worst outcome here is that the owners then take the responsibility into their own hands again.

The development of systems for staff to follow is vital, but so often overlooked. Systems enable the owners to confidently let go of some day-to-day tasks themselves and instead monitor the implementation of those tasks. Time needs to be invested in putting systems in place and training the staff in their use. No matter how experienced in the industry an employee is, some level of training is essential in ensuring that they learn how to operate in their new organisation. The earlier in the life of the business that these systems are developed, the better it is in terms of gaining staff acceptance.

Drawing up an organisational chart at an early stage allows the owner to consider lines of responsibility and reporting for the future. It also assists in identifying each different facet of the business, to ensure that all tasks have been allocated to someone in the organisation, and that there are no gaps. There is no reason why an organisation chart cannot be drawn up before the business commences. In a one man business, one name appears in all the boxes but it helps enormously to clarify roles when the first and second employees are taken on.

Even after considering all of this, the timing of recruitment can be a difficult balancing act. Any increase in employees will also bring an increase in the cost base, which needs to be financed. In the early stages of growth this can be a significant problem, with manpower shortages stifling growth, but with the owners feeling it is not possible to take on additional resources because of the short-term funding issues. It is important to identify all of the likely cost increases as a result of the potential employee. These are likely to include:

- salary and National Insurance costs;

- fringe benefit costs (e.g., a company car or pension);

- employment advertising or agency costs;

- additional overheads (e.g., stationery, motor expenses and telephone).

Even when the business feels it is the right time to employ additional resources, it is vital that the right people are employed. Recruitment is a long, time-consuming and expensive process. Finding out three months down the line that the employee is not right for the business can be costly as the process starts again.

The specific areas that require consideration are:

(a) *level of skill* – does the position require any special skills, such as specific industry expertise? If the owners already have the capability to carry out the job, is it practical to take on an untrained individual and train them? Will the owners have time?

(b) *experience* – does the work require the individual to have previous experience, and if so, what experience is important? Will the position require a high degree of responsibility and judgement?

(c) *temporary or permanent* – is the job definitely a permanent position or would a temporary contract solve the current problem?

(d) *the job* – it is useful to list all of the tasks that will be required of the individual. During the recruitment process, it is vital to give the potential employees all the facts regarding the position. Dressing up the position through the omission of mundane aspects of the job is likely to lead to a demotivated employee, who may well leave after a short spell of time, after time and money have been invested in them.

(e) *the future* – how are the owners expecting the role to develop as the business grows? Considering this at an early stage is important in the assessment of whether individuals are capable of growing with the business and taking on further responsibility.

Building these elements into a written job specification is a useful exercise.

Meeting promises made to customers

In many new businesses there is a temptation to promise the earth to customers or potential customers.

From the customer's point of view, there is rarely a larger let-down in business life than a supplier not delivering the goods or services on time and at the level of quality expected or promised. At this stage reputations are at stake, and repeat business from a customer who feels let down is unlikely. Therefore, at best, over-promising can be unproductive and, at worst, can be very damaging to the business's reputation in the marketplace. Once this happens, it makes it even more difficult to win new customers.

Dealing with the unforeseen

Many things can go wrong in a business, and if there are no plans in place to deal with them, the business will suffer unduly. Examples of such problems are:

- systems breakdown;
- loss of a key employee;
- loss of a key customer;
- loss of a key supplier;
- suddenly doubling turnover overnight.

All potential problems need thinking through in advance and systems put in place to cope with them. Chapter 7 'Seeing Around Corners' looks at the process of planning, evaluating and addressing risk.

The start-up survey identified a number of perceived risk areas. The top 10 are shown in Figure 3.10.

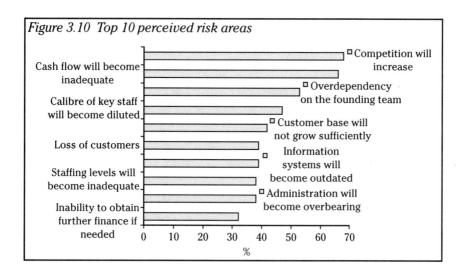

Figure 3.10 Top 10 perceived risk areas

Conclusion

A few final messages from the start-up survey are shown in Figure 3.11.

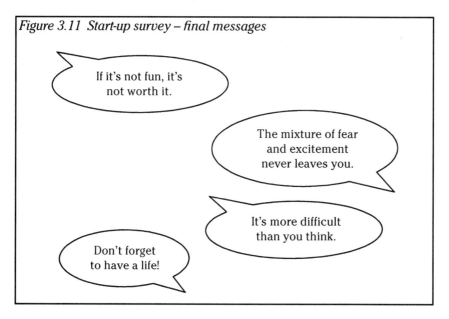

Figure 3.11 Start-up survey – final messages

Now that the dreaming and initiating stages have been successfully completed, it is time to move on to the attacking stage. That is, dealing with the first problems of growth and coping with growing up.

4

Focus focus focus

Introduction

Why should a business concern itself with having clear objectives or targeting specific customer segments, and why do so many businesses suffer from not being clear on how they intend to grow?

In this chapter we examine the reasons why, once the business has established itself, it must focus all its energies on maximising commercial advantage through its products and services, market positioning, channels of distribution, or any other factors by which it can gain a competitive edge.

Focus is the key to achieving successful and profitable growth. Without a clear focus on the characteristics which give a substainable advantage over competitors, the business may fail to live up to the potential it identified in the earlier stages of its growth.

To ensure success, the business needs to:

(a) focus on the use and control of business resources, including people, systems and working capital;

(b) focus on how customers are targeted and won; and

(c) focus on those features of the business which provide a distinct competitive advantage.

Focus, focus, focus is the clear message of this chapter. Without it, business failure may be just around the corner.

The business needs to tackle the principal issues facing it at this stage of growth, which include:

- developing a focused marketing plan;

- making effective use of IT;

- managing cash and working capital; and

- ensuring the business plan remains on course.

The attacking stage

By the time a company passes through the initial phases of growth and enters the attacking phase of our model, the business has overcome the hurdles of turning its business idea into a reality and has commenced trading.

At the attacking stage, the business has excellent potential and could be a major player in the markets which it serves. On the other hand, the business may not perform in the way its owners/managers expect and this could lead to business stagnation, and, at worst, there remains the real threat of business failure, even at this exciting stage of growth (see Figure 4.1).

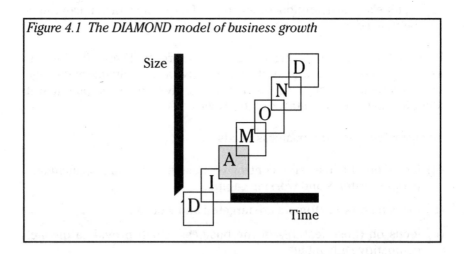

Figure 4.1 The DIAMOND model of business growth

Characteristics

The characteristics of businesses at the attacking stage of growth are summarised below:

- basic systems established but not settled

- constrained by initial IT selection

- administration overload

- overdependency on the founding team

- staff are loyal to the company and one another

- flat business organisation

- business is responsive and flexible

At the attacking stage, the business has the systems to survive and can provide its owners and managers with a good living. However, its business foundations are not sufficiently robust to sustain a major change in market or operating conditions. In addition, its long-term prospects are restricted by the ability to manage working capital and cash flow and the size of its customer base. As the business passes through the attacking stage, the pressures for growth accelerate. This leads to strains on the business which need to be tackled, otherwise there is a risk that the business could fail.

Rycon Business Solutions illustrates some of the issues facing a business at the attacking stage of the DIAMOND model.

RYCON BUSINESS SOLUTIONS

Richard Fulford and Simon Whitfield set up Rycon in October 1995. Previously, they had been computer consultants. On hearing that IBM were to launch a new product, Concorde XAL, into the UK market, the two became very interested in the opportunity to make a good living, work for themselves and work nearer to home.

Concorde XAL had been successfully launched in Scandinavia so they knew that the product was a quality software package. The software offers comprehensive business solutions and has the backing and development of IBM in its 'off-the-peg' form but can be tailored to suit the specific needs of clients' systems and businesses.

IBM undertook a stringent vetting procedure for the would-be suppliers of the software. At first, only two were chosen – Rycon being one of them. Today, there are about 15 authorised dealers in the UK.

Rycon set out with a detailed business plan on the back of which they were able to secure a small British Coal Enterprise Loan as part of the start-up capital. Other capital was supplied by the two executive directors and two 'business angels' who became non-executive directors.

By September 1996 Rycon had grown to a position where the business angels were able to be bought out.

Working capital

From the start Rycon knew that close management of cash flow and working capital was a key to their success. During the initiating stage of their business the two executive directors carried out some consultancy projects in order to assist cash flow whilst the product took off.

Rycon negotiated payment terms with suppliers so that cash was received up front for installations in order to ease cash flow pressures. This was necessary as the business costs are principally fixed monthly salaries and, consequently, sufficient and steady cash flows were required to pay the staff. Rycon has always been effective at doing this and has never needed an overdraft.

Marketing

The bulk of the marketing of the product is through direct mailing and telesales. This is supported through advertisements in appropriate journals and exhibitions. There is also direct marketing from IBM.

Rycon has taken the step of developing strategic alliances with most of its competitors. The ethos is that the product is competing against other products available. One of the selling points of the product is that it can be effectively supported by any UK distributor and thus buyers are not tied to using one supplier for the lifetime of the software.

A consequence of this is that Rycon has to compete against other distributors of the same product. Rycon does this by focusing on client service, recruiting the best staff and exploiting its experience as the longest established supplier.

Recruiting staff

One of the key barriers to growth during the attacking stage had been the difficulty in recruiting the best staff in order to give the highest level of service possible. Tailoring and developing the software to fit client needs requires a high level of skill. Rycon has taken the view that the right staff are essential, no matter the cost and has even imported skills from other countries such as Iceland.

The future

Rycon has had exceptional growth so far at 130 to 140 per cent turnover growth per annum and now employs over 20 staff. The directors are aware that the business is entering the maturing phase and are in the process of establishing systems. At present, the business has a number of significant growth opportunities but is faced with two principal growth barriers – capital and recruitment.

The two are interlinked as growth capital is required for investment in new staff and staff development. Recruitment of staff of the right calibre to maintain the high service levels is difficult and a good deal of management time is spent tackling the problem. Despite this, the directors are very confident of the future prospects for the business.

Transitional issues

The transitional issues confronting organisations at this stage include:

- not being robust enough to survive major change

- identifying skill deficiencies

- no contingency planning

- communication lines being stretched or inadequate

Systems for arranging customer requests and orders, maintenance of financial records and basic administration systems are now established but are not very settled. In the early stages of growth, the company will have made decisions about whether or not to invest in information technology. At this stage the business will be starting from a position of no IT or basic packaged software that provides the fundamental ledgers, i.e., sales ledger, purchase ledger and nominal ledger.

Commonly, there is limited or crude control over critical components of working capital such as stock and cash. The initial IT system selection is likely to be a constraint to the further growth of the business and it is quite probable that the administrative systems of the business are struggling to keep up with the drive to obtain and process more business. For example, as the number of employees and customers increases, the business may wish to share information more widely across the organisation and to network its PCs and/or introduce PCs more widely throughout the organisation. This will require a re-think of

51

the IT systems within the business and may act as a catalyst for an overall review of IT needs.

As the level of sales growth increases, the original administrative systems will start to buckle. The company will find it increasingly difficult to deal with the volume of customer leads and sales and mistakes are likely to be made. Furthermore, although a number of new employees have come on board, the business is still heavily reliant on the founding team and gaps are likely to exist within the skills base of the management team. On the positive side, however, the organisational structure is still relatively flat and can respond quickly to market pressures.

As with every stage of growth, people-related issues form a critical and vital business dynamic. At least three of the key characteristics we identify at the attacking stage have a people dimension.

The skills and abilities of the management team lie at the heart of the business's ability to succeed at each stage of growth. In the earlier stages of growth, and sometimes well beyond, it is not unusual to find a management team which lacks the complete range of skills and competencies required to successfully manage and operate a business. We will look at the importance of teams in Chapter 5.

A further example of a business coping with the issues facing organisations at the attacking stage is illustrated by Rimmer Bros, the market leader and largest supplier of Triumph and old Rover spares in the world.

RIMMER BROS

Bill and Graham Rimmer had been Triumph and Rover enthusiasts since they were teenagers, owning, driving and restoring old British Leyland cars. Both brothers had graduated in mechanical engineering and had worked for a couple of years when they decided to take their hobby and turn it into a business. They set up with only £3,000 of working capital from some old farm buildings at their father's house in Lincolnshire.

The business was initially based around the restoration and selling of spare parts, both new and second-hand. With their experience as enthusiasts, the brothers knew where the few inherent weaknesses were in the cars and so knew which parts to stock as spares. Over time, their reputation grew and work levels were buoyant.

Then, when the TR7 went out of production Rimmer Bros were able to buy up large amounts of unwanted stock at knock-down prices. This was a real turning point for the business and the volume of time spent sourcing these new stock items meant that the restoration and second-hand businesses were disbanded. The business was now in the niche market of selling new spare parts for Triumph and Rover cars by mail order.

Rimmer Bros put their early successes down to a knowledge of the product, carefully considered and focused advertising and listening to the market and their customers. If people were ringing up in numbers for parts which they did not stock there was an obvious market there to be tapped into.

Rimmer Bros focused on providing a first rate service to customers which entailed having a knowledgeable sales team, dealing with problems quickly and knowing their customer. Eighty per cent of sales are direct to end-users who need the parts for emergency reasons in many instances, for example, if their car has broken down. Rimmer Bros focused on being able to provide an overnight delivery mail order service.

The business started to grow successfully but was faced with a number of hurdles.

Working capital

In a spare parts business, growth is limited to a large extent by how many product lines you can carry. To buy in these product lines requires working capital which can be tied up in stock over a long period. Thus, growth was inhibited by a lack of funding for a couple of years. After taking professional advice, Rimmer Bros decided to incorporate the business and they were then able to obtain a debenture loan against the stock. This significantly facilitated the business's growth.

During the times when working capital was tight, the business sometimes had problems paying suppliers on time. Rimmer Bros took the view that rather than ignore the situation they would be upfront with their suppliers, tell them they would pay and agree payment terms. As some of the suppliers were manufacturers of highly specialised parts, this process of building relationships was essential to secure product supplies.

Marketing

As a young business there are usually problems in gaining new customers. Rimmer Bros had found that historically there had been little supplier loyalty as, when customers needed products delivering next day they kept ringing round until they found someone who could meet this particular need. Consequently, Rimmer Bros focused on this requirement by adapting their stocking policies and, with their expert advisory team, the business was able to generate customer loyalty.

Rimmer Bros also spent a considerable amount of time producing catalogues of their product lines for each vehicle type in an immense amount of detail which meant that their customers were able to pick the exact part they needed every time. Although this was relatively costly to the business, the customer loyalty generated far outweighed these costs.

Staff availability

In order to maintain the level of customer service Rimmer Bros believed was fuelling their growth, they had to recruit skilled and knowledgeable people. Being based in Lincolnshire with a relatively low population this was not easy. However, Rimmer Bros managed to do this by recruiting a mix of parts specialists and car enthusiasts which led to a cross-fertilisation of knowledge and techniques. This, combined with on-the-job training, ensured that the level of service provided remained very high.

The final key to success for Rimmer Bros in the attacking phase came with the use of IT. The business was one of the first in its industry to introduce a computerised inventory and warehousing system. This led to the ability to guarantee delivery over the phone, monitor stock levels more accurately and thus control working capital more effectively.

Today, the business is the market leader and is the largest supplier of Triumph and Rover spares in the world. The business is maturing with established structures and systems. Rimmer Bros, though, are still looking to the future, and to further growth opportunities.

Rimmer Bros have identified the need to increase their management skills and are taking advice, including that from BDO Stoy Hayward, on how to achieve this. Planning has also become a prime focus as the business tries to improve control over its direction. Furthermore, Rimmer Bros are looking to reduce some of the risk of surviving a major change in their niche market by looking to new products and services deliverable from their core skills base.

Developing a focused marketing plan

The Chartered Institute of Marketing definition of marketing is as follows:

> The management process responsible for identifying, anticipating and satisfying customer requirements profitably.

By definition, this involves the *promotion* of the right *product/service*, at the right *price*, in the right *place*. The degree of success will also be dependent on the efficiency of the business's *processes*, the quality of *people* employed and the ability to exhibit *physical evidence* of competence to deliver exactly what the customer wants. These factors are often referred to as 'the marketing mix'.

We will examine the marketing planning and execution process in five discrete stages, as identified by Wilson, Gilligan & Pearson in their book *Strategic Marketing Management*. The process is illustrated diagramatically in Figure 4.2.

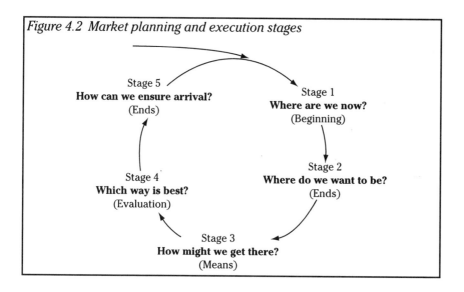

Figure 4.2 *Market planning and execution stages*

Stage 5
How can we ensure arrival?
(Ends)

Stage 1
Where are we now?
(Beginning)

Stage 2
Where do we want to be?
(Ends)

Stage 4
Which way is best?
(Evaluation)

Stage 3
How might we get there?
(Means)

Stage 1 – Where are we now?

The starting point for determining the directional focus of future marketing activity is the marketing audit. This is an in-depth analysis of the current position of the business in terms of product and service offering, production capacity, financial stability, and the effectiveness of marketing activity to date.

It is essentially a critique of the marketing mix and will enable identification of any changes that may need to be implemented in a business to cope with social, legal, economic, political or legislative changes in the future as the business goes forward to attack the market.

If you think you are already good at marketing, remember this review of marketing effectiveness could result in improving performance from good to excellent!

The marketing audit should utilise techniques such as competitor profiling to measure performance against other companies in related industries, market and marketing research, an analysis of why customers buy your products, how they use them, and who influences the purchase decision.

This will provide you with a detailed SWOT analysis of your current marketing strategy, highlighting internal strengths and weaknesses, and an external analysis of opportunities and threats from which to develop future marketing action plans.

When carrying out this audit there is an abundance of data sources which can be referred to first. Some are as listed in Figure 4.3 and can be categorised into primary and secondary research sources. Secondary sources are those that are readily available, and primary sources are those where specific research has been commissioned because secondary sources were not available or suitable.

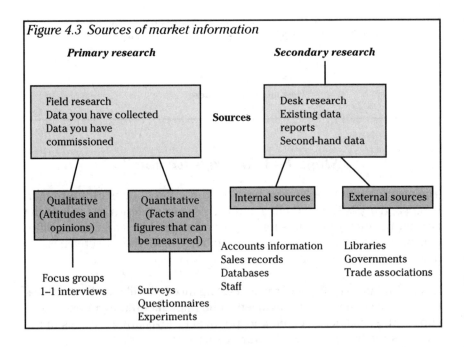

Figure 4.3 Sources of market information

When conducting research it is wise firstly to identify the problem or question that needs to be addressed and determine what information is required. It is then advisable to establish which is the most cost-effective way to gather this information. There are advantages in conducting your own primary research as the outcome will exactly match your requirements, but costs may be expensive. Secondary research, on the other hand, is readily available and may negate the need to conduct primary research. Always check the reliability, age and bias of secondary research.

Table 4.1 should help in deciding on the need to conduct primary or secondary research.

If there are still gaps in knowledge, or there are insufficient internal resources to do the research cost-effectively, a market research agency may have to be commissioned to carry out primary research. If this is required, a brief which gives a résumé of the business and clearly identifies the research objectives will need to be drafted to give to agencies. The Market Research Society will be able to suggest suitable agencies to contact.

Try to give all agencies the same brief so they can be compared on a like-for-like basis. Selection of the best agency should be based on their ability to suggest a research method that is going to meet the objectives, personal relationships, confidentiality needs and any budget or timing constraints of the business.

Stage 2 – Where do we want to be?

Once the research has been completed it should have identified areas to list under each heading in the marketing SWOT analysis. Decisions can be taken on how marketing can help the business to capitalise on its strengths, take advantage of opportunities, counteract threats and reduce weaknesses.

Action may not be possible in all areas immediately, but each area can be prioritised in terms of importance and the ability of existing marketing resources to influence and implement the changes required.

It is not enough to say that the objective is to increase sales or reduce a weakness in service delivery. There needs to be some kind of qualitative measurement which is set over a defined time span so that actual performance can be measured and evaluated against the objectives set. The marketing objectives must also be realistic and achievable in terms of the environment in which the business operates. A new entrant to the market might be able to gain market share quite quickly, whereas for a

Table 4.1 *Primary or secondary research?*

Area to be researched	Some typical questions	Sources of data
Target market	Size of market, market share, market trends? Who buys the product?	Electoral rolls, list brokers, industry bodies, trade associations, government, libraries, Internet sites. Internal databases, customer questionnaires.
Economic/political trends	How stable is the economy? Regulation or legislation changes, social trends, industry trends.	Trade association reports, government papers, newspapers, general instinct!
Promotional	Which promotional tool or activity works? How is my business perceived? Does the packaging work?	Use internal IT systems to compare sales figures against marketing budget, identify sources of new business. Interview new and existing customers and suppliers.
Sales	Is the sales force effective? Do they need additional support? Are they incentivised?	Use invoices and sales forecasts to compare sales force performance, interview sales force and customers.
Products and services	Why are products purchased? What are they used for? Do they need improvement? Are they still profitable? Are any new products needed?	Customer interviews and questionnaires, new product experiment results, sales profitability records. Interviews with sales staff. Analysis of competitor products.

Price	Are my prices right?	Test customer attitudes to different prices, compare to competitors, evaluate break-even profit percentages.
Distribution	Are my products available in the right geographic areas, are retail/wholesale outlets well placed, can service levels be met efficiently? Where else could we sell from?	Interview staff and customers, review economic reports for growth areas, look at social trends, assess where competitors sell. Assess where existing customers travel from.
Physical evidence	What is my corporate image, how is my company perceived, condition of buildings, offices, vehicles, uniforms, stationery, literature?	Interview customers, suppliers and staff, conduct quality reviews.
Processes	Is my company easy to buy from? Does IT need improvement? Are my staff knowledgeable and well trained?	Interview customers, see how quickly telephone is answered. Review the sales ordering system, conduct staff appraisals, review management and marketing information reports.
Competitors	Who are my competitors? What do they sell? How do they market themselves? How are they structured? What are their sales figures? What makes them successful? Why do their customers buy from them?	Industry knowledge, sales staff, customers, your suppliers, company reports, newspaper stories.

59

more established business or product market share might be harder to gain.

Marketing objectives should follow from the corporate objectives of the business and, whilst these might refer to measurements related to profits and return on capital, marketing objectives refer to increases in market share, sales volume, number of distributors, retail outlets or the number of new products/services. Examples of marketing objectives include:

- improve service delivery to 95 per cent within six months and 98 per cent within three years;
- increase sales of Product A from 50 units up to 75 per month in the next 12 months;
- open four new shops over next 24 months;
- increase name awareness from one in ten people to five in ten within 12 months;
- introduce two new products within 12 months;
- increase market share by 4 per cent within three years.

Stage 3 – How might we get there?

Once the business has determined its marketing objectives, decisions regarding marketing strategy are necessary in order to decide the best approach to ensure objectives are met. As with all plans, it is important to communicate this strategy to all employees to ensure that everyone is following the same plans and strategies. Failure to do so could mean some veer off on to the wrong track and long-term plans will falter.

To choose the strategies capable of producing sustained growth involves identification of the types of customers to which the business should be selling products and services and ensuring these strategies will position the company on the shortlist of potential suppliers when a purchase decision is being made.

Regardless of how good a business's products or services are, there tends to be a natural erosion in the number of buying customers. This could be due to customers moving out of the area or choosing to buy alternatives. Whatever the reason, businesses need to know how they are going to find new customers to replace them, and others besides, to continue a healthy rise in growth.

You have to sell something to someone to exist as a business.

Two models frequently used to determine strategies for growth are Ansoff's Growth Vector Matrix (Figure 4.4) and Porter's three generic competitive strategies (see *Strategic Marketing Management*) (Figure 4.5).

Figure 4.4 The Ansoff Growth Vector Matrix

The Ansoff matrix defines four basic strategies for growth:

Market development
Selling existing products to new markets. These could be new geographic locations or new customer groups. For example, a company selling fastenings to the textile industry might appoint new sales people for new geographic areas or decide to sell the same products to businesses in different industries.

Product development
The improvement of existing products or launch of new products to existing customers. For example, new improved formula products, Mk1 and Mk2 versions of motor cars, etc.

Market penetration
Selling more of the existing product to existing users, or attracting customers from the competition – for example, buy one and get one free and multi-pack purchases are all techniques to achieve market penetration. It is important to bear in mind that a strategy to increase market share by lowering prices could be very short-term and lead to competitors being able to regain their customers fairly easily once the offer has finished.

Diversification
A diversification strategy is often selected in circumstances where the profits of an existing product line are declining and a change is needed to sustain the profitability of the business. This may be done, for example, by using existing manufacturing equipment to make new products, or by acquisition of other companies to grow the new activity whilst the old core business is sold off or left to decline.

Source: Adapted from Igor Ansoff 'Strategies for Diversification', *Harvard Business Review*.

Figure 4.5 Porter's three generic competitive strategies

The strategies suggested by Michael Porter are:

Focus or niche
A focus or niche strategy is based on dividing the market into a number of market segments and concentrating on one particular sector or niche market, i.e., a tour operator who specialises in coach trips for the over-sixties.

This strategy is fine as long as the segment is large enough to sustain long-term profitability and growth. This is where information from the marketing audit becomes a useful aid to decision making.

Differentiation
This is based on raising the quality or perceived quality of the product and thus its cost and sale price. In other words, the business is making what it offers different to its competitors.

This can be differences in the product, price, promotional techniques, customer service or places where the product is available. For example, you would only find a Rolex watch for sale in selected jewellers. Therefore, Rolex maintain their differentiation on price and the exclusivity of outlet.

It is essential to note here that, whatever improvements are made, they must be viewed as important by the customer. Also, it is important to remember that a competitor may soon make the same improvements and the competitive advantage may be quickly eroded. Therefore, it is essential to balance the costs of improvements against the time-scale and likely increase in revenue and profits.

Cost leadership
A cost leadership strategy requires the mass production of a product and the ability to bulk buy favourably-priced raw materials or technology to achieve economies of scale. Pricing is very aggressive and it requires a lot of capital up-front. This is often used to build up market share very quickly. However, adoption of this strategy means vulnerability to price attack from lower-cost-based competitors and may devalue the image of products or services.

These models suggest alternative strategies for growth. However, over a period of three to five years the business may need a progression of strategies. For example, having selected a focus or niche strategy to launch a new product or service, a market development strategy may be required to attack new geographic locations.

At this stage only tentative decisions regarding strategy can be made pending the outcome of the segmentation, targeting and positioning analysis. The results of research into buyer behaviour will be invaluable at this stage.

When marketers refer to positioning, this simply refers to the images that come to mind in the eye of the customer when they think about a business and its products or services. The position is usually based on the key criteria that a customer uses to judge a specific product or service against those being offered by its competitors. A business can also utilise these criteria when looking for a gap in the market that is not as yet being met.

The process of identifying the best position for the business's products and selection of the ideal target audience will have a substantial bearing on choice of strategy and on how promotional campaigns are developed.

Figure 4.6 illustrates how a potential target market might be broken down into different market segments.

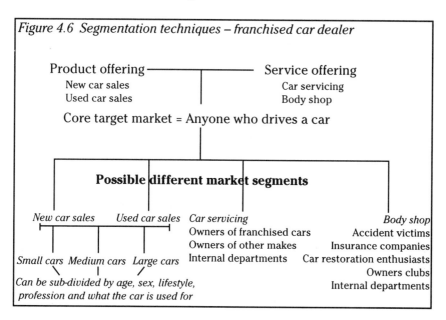

Figure 4.6 Segmentation techniques – franchised car dealer

Product offering ———————— Service offering
New car sales   Car servicing
Used car sales   Body shop

Core target market = Anyone who drives a car

Possible different market segments

New car sales Used car sales Car servicing   Body shop
           Owners of franchised cars Accident victims
           Owners of other makes Insurance companies
Small cars Medium cars Large cars Internal departments Car restoration enthusiasts
                      Owners clubs
Can be sub-divided by age, sex, lifestyle,   Internal departments
profession and what the car is used for

Other segmentation variables include industrial classifications such as business type or size, geographic location, position of purchase decision-maker, level of usage, benefits sought and consumer classifications such as age, sex, lifestyle, occupation, county, neighbourhood, lifestyle, attitude and cultures.

It is critical to marketing effectiveness that each target is clearly defined and segments are prioritised in terms of attractiveness using the following guidelines:

- *Accessibility* – Can you reach the target audience profitably with promotional messages?

- *Measurability* – Can you quantify what your likely market share will be and will returns justify marketing effort?

- *Size* – Is the segment large enough to sustain long-term profitability?

The key is to know the customer and have an understanding and appreciation of the decision-making processes. This is sometimes called the decision-making unit and this consists of those who actually make the purchase, others who may use the product or service and therefore influence the decision, and friends, colleagues or relations whose opinions are sought prior to, or after, the purchase.

It is also important to decide whether to be market-led or product-led in approaches to marketing strategy. A market-led strategy identifies specific groups of customers to which products and services can be sold. It can relate to industrial classifications like farmers or builders, or lifestyle classifications, for example, the newly married, the retired or growing businesses. A product- or service-led strategy is where a company specialises in a particular product or service, for example, accountancy services, grain, bricks, wedding gifts or coach holidays, and concentrates on providing these products or services to a wide range of consumers.

Stage 4 – Which way is best?

The analysis carried out as part of the marketing audit will have identified key areas within the marketing mix which need to be addressed. It may be a review of products and services, a change in corporate image, training needs, development of information systems or changes to distribution channels. One area that cannot avoid close scrutiny is the range of products and services.

Whatever the business sells, it will have a life cycle. This could be very short-lived as a result of a current fashion trend, or a cycle which is seemingly everlasting. However long the cycle, it is always advisable to keep a close eye on the product's current and likely future position according to the product life cycle map illustrated in Figure 4.7. The business will need to ensure that it has sufficient products or services in other stages of development to counteract the reduction in sales from any product or services nearing a period of decline.

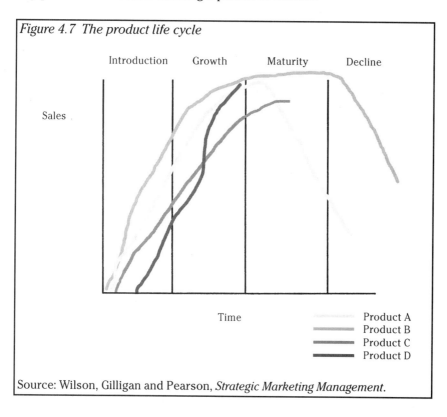

Figure 4.7 The product life cycle

Source: Wilson, Gilligan and Pearson, *Strategic Marketing Management.*

Promotional techniques

When developing a promotional plan for products or services at various stages of the product life cycle, a similar planning approach can be adopted. One can conduct a situational analysis to assess how aware a target audience currently is of the product or service, and then the business can set objectives for what these levels should be after the promotional campaign.

Using the segmentation criteria and depending on the budget and

Figure 4.8 The product life cycle

Introduction

This is a period of slow sales growth when profits are low because of the high costs incurred in launching the product or service. Communication techniques are usually designed to promote awareness and include advertising, direct mail and product launch exhibitions. This is the question mark stage when there is uncertainty as to whether the product will become profitable or die.

Growth

The growth period is where the product becomes a star as the market accepts the product and it enters a period of growth and increasing profits. There is also a switch from communication techniques which raise levels of awareness to those which will stimulate purchase, like money-off coupons, packaging and point of sale merchandise. These products can be associated with the latest innovations which are popular but still need a lot of investment in promotion.

Maturity

The majority of products on the market are at the maturity stage with a stable income. These are your cash cows and are usually the most popular products in your range. The business will find that in order to sustain the life of the product, marketers adopt approaches which improve product or service quality and focus on processes, people and branding – i.e., their reputation for reliability, quality, etc. PR, advertising and direct mail are common techniques at this stage.

Decline

The final stage is the decline stage, the period when sales show a strong downward trend with declining profit margins. The decision has to be made whether it is still viable to continue to offer the product or service and whether or not to incur additional promotional expenditure to try to boost declining sales.

resources available, a decision has to be made as to which is the best segment to target in order to achieve the desired objectives. Of course, if sufficient resources are available, separate promotional plans for each target group can be implemented.

In order to be cost-effective, many successful marketing campaigns have used a progression of promotional tools. This is called integrated marketing and involves using a selection of promotional tools to achieve a common aim. For example, an attractive eye-catching glossy mailer sent by direct mail might be used to attract people to exhibitions, be supported by adverts in local press and followed up with telemarketing the leads gained by the sales team at the exhibition.

Figure 4.9 is a list of the most common promotional techniques used by companies.

How much to spend?

There is no correct way of determining how much to spend on marketing. When calculating the amount to allocate to a marketing budget one of the following methods can be used:

- **task-based**

  The objectives and methods are defined and a specific project budget is costed accordingly in order to meet those objectives.

- **percentage of sales**

  Sales volume is anticipated and a percentage of turnover is devoted to promotion.

- **competitor matching**

  Find out how much competitors spend and allocate accordingly.

- **experience**

  An experienced marketer will have some prior knowledge of what resources a promotional campaign will require and, most importantly, will use past experience to concentrate on activities that have proved themselves to be successful.

Stage 5 – How can we ensure arrival?

Each marketing plan relates very much to the individual circumstances of a business and should reflect the financial, production, sales, marketing and distribution resources of the business.

Figure 4.9 The most common promotional techniques

Advertising

This includes 'paid for' adverts in local papers, magazines, bus backs, cinema, posters, radio and television commercials.

Exhibitions or seminars

Some businesses choose to display their products or services at exhibitions, or hold seminars on topics related to the products or services they can offer.

Sponsorship

Sponsorship takes many forms. It can be 'outright sponsorship' of an event to gain benefits like added media coverage, or 'patronage sponsorship', whereby the sponsor has no other motive than being the provider of funds to make something happen. An 'endorsement sponsorship' is where the business gets a team to use and endorse their products or services.

Sales promotion techniques, point of sale material, merchandising, packaging

Sales promotion methods include money-off coupons, and buy-one-get-one-free type offers. They act as a buying stimulus at the point of sale and are often done in tandem with attractive packaging designs and point of sale displays.

Public relations (PR)

Public relations involves managing the goodwill between your company and the people who influence its success. These 'publics' include employees, customers, suppliers, financiers and opinion formers. PR techniques include press interviews, articles and press releases which make announcements to ensure that the 'publics' are aware about the developments within a business and any new or improved products or services.

Direct marketing

Direct marketing brings your products or services to the potential purchaser instead of them having to go out to buy them. Techniques include telemarketing, direct mail, and adverts with your telephone number or e-mail address that are intended to stimulate direct action or response from the customer. These techniques also have secondary power of enabling a business to set up a mailing database for future use which can also help it to build a profile of customers and the reasons why they buy from that business.

Personal selling

Personal selling is often used in technical environments where a brochure cannot clearly illustrate all the benefits. A salesperson can also build up personal relationships and encourage loyalty.

Word of mouth

Many successful businesses have grown as a result of their reputation and from recommendations from others. Remember, a bad word travels faster than a good one, so incentives to reward those who recommend a business are growing in popularity.

Literature and brochures

Often used as an aid to personal selling, exhibitions and direct mail. They will be highly visual, illustrate the product and can detail technical specifications.

There is little point developing a marketing plan and setting objectives if control mechanisms are not set up to monitor on an ongoing basis the success or otherwise of marketing activities. This can be achieved by measuring the effect of promotional activity on turnover/sales, and levels of corporate brand name awareness in each target market.

With the amount of information technology that is available today, businesses should be able to integrate customer databases, sales, and management information systems to provide reliable research data which can be used to make accurate recommendations and decisions about future marketing activities.

The completion of a marketing audit provides the business with a degree of certainty that it is making the best use of its marketing budget and targeting its promotional activities to the right audience. However, there are additional evaluation and control procedures that can help a business ensure all the set objectives are achieved. Some techniques that will aid effective evaluation and successful implementation are listed below:

(a) Developing an attitude where everyone is encouraged to consider customer needs first and foremost will help towards ensuring the entire business is working to a common goal.

(b) Appointing a person with dedicated marketing responsibility is a starting point. However, development of a marketing-oriented culture and a philosophy where people at all levels accept responsibility for promoting the business will ensure marketing is far more effective.

(c) Ensuring everyone knows who has the final authority over marketing decisions and use of corporate guidelines will help maintain consistency of marketing messages and corporate identity.

(d) Use of IT to set up databases to record details of sales and enquiries from prospective customers and from where they originated will help evaluation of each promotional tool and sales force efficiency.

(e) Use of information on databases to evaluate the effectiveness of media choice in terms of increases in sales volume or brand awareness, which can then be used to enhance effectiveness of future campaigns.

(f) Tight control and monitoring of the marketing budget, by product, business unit and media choice will highlight whether resources need increasing or allocating to different areas.

The list is not exhaustive and the ability to implement any kind of evaluation system successfully will vary from business to business. It will be dependent on the attitudes of employees, the culture of the business, how management and business units are structured, how restrictive or open internal policies are, and how budget and human resources are allocated between each department.

As the business grows there may be resource constraints both in terms of the marketing budget that is available and the number of personnel with a specialism or interest in marketing. Again, this requires a close scrutiny of current human resource capacity and development of a marketing strategy and objectives that reflect the resources that are available.

Also, the ability to make any kind of improvements may be subject to any prevalent economic factors, for example, a recessionary period may create feelings of job insecurity, and innovation may become dampened as the business becomes averse to taking risks. In contrast, during buoyant times the business is likely to be more adventurous and full of innovative ideas they wish to bring to the market.

Regardless of the economic position it is vital that there is a high degree of consensus between management and employees as this will influence the business's ability to achieve marketing objectives. Clearly, if management have a different set of objectives to employees, attitudes need to be influenced, communication needs to be enhanced and internal policies and structures reviewed before marketing can be truly effective.

A list of contacts which may be helpful in obtaining market information and on the use of marketing techniques is included at Appendix 7.

Making effective use of IT

In the attacking stage, there is a need to have an effective means of communicating within the business. However, the necessary infrastructure to achieve this efficiently may not be present.

Areas where IT can assist in the attacking stage include stock control, order processing, measuring the throughput of work and management reporting and control. Also, IT can facilitate cash flow monitoring and forecasting, effective control of working capital, recording leads for future work, management of prospective customers and improved communications internally and externally.

Working capital is the lifeblood of the company and effective control of working capital is essential. The growing business must ensure a fast throughput of work. The use of a computer system to track the progress of the entire cycle from sales lead through to receipt of cash can improve the efficiency and the management of working capital, as well as give a competitive advantage through which to win new business. For example, a mobile phone company appointed a courier company to deliver replacement phones in 24 hours based on the courier's unique software package, which enables it to track the exact whereabouts of parcels in the delivery system.

Use of the correct computer system makes it possible to prevent build-ups of work in progress and ensures fast movement through each stage of the business cycle.

In addition, the availability of timely and accurate management information is a key requirement of any business. The accounting system must enable the timely production of the following financial statements:

- profit and loss account;
- balance sheet;

- cash flow forecast.

Capturing information about sales enquiries and leads is fundamental to receiving cash. Many opportunities are lost even before businesses become aware of them. Effective means of capturing leads, following up sales calls and tracking conversion of leads to sales give a useful edge to the ability of a business to stand up effectively against the competition.

A good IT system can be invaluable in this process, since it can provide the means to store this data, generate prompts to follow up each lead, with escalation as time progresses, and, more importantly, enable the entire process to be tracked and monitored for reporting purposes.

Once a business gets beyond the initial stages of growth, communication channels become more complex and difficult to manage. Previously, everyone was within earshot and immediately available, but now there are people who are rarely around – sales representatives are on the road, offices are on the other side of the building, and people are often in meetings. The use of an effective e-mail system such as Lotus Notes or Microsoft Outlook is a valuable factor in speeding up communications throughout the business.

These communication systems can enable the sales representative on the road to transfer a customer's order back to the office from a laptop via a mobile phone modem. The goods can then be delivered the same day, so improving service response to customer requirements. In an era when time is money and delay can result in loss of business, anything that can cut time from the delivery cycle is a valuable weapon in the corporate armoury.

Customers can come from far and wide, but the promotional budgets are unlikely to cover such a wide area. Through use of the Internet it is possible to reach a worldwide marketplace. This can be started in a small way then later scaled up. For less than £200 a year, a business can start a website that invites e-mailed orders or telephone enquiries. Once proven as a source of leads, an interactive site that records customer orders can be set up. This can then be extended to provide what is effectively an EDI (Electronic Data Interchange) system, whereby the orders can be linked into the business's order entry module in the main accounting system.

There are, however, a number of common issues or problems faced at identifiable stages within the process of using and implementing IT. These stages exist in any organisation and BDO Stoy Hayward have adopted them as a review framework which can be utilised by any business. The system stages are depicted in Figure 4.10.

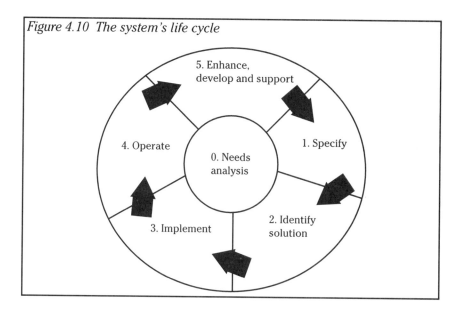

Figure 4.10 The system's life cycle

Needs analysis – life cycle stage 0

The life cycle of any system starts with the needs analysis. No system will ever achieve its objectives unless these have been properly defined at the outset. These objectives will, of course, be constantly referred to and modified as the business progresses through its life cycle stages.

The process by which any business assesses and modifies its needs for IT lies at the core of its most common problems. You would no more invest in information technology without first performing a needs analysis than you would buy a two-seater sports car without giving consideration to the fact that you regularly need to carry a four-person family plus a large pet. You would soon discover you have made an unsuitable investment – as your family would not hesitate to point out to you!

System specification – life cycle stage 1

One needs to start by answering very basic and fundamental questions such as: 'why do we need IT' and 'what exactly do we want to use it for?'

The answers may seem all too evident, but they are a good starting point when developing the first needs analysis criteria.

An IT needs analysis must therefore reflect a business's overall long-term direction and priorities. All too often, a needs analysis ends up focusing on short-term firefighting, and does not address long-term strategic questions. This is typical behaviour at the dreaming and initiating stages of growth.

Some businesses make the mistake of believing that they need large and sophisticated IT systems, such as an NT server or a Novel Network or an AS400. The starting point is what system does the business need to carry out the tasks and processes that are needed effectively to run and continue to grow the business. The system may be manual, it may be computerised, and it may be a combination of both. This may be a particular package, a bespoke program, or a manual system such as Kalamazoo.

Supplier selection – life cycle Stage 2

Amongst user organisations, it is our experience that there is an unjustified belief in the uniqueness of the needs, and a desire for the perfect solution, which drives businesses towards bespoke/customised solutions – thus narrowing down the choice of supplier. The supplier selection process also lacks rigour and is rather haphazard. Some business processes may need to be adapted to fit in with system offerings – this may, however, give the business a wider choice in selection.

System implementation – life cycle stage 3

Many businesses also adopt an unstructured approach to the IT implementation process – an approach which is reflected in the words 'a wish and a prayer'! In large part, the approach reflects the heavily cost-conscious environments in which many businesses are investing in IT. Our research has identified that IT implementation tends to be dominated by physical/technical concerns ('when and where shall we plug it in?') and, as a result, important issues are missed or ignored.

Often, absolutely no planning goes into the implementation process, and mid-sized businesses put themselves at the mercy of suppliers. There is also a tendency to minimise or pare implementation costs to the bone in order to get within budget – unavoidable but undeclared costs then come as a nasty surprise.

The interdependency of IT and business issues is also often insufficiently thought through – such as the knock-on effects on key business activities such as sales cycles; and little forethought given to dual running issues (i.e., how to approach handover from a manual to an IT system or one IT system to another).

Poor planning leads to crisis after crisis in which external support is used to patch up the problems. This can lead to expensive dependency on outside resources.

Operation, enhancement and development – life cycle stages 4 and 5

The problems and issues which seem to arise in these two final and consecutive stages of the system's life cycle reveal the close interrelationship of all stages: it is very difficult to draw lines between them and attribute a problem to any one particular point in the process. For example, a computer sizing problem may be seen to lie at the door of the needs analysis, or system specification, or supplier performance.

Growing businesses generally underestimate how demand for, and use of, the system will increase, and this often leads to hardware pressures in terms of:

- early demand for upgrades;
- power of planned upgrades being absorbed too quickly;
- performance degradation;
- poor response times;
- need for more terminals to meet increasing user demand;
- need for more data storage capacity;
- configuration and resilience issues.

An absence of in-house IT skills and expertise also emerges as a barrier to progress.

So how does a business ensure that it successfully uses IT to gain a business advantage? Based on our experience, successful IT seems to be more likely to occur where the following factors are present:

- IT meets business priorities (client pressure, competitive pressure, etc.)

- IT sparks the imagination and commitment of senior management and decision-makers

- the use of IT has been properly planned and its current status/enhancement opportunities are constantly being revisited

- use of the system is supported by good user involvement in its development

- the users find the system 'obviously beneficial'

- the users perceive the system to be close to their work or their perceived mission

- realistic expectations of the technology have been set

- the systems in use have been chosen because of software functionality, operational expandability and supplier synergy, not because the hardware is leading-edge

- the people who use the system see it as their system

No successful business can truly afford to be without IT today. Computers rank alongside quality management skills and human resources in terms of value to the business (and sometimes ahead of these factors). Therefore, choosing the wrong system – wrong for the particular business – or a system which does not match its needs, will not only cost money, but will put the business at a competitive disadvantage.

A summary of the rules or guidelines to be observed at each stage of the life cycle are shown at Appendix 8.

Managing cash and working capital

Cash and profit are not the same. Profitable businesses can fail due to problems in managing cash. Similarly, some businesses can generate cash in the short term without being profitable. In order to achieve successful growth, however, it is essential that both cash and profit are managed effectively.

In this section, we focus on cash. In simple terms, effective cash management is about making sure that, where possible, you receive cash before you spend it. In order to ensure that problems are not encountered with breaching overdraft limits, etc., it is essential that the flows of cash in and out of the business are accurately forecast. Most people in business fear the situation where the bank manager has to personally authorise all their payments because the business has exceeded its overdraft limits. This also has the disadvantage of consuming a lot of management time, which is spent dealing with the bank and therefore not working in the business. The best way of guaranteeing that this does not happen is to manage cash effectively and ensure that the bank manager knows what is happening.

Cash management also impacts on profitability. Running an overdraft means paying interest on the balance outstanding, so the higher the overdraft the higher the interest cost to the business. Equally, ineffective management of positive cash balances in a business means that interest income is forgone.

Cash flows

In order to be able to forecast cash flows for the business accurately, one must first understand the cash cycle for the trading activities. The cash cycle maps out the flows of cash over time from initiating production or delivering a service, through to receipt of cash. Example 4.1 looks at a manufacturing business.

EXAMPLE I

An order is received on 1 January from a customer for widgets with a sales price of £100,000. The parts to assemble the widgets are ordered on the same day at a cost of £50,000. The parts are received on 7 January together with the invoice which is due for payment at the end of the month.

The assembly process takes place from 10 January and takes 28 days to complete. Employee costs of £20,000 are incurred in the assembly over the period with employees being paid weekly in arrears.

The widgets are sent to the customer on 7 February together with the invoice. The customer then pays at the end of the following month.

The cash cycle is as follows:

Event	Date	Days from first payment	Cash flow £	Net cumulative cash flow £
Assembly wages (week 1)	17 January	0	(5,000)	(5,000)
Assembly wages (week 2)	24 January	7	(5,000)	(10,000)
Assembly wages (week 3)	31 January	14	(5,000)	(15,000)
Payment for parts	31 January	14	(50,000)	(65,000)
Assembly wages (week 4)	7 February	21	(5,000)	(70,000)
Cash received from customer	31 March	73	100,000	30,000

The cash cycle is 73 days for the process shown above. This means that in order to make a profitable sale, the business needs to have £70,000 of cash available to make the sale possible.

Suppose the business made 12 such sales per year, and on average customers take 60 days to pay and the business takes 30 days to pay its suppliers. The average debtors figure will be £197,000 (£1,200,000 × 60 days/365 days) and the average trade creditors figure £49,000 (£600,000 × 30 days/365 days). Thus, the average positive cash balances required to manage debtors and creditors is £148,000. This excludes the assembly wages. At an interest rate of, say, 8 per cent per annum, this costs the business almost £12,000 per year.

If in this simple illustration we suppose that the business negotiates with its customers and agrees payment terms of within 30 days, the average debtors outstanding falls to £99,000 and the cash requirement falls to £50,000. The resultant interest cost to the business thereby reduces to £4,000, **a saving of nearly £8,000 per year**.

Whilst it is essential to understand the cash cycle, there are also a number of other non-trading-related business processes which impact on cash such as interest, taxation and capital movements.

When constructing cash flow forecasts for a business, there are many factors to be considered.

Debtors

In order to monitor and forecast the timing of receipts from your customers, it is useful to identify the average time they take to pay from the date of invoice, commonly known as debtor days. Debtor days are calculated as follows:

$$\text{Debtor days} = \frac{\text{Average trade debtors} \times 365 \text{ days}}{\text{Annual sales (incl. VAT)}}$$

Good credit control procedures are important in ensuring that any late payers are chased efficiently. To achieve this, individual responsibilities for credit control must be identified. Often one individual or team will be responsible, in which case systems must be in place so that all the information they need in order to chase debtors effectively, and sensitively, is available to them. Targets should be set for debtor day performance, and procedures for chasing late payers should be put in place.

In certain circumstances, it may be appropriate to offer discounts for early settlement of debts, although this can eat into profits. Alternatively, it may be possible to employ some form of debt factoring, where debts are sold to a factoring house. Here, cash is received for a negotiated proportion of the invoice value, on the date the invoice is raised for the customer. Some forms of debt factoring can create bad feeling with customers, although this point is now largely historic. Factoring and related products have in recent years enjoyed a massive surge in popularity.

Creditors

From a simple cash flow perspective, it is preferable to maximise creditor days, that is, the time it takes to pay suppliers. The main problem with stretching payments to suppliers is that relationships can be damaged. This may mean that the business does not achieve the best prices on its purchases. Equally, if the supplier has a scarce resource which could be sold to a number of customers, the business may not be its preferred customer if it has a history of slow paying. Creditor days are calculated as follows:

$$\text{Creditor days} = \frac{\text{Average trade creditors} \times 365 \text{ days}}{\text{Total trade credit purchases (incl. VAT)}}$$

Suppliers may offer early settlement discounts. The decision on whether or not to take these should be based on the relative interest cost, compared to the level of discount offered.

The CBI have recommended a prompt payment policy which states that all creditors should be paid within 30 days. However, in reality payment periods differ significantly from industry to industry. The Government has now introduced new legislation on late payment. The Late Payment of Commercial Debts (Interest) Act 1998 is aimed at forcing big companies to pay their bills on time and came into effect in November 1998. Under the terms of the Act, small businesses (with 50 or fewer staff) can collect interest at base rate plus 8 per cent for the length of time invoices are unpaid beyond a contractually agreed credit period.

Stock

Holding stock ties up cash. Consequently, all businesses should aim to hold the lowest amount of stock possible to meet the needs of their product or service delivery. Many complex stock management systems are available. However, an effective stock-holding policy can be derived from considering and planning for the following factors:

- delivery lead time – how long it takes your suppliers to supply you with the item;
- volume discounts – suppliers may give lower prices for bulk purchases;
- usage levels – how much of the stock you anticipate using;
- buffer stocks – how much 'safety' stock to keep in case demand levels exceed those forecast, or if there is a problem with further supplies.

Stock usage can be measured using the stock turnover ratio, which is calculated as follows:

$$\text{Stock turnover} = \frac{\text{Cost of goods sold}}{\text{Average stock value}}$$

The higher the turnover rate, the more efficient use you are making of your cash.

80

Labour costs

Planning for labour costs is made easier by the fact that most employees are paid on a weekly or monthly basis. Also, for many businesses labour costs are a relatively fixed cost, with a constant core team of staff employed. Extra labour costs are incurred with overtime, employment of new staff and the use of temporary staff. This is likely to vary with the level of business activity.

In many service industries, labour is the prime business cost. As employees are normally paid at regular intervals, and generally at a fixed rate, there is a reduced opportunity for flexing this cost to meet working capital requirements. Consequently, the effective management of working capital is often more important for service-based businesses.

For example, firms of accountants pay most of their employees a salary on a monthly basis. The seasonality of the average accountancy firm has historically tended to be biased towards the first half of the year, with client businesses having December and March year ends. As such, there is a marked cash inflow in the first six months with a lesser cash inflow in the second half of the year. Generally speaking, salary levels remain constant throughout. Effective cash management is therefore essential.

Overheads

In order to prepare an effective cash forecast, it is essential that all overhead cash flows are included. Cash outflows can be smoothed over the year with effective planning. For example, payments for such items as rent, business rates and professional fees can often, by agreement, be spread using monthly or quarterly direct debits.

Capital expenditure

Purchases of items of a capital nature such as plant, premises, computer hardware, equipment and fixtures and fittings need to be included in cash flow forecasts. Although the cost of these items is spread over the life of the asset through the depreciation charge in the profit and loss account, they impact in full on cash when they are paid for. The timing of capital expenditure needs to be carefully considered therefore.

Before making the acquisition, the issue of whether it is better for the business to lease or buy the asset should be addressed. If the buy decision is taken, then in many instances the cash outflow can be spread, using hire purchase or a specific loan against the asset. As a rule of thumb, the period of financing for such a purchase should match the useful life of the asset (the length of time over which the asset is used by the business).

Taxation

Taxation cash flows tend to be relatively easy to determine. PAYE and NI are payable monthly, VAT usually quarterly, and corporation tax annually. Taxation payments can be managed to some extent with effective tax planning. There are many ways in which this can be achieved with good professional advice.

For example, seasonal businesses may find it beneficial to change their year ends, so that the corporation tax is paid at a time of year when the business is relatively cash-rich. Businesses with frequent bad debts or very long cash cycles and who have turnover of less than £350,000 per annum can opt to account for VAT under a cash accounting scheme. This enables VAT to be accounted for on cash received or paid rather than on invoices.

Drawings, dividends and directors' salaries

The amount of money that directors and shareholders take out of the business can often be adapted to meet the needs of the business, both in terms of when and how much. However, it is still an essential item for inclusion in the forecasts.

An example of a useful format for forecasting cash flow is shown at Figure 4.11.

Keeping control of cash is essential for all businesses. It is crucial for businesses in the attacking phase of growth. During this growth stage, working capital pressures can be very significant. A long cash cycle can lead to serious cash flow problems as more sales are made. This is known as over-trading.

To illustrate this with the previous example (Example 1), if the business in question were to double its turnover from £1,200,000 to £2,400,000 with debtor and creditor days remaining at 60 and 30 respectively, the cash requirement to fund the trading would rise from £148,000 to £296,000. If the business was restricted to an overdraft limit of £200,000, this growth could cause significant problems for business continuity.

Furthermore, during the attacking stage there is often a temptation for businesses to try to win customers by offering a more attractive package than competitors. The cash implications of this must be considered carefully as, for example, offering them longer credit terms may seriously damage the business.

Ensuring the business plan remains on course

When a business is preparing a three or five year strategic business plan, it may feel like it is gazing into a crystal ball and trying to forecast business targets and outcomes that the organisation cannot even comprehend. The process of updating and replanning aims to try and help in keeping the business plan up to date, in order that it reflects the current circumstances of the business. This allows management to redefine targets and outcomes if the desired strategies are not realistic or cannot be attained.

Therefore, the process of updating and replanning is essential in helping a business keep 'on track' and ensuring that the business plan remains a 'live' document, and does not get left on the shelf, never to be looked at again.

If replanning is not carried out on a regular basis, the energy and effort expended in preparing the original plan will simply be wasted. Business planning is not intended to be a one-off exercise, but rather part of an overall planning process which helps the business to focus itself. This is essential at the attacking stage of growth, where the business constantly needs to keep track of progress. The business needs to assess how successful it has been in achieving its desired strategies of attacking the marketplace. Also, it needs to consider whether or not there is a need to revise the strategic direction of the business, to reflect changes in the business environment/customer base. Without a regular review of planned activities, there is a real risk that the business's intended growth plans will not be fully realised.

Who should do it? In most cases, the management team should be responsible for making the business plan work and ensuring it is updated. Each member of the team could take responsibility for a specific aspect of the plan, and get together through management team meetings to disseminate action plans. The advantage of involving the

Figure 4.11 XYZ Limited – cash flow forecast for the year ended 30 April XX					
	MAY	JUN	JUL	AUG	SEP
RECEIPTS					
Sales	35980	45290	42580	46890	42000
Bank loan		70000			
VAT on sales	6297	7926	7452	8206	7350
	42277	123216	50032	55096	49350
PAYMENTS					
Direct costs	23906	48906	42500	35000	33750
Wages	7714	7714	13316	13315	13315
Salaries	1833	1833	1833	1833	1833
Directors' remuneration	4041	4041	4041	4041	4041
Rent			2680		
Rates, light and heat	446	446	446	446	446
Insurance	375	375	375	375	375
Repairs	335	335	335	335	335
Telephone	340	340	340	340	340
Postage & stationery	175	175	175	175	175
Advertising	50	50	50	50	50
Entertaining	50	50	50	50	50
Motor & travel	1500	2500	2000	2000	2000
Vehicle hire	170	170	170	170	170
Accountancy			2100		
Legal fees			500		
Bank charges			500		
Bad debts	949	664	664	617	617
Sundry	200	200	200	200	200
Bank loan interest			2000		
HP interest	54	54	54	54	54
HP capital	264	264	264	264	264
VAT on costs	4689	9239	8955	6718	6500
VAT paid to/(by) Customs	(1046)			1209	
Bank loan repayments	119	1285	1285	1285	1285
	46163	78641	84833	68478	65800
Opening bank	−30457	−34344	10231	−24571	−37953
Receipts less payments	−3887	44575	−34802	−13382	−16450
Closing bank	−34344	10231	−24571	−37953	−54403
Agreed overdraft	50000	50000	50000	50000	50000
Surplus/(deficit)	15656	60231	25429	12047	(4403)

OCT	NOV	DEC	JAN	FEB	MAR	APR	TOTAL
63000	65000	65000	62580	62580	65000	50000	645900
							70000
11025	11375	11375	10952	10952	11375	8750	113033
74025	76375	76375	73532	73532	76375	58750	828933
32500	32500	32500	32500	32500	28750	26250	401561
7714	7714	7714	7714	7714	7714	7714	109372
1833	1833	1833	1833	1833	1833	1833	21996
4041	4041	4041	4041	4041	4041	4041	48492
2680			2680			2680	10720
446	446	446	446	446	446	446	5352
375	375	375	375	375	375	375	4500
335	335	335	335	335	335	335	4020
340	340	340	340	340	340	340	4080
175	175	175	175	175	175	175	2100
50	50	50	50	50	50	50	600
50	50	50	50	50	50	50	600
2000	2000	2000	2000	2000	2000	2000	24000
170	170	170	170	170	170	170	2040
2000			1000			1000	6100
		600					1100
500			500			500	2000
617	617	617	617	474	522	617	7591
200	200	200	200	200	200	200	2400
1897			1793			1689	73789
54	54	54	54	54	54	54	648
264	264	264	264	264	264	264	3168
7100	6281	6386	6925	6281	5625	5831	80528
	(6263)			(14110)			(20210)
1285	1285	1285	1285	1285	1285	1285	14257
66625	52467	59435	65347	44477	54229	57899	744394
−54403	−47003	−23094	−6154	2031	31085	53231	−30457
7400	23908	16940	8185	29054	22146	851	84539
−47003	−23094	−6154	2031	31085	53231	54082	54082
50000	50000	50000	50000	50000	50000	50000	50000
2997	26906	43846	52031	81085	103231	104082	104082

management team is that it provides ownership of the plan at a wide level.

A more formalised system for reviewing the business plan can be adopted. Formalised planning systems involve putting procedures in place which regulate the individuals who will contribute to the planning process, what contributions they are expected to make and the timing and frequency of their involvement. This is likely to be documented as a part of an internal procedures manual. Such systems are typical of businesses at the maturing stage of growth.

However, in circumstances where the degree of change is likely to be high, corporate planning systems are likely to be inflexible. In the attacking stage, where growth may be achieved very quickly, this could lead to problems. A planning system is required which can react quickly to internal or external pressures. Therefore, ad hoc arrangements may be the most appropriate to use, with the organisation reacting quickly to environmental changes by putting together the relevant team, as and when they are required.

Like any system, informal or ad hoc systems do have their weaknesses. If attention is diverted away from the planning process for too long, the business plan can become obsolete very quickly, and become a relatively blunt instrument of management. In addition, without regular phases of performance review, it becomes impossible to keep track of progress against pre-defined plans and targets. Altering the timing of these ad hoc checks can help in mitigating against this.

What do we measure? Clearly, the business is going to require financial information to establish whether sales targets have been achieved, and whether profits were as forecast. Information will also be required on customers, both in terms of whether target customers have been secured, what contribution to sales and profits individual customers make, and whether the product/services provided by the business are meeting customer needs.

It is always useful to keep track of competitors, to see whether new competitors are emerging, whether existing competitors are succeeding in existing or new markets, and to understand what factors give a business a sustainable competitive advantage over its competitors.

To some extent, this information-gathering process can be tied together with a revisit to the SWOT analysis, which would have formed a part of the business planning process undertaken at the early stages of growth.

In financial terms, measurement against budgets is clearly essential. There may be good reasons why the business has under-performed or over-performed against the budgets included in the business plan. In terms of customers and markets, the business should be looking to measure market share, customer satisfaction and how quickly it can get products and services to the marketplace.

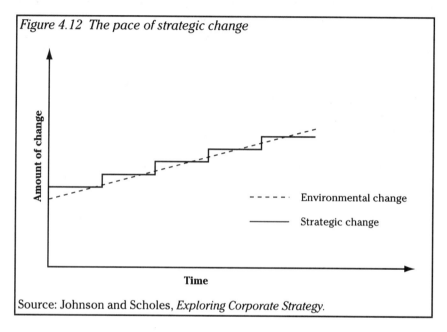

Figure 4.12 The pace of strategic change

Source: Johnson and Scholes, *Exploring Corporate Strategy.*

If the pace of environmental or external change in the business is relatively modest and reasonably predictable, it is then entirely reasonable to have a strategic replanning process which is pre-defined and occurs on a reasonably infrequent basis, perhaps six-monthly or annually. This situation is depicted in Figure 4.12. The dotted line represents the rate of external change, with time on the horizontal axis and the rate of change on the vertical axis. The level of strategic change required by the business is represented by the solid line, which keeps pace with changes in the environment by replanning on a regular and systematic basis.

However, if the pace of external change is irregular and significant, such a replanning mechanism may not work and there is a risk of what is called 'strategic drift'.

Strategic drift occurs where an organisation is familiar with taking incremental step changes in strategy on a regular basis and is then faced with a more steep pace of external change. This could result from the introduction of new competitors, new legislation or alternative products in the market.

Therefore, 'strategic drift' occurs where an organisation continues to plan on an historic basis, without paying proper regard to changes in the external environment. In this example, the organisation goes through a period of flux, where it reappraises its strategy, in the light of changing circumstances, and then makes a quantum change in strategy to correspond to the current environment. This is known as transformational change. As Figure 4.13 indicates, if the organisation does not make this change, it runs a risk of failing. This is a real risk to businesses at the attacking stage of growth. Change can occur at a rapid pace, particularly in new and emerging markets, and business owner/managers need to maintain close contact with the marketplace.

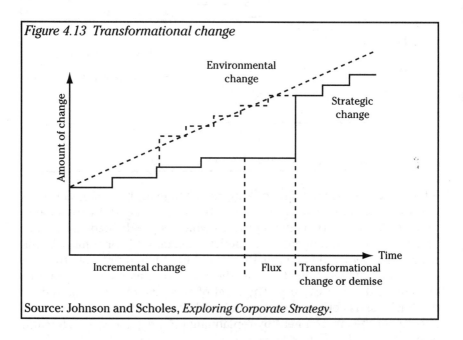

Figure 4.13 Transformational change

Source: Johnson and Scholes, *Exploring Corporate Strategy.*

It is essential, therefore, that whatever systems are in place in the business for updating and replanning are sufficiently flexible to react to changes in the external environment (or internal factors for that matter), in order that 'strategic drift' and all its consequences are avoided.

Conclusion

The business may remain in the attacking stage for some time, as it seeks to establish a strong presence in several market segments, and pursues a number of different opportunities. There are no guidelines as to how long a business spends in the attacking stage – this is really dependent on how quickly the business overcomes the transitional issues at this stage of growth and starts to display the characteristics of a business at the next stage of the DIAMOND model.

The next chapter looks at the fourth stage of the model, the maturing phase, and examines in some depth one of the most important issues facing the growing business – building and maintaining an effective team.

5

The art of letting go

Introduction

In the last chapter we looked at the attacking phase of the DIAMOND model. Businesses may remain at this stage for a number of years but, over a period of time, business systems and procedures start to mature.

This reflects the experience of the business in managing many of its activities. For example, budget planning becomes a regular annual activity, and the business looks for incremental growth. The outlook of the business is relatively risk-averse, and its decisions are based on previous experience and a tried and tested way of doing things.

On the positive side, business procedures are clear and well defined. Employees can refer to procedures, and systems have been developed to deal with most eventualities. Control is an important feature, and the business is a disciplined and fairly predictable organisation. Management is professionalised in order to deal with the size and complexity of the customer base and the organisational structure of the business.

Potential weaknesses in such structures largely arise from the rigidity brought about through the introduction of standard systems and processes for all aspects of the business. The business can become unresponsive to changes in market conditions and internally focused, concerned with maintaining established systems and procedures. Some employees can become frustrated in this type of environment and leave to seek new, more exciting opportunities elsewhere.

The maturing stage

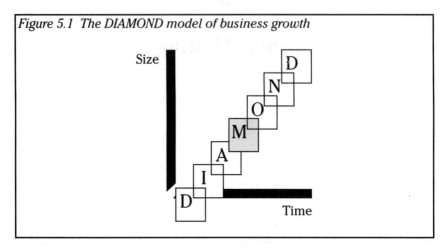

Figure 5.1 The DIAMOND model of business growth

Characteristics

Businesses that reach the maturing stage of the DIAMOND model share a number of common characteristics:

- established controls and systems for managing the business

- new people, new skills, new approaches and disciplines

- widespread planning

- formalised communications

Established systems

By the time it reaches the maturing stage, the business is likely to have well established systems for all key business processes. In addition, it is likely to have a clear organisational structure, which is typically hier-archical in nature. The systems are understood by the business's employees and reflect custom and practice in the organisation.

The systems enable the business to perform routine processes effectively and regularise tasks which were carried out (haphazardly) during the attacking stage. IT may form an important part of these systems.

Mature systems, whether manual or computerised, can become entrenched within a business and may not be flexible enough to deal with change.

People and skills

Individuality and freedom of action give way to clearly defined roles and structures. Whilst each of these characteristics exists in all organisations, the latter is more predominant in this phase of growth.

As the business grows, it will need to establish protocols for induction and provide a career path for its employees. In larger businesses, there will be a regular throughput of new staff. One of the key challenges for the business at the maturing phase is the ability to maintain and maximise the performance of its employees.

Much of this chapter is dedicated to the role of individuals and teams in the growing business. People are the key asset of any business. Whether it is senior management, salesmen or junior clerical staff, employees are the lifeblood of any organisation.

Planning

As a business becomes familiar with its commercial and legislative environment, and gains a good understanding of its marketplace, planning, rather than being a means to an end, can become an end in itself. Sophisticated planning processes can be introduced which seek to direct the activities of the business in a prescriptive manner. These planning guidelines can become quickly outdated – and soon the business is out of touch with its customers and markets alike.

Communication

The process of communication becomes increasingly formalised at the maturing stage. Unlike earlier stages of growth, defined channels of communication are likely to exist. Whilst this may in part reflect the size of the organisation, a structured and ordered way of doing things is the norm.

This formality in communication allows control to be exercised more readily, although shorter lines of communication may be lost.

Transitional issues

The transitional issues confronting businesses at the maturing stage include:

- management surpassing leadership

- losing touch with the market

- executives not incentivised or motivated correctly

- innovation dampened

Management surpasses leadership

As organisations grow, professional managers are introduced to run the day-to-day business. With these new managers come new skills and qualifications, and perhaps a different style. This may be at odds with the accepted leadership style adopted throughout the business's previous development.

The professional manager's approach may clash directly or indirectly with the traditional style of leadership, which created the successful business entity at the outset. The following business issues are worthwhile considering at this point, namely that:

- management are now seen to be the real experts;

- management are able to introduce a new business culture with associated values, ideas and a different customer focus;

- management seek to be properly rewarded for their efforts;

- management are more focused on the customer rather than the internal organisation.

The leader, in the form of the founding shareholder/manager, may find it difficult to continue to manage the business effectively beyond the early years of growth.

One of the key issues facing the leader is when to 'let go' of the business. This may relate to succession issues and his replacement at the helm by a professional manager. Alternatively, letting go of a controlling equity interest in the business the leader founded is equally difficult.

The business loses touch with the market

As the business matures, its internal systems can become bureaucratic and unresponsive to changes in the external environment. Planning is based upon historic experience rather than a critical analysis of current and future developments. The pace of change in the external environment is often frightening. Businesses constantly need to address the impact of changes in customer preferences, competition, etc. on their product and service offerings.

The position of IBM in the early days of the personal computer market is often quoted as a good example of losing touch with the external market.

> Bureaucratic and cumbersome decision-making processes in product and service development can stifle technical competence. One of the reasons often cited for why IBM failed to dominate the personal computer market in spite of setting the standard for such products is that they were outwitted by smaller, more agile and sharper rivals. Often products just arrived on the market too late. Products would arrive a year or so after they would have been a really good idea.

Tony Broughton in *Operations Management*

Clearly, there is still potential for the David to challenge the corporate Goliath! Businesses at the maturing phase can become shortsighted and ignore major shifts in the external environment after many years of market domination. This provides an opportunity for younger, more agile businesses to challenge the position of the market leaders.

Executives not incentivised or motivated currently

People are central to the success of any growing business, in particular those individuals who contribute most significantly to wealth creation in the business. Without these key individuals, who are most likely to be in senior positions in the organisation, business success and growth is unlikely to be achieved.

It is these key executives who need to be appropriately incentivised to ensure that their performance contributes to the growth of the business.

At the maturing stage, these senior executives may feel that their contribution to business performance is not being valued or rewarded correctly. Instead, the founder shareholder/managers are reaping the benefits of success, for what may appear to be limited input.

Incentivisation is, therefore, critical to ongoing growth. Common mistakes are made in incentivisation in:

- rewarding the wrong people;
- providing the wrong form of incentive;
- cynical or crude use of incentives;
- confusing financial incentives with money incentives.

Many businesses fail to get off the starting block of incentivisation – pedestrian businesses populated by unambitious employees with stagnant products and limited growth opportunities.

Incentivisation alone cannot cure all these ills, but a careful programme of implementation can give a clear sense of purpose to even the most challenged environment.

Proper incentivisation coupled with real people values can and should:

- target the individuals on whom the business relies;
- assess their most beneficial measure of reward;
- provide the individual with a mechanism to control a significant element of their income or wealth;
- retain important key players in the business with a renewed sense of purpose.

Incentives are important in all businesses but if a business is seeking to protect and extend a market position, or wishing to create and retain the best teams, then incentives are essential. A well written incentive plan – more likely an overall company strategy – will at worst help you to assess the real profit generators in the team. At best, it can create new entrepreneurs to capture the hunger of the business characterised at the attacking stage and bring wider scope to the business.

No incentivisation should be the result of anything less than a critical analysis of the key drivers within the business. Good incentivisation plans will be successful in varying circumstances and will aim to take the business forward as a team.

Incentivisation takes many forms, some of which are not financial at all. It can involve conferring well deserved status to individuals, or the creation of defined roles to allow successful employees to properly see their career path.

Other approaches naturally and mainly emphasise controllable financial reward – with the emphasis on controllable. The business must control the reward in the context of:

- its scale;

- its profit impact (poor incentives can reduce profits);

- the comparative impact between employees;

- the mix between basic and incentive remuneration;

- the creation of rewards for employees who are entrepreneurs in their own right – and therefore demand capital.

Employees must feel that they can control the incentive to the extent that they truly own the measure – that their actions really have an influence over the ultimate rewards they receive.

The essential ingredient of all good incentivisation schemes is that they must be directed towards those who can really influence the success of the business.

Although it is true to say that every employee within a business in some way contributes to its success, good incentive plans must recognise that the real levers of profitability are in the hands of a very few people. There is an essential difference between blanket incentivisation which rewards all employees and rewarding directly the personal performance of an individual. There, the effects should be to create and retain a motivated employee wanting more reward linked to further success.

A further distinct group is those individuals who display entrepreneurial characteristics, and who must be retained within the business. These people, employed at various times in every successful growing business, will not only be a potential loss to the business if they leave but may be the most logical and natural competitors if their creative corporate talents are unleashed. Keeping them will mean making sure that they participate not only in monetary reward, but also in the capital growth of the business itself. Forms of capital incentive – wise if measured and controlled – are the preserve of the very few stars the business will nurture and grow.

The golden rules of incentivisation, distilled from many years' experience balancing the carrot and the stick, are:

- to avoid unfocused incentivisation techniques – this is the best way to unwittingly spend profits for no measurable or consistent return;

- to identify opportunities within the business for real reward systems, not only confined to sales-related functions;

- to consider all forms of non-monetary rewards, e.g., titles and responsibility. These judgemental issues mean a great deal to career-minded individuals;

- to provide self-financing initiatives wherever possible: remember that a proper incentive, creating more profits, theoretically has *no* cost;

- to be wary of the trap of the bonus structure: bonus-led employees tend to have consistent leaving dates – immediately after that bonus has been paid! Be prepared to make bonus payments by instalments to ensure maximum employee retention;

- to preserve capital incentives for the few who deserve them

The following list identifies – from lowest capital cost to highest – the strata of many incentivisation schemes and plans. This should be used to distill where your company strategy most fruitfully lies.

- simple profit-related incentivisation

- phantom options or deferred bonus schemes

- executive share options

- personal share options

- general capital involvement schemes

- allocation of capital

Capital incentives can have a real beneficial impact on the business, but one should understand the dynamics and the issues that they can create if not properly implemented and communicated.

Capital incentives, which involve letting an employee have a right to part of the shares in the business – are admittedly an alien concept to most private business owners. But most private business owners who have employed a star manager have suffered when he or she left, perhaps to join a competitor or to start a business of their own.

These experienced people are usually only invigorated by the prospect of an involvement in the growth of wealth in the business. How can such an incentive be provided without giving away the wealth the founder shareholders have created? How can an employee be expected to produce the level of capital necessary to buy a significant holding in the business without access to private wealth or unrealistically high borrowings?

To the rescue in many situations comes the unapproved share option. This simple document, enacted properly, includes a number of valuable attributes:

(a) it provides the right to buy a proportion of capital at today's value (or at a discounted value if you choose) at any time up to 10 years in the future;

(b) it does not require capital resources when granted;

(c) it allows the option holder to participate in any subsequent disposal, or to use the option as the first rung on the ladder of a management buyout;

(d) the right to capital lapses if the employee leaves the business;

(e) if the option has been exercised and shares bought, the shares must be resold if the employee departs from the business.

A word of warning – options are a powerful tool and if misused they can be dangerous: they are the trigger to a change in ownership of the business in the future.

Research on UK executive pay carried out by McKnight and Tomkins (adapted from *Director Magazine*, December 1998), showed that between 1993 and 1996 average remuneration in the form of share options grew by 140 per cent. Share options now represent over 60 per cent of the average board director's total emoluments.

There have been many windfall gains from the use of share options. A celebrated example is that of Michael Eisner. In December 1997, as chairman and CEO of Disney, he exercised 7.3 million share options, then sold 4 million options on the open market. He made around $500 million!

A good example of the use of incentivisation techniques to motivate employees is provided by Richer Sounds.

INCENTIVISATION AT RICHER SOUNDS

In the early 1970s Julian Richer was cutting his entrepreneurial teeth in his native Bristol. By the age of 19 he had opened up his first hi-fi store in London. By 1998 the turnover at Richer Sounds was in the region of £45 million. What makes this even more staggering is that this has been achieved with only 200 staff. The most obvious feature of his success is the ability to generate turnover in a restricted floor space – in 1997 a staggering £5,500 per square foot, compared with £630 from PC World and £530 from Currys. This has earned Richer a place in the Guinness Book of Records.

The ability to recruit, motivate and develop staff has caught the eye of the likes of Sears, Asda and the Halifax amongst others to help focus their own policies in this area. As a result, Richer is now firmly ensconced on the consultancy circuit and his book *The Richer Way* is proving to be a market success.

Richer is devoted to a clear and defined policy that gives his employees scope for personal and career growth at any level. Employees in his shops wear a trainee badge regardless of their status, until they feel competent and are in tune with the culture around them. This also protects them from technical questions and process queries from customers who may initially feel that they are dealing with an idiot. Their progression is based upon a rigid and objective customer survey based on invoices and sales dockets. Until they reach the 'excellent' category, the badge stays on. To support this Richer firmly believes that:

> **You cannot give good service without friendly, helpful and knowledgeable people.**

Richer's gospel in terms of customer service is also reflected in his reward policy. This does not apply only to actual performance, but to social issues such as smoking, for example. The bonus system for employees pays out three times a year, enhanced by small increments from results of customer surveys. Directors get an annual bonus linked to audited results. All of this information is openly available.

Store and departmental performance is rewarded by the use of a Bentley or a Jaguar for a month. Employee suggestions are also taken seriously, with even the smallest idea rewarded with a £10 cheque; this may be enhanced if the idea is picked up and used further. All suggestions are personally acknowledged.

Richer is also aware that not everyone can be a star. Staff with five years' service, at any level, are rewarded with a meal in the West End and a short holiday. As a result staff retention is high. Promotion for Richer is also seen to be an internal process – all eight of his consultancy associates have been appointed from within the organisation.

Source: Godfrey Golzen 'King of Hi Fi', *Enterprise.*

Innovation is stifled by inflexibility

Businesses at the maturing stage are typically more bureaucratic in their approach. This can create inherent rigidities in the business which can stifle innovative thinking and approaches.

Without innovation a business cannot thrive and grow. Innovation, whether in the form of product development or working practices, is crucial to keeping in step with changes in the external environment.

Peter Drucker, the accomplished management thinker, sees innovation as providing a significant business opportunity. These opportunities arise from the purposeful exploitation of a number of unrelated events or requirements, which comprise:

(a) *unexpected occurrences* – sometimes, where a particular product fails in the marketplace for a number of reasons, there may be a more suitable market elsewhere. The use of local anaesthetic, which was unsuitable for general surgery but short-term enough for dental surgery, is a simple example here;

(b) *inconsistency* – a process or activity which goes against the grain is often overlooked and found to be unsuitable. However, within this lies an opportunity to innovate. The brewing industry is now able to market a wide range of products as off-shoots of the main brewing process;

(c) *industrial needs and requirements* – the birth of advertising to support the production of newspapers, and reduce costs accordingly, can be seen to be the best example of a need to support an industrial requirement;

(d) *industry and market changes* – the climate within which businesses now operate changes rapidly and this can affect structure immediately. The growth of the private medical care market is an example of businesses which have grown to address changes in perception about choice in medical service provision.

In terms of the external environment, there are three further sources of innovation open to an organisation, those of:

- *demography*

  The focus on the change in lifestyle patterns and resulting behaviour can be seen to be an opportunity to innovate. In recent years there has been a huge growth in companies providing combined wedding/honeymoon packages abroad.

- *perception*

  Innovation can be characterised by an individual looking at a glass. It can either be half empty or half full. This interpretation turns the innovator into an opportunist. These opportunities may be simple, like the invention of the 'cat's eye' for road safety, or not so obvious as the 'Post-it' note, which evolved from the use of end cuts from the paper production process.

- *knowledge*

  This is a precious commodity. The application of new technologies in business areas is the result of long and necessary research. The short-term benefits cannot easily be identified – the personal computer endured through many years of research and the overturning of the original idea that computers were only affordable in large organisations.

Innovation is central to gaining competitive advantage in the marketplace. At the maturing stage, the opportunities for applying innovative practices, as outlined above, should be sought out regularly. Innovation is the responsibility of all managers and should form a part of their planning processes. Innovation begins with a conscious search for opportunities. This activity should be instilled in the culture of the organisation, so it becomes a natural part of business activity, rather than something which is forced upon the business.

Businesses should use the triggers identified by Drucker to act as a prompt for action.

The concept of empowerment

Empowerment can be seen to be:

The ability to make decisions within one's area of operations without having to get approval from anyone else.

Fred Luthans

This definition underpins the thinking behind empowerment as a management tool. Empowerment permits elements of the decision-making process to be delegated, and can be seen to be unique, as Luthans continues, as it has two further characteristics.

Firstly, staff are free to use their own initiative – just get on with it! And secondly, the staff are not only given authority, but also the support services and resources to go with it. For example, if a customer telephones a mobile phone company and says that the cellular phone they received that morning does not work, the empowered employee would be able to get a replacement delivered immediately and the original returned. To support this there would be a follow-up call to ensure that the replacement phone worked. This approach generates tangible benefits in terms of customer retention and business reputation.

To emphasise this process further, empowerment must evolve around the following key elements:

- participation – **everyone** is willing to improve their daily work schedule and be open and flexible to new ideas and relationships;

- innovation – **everyone** has the authority to investigate new ideas;

- access to information – **everyone** can access data to support their work, and can be trained if required to interpret data which increases their efficiency and effectiveness;

- accountability – **everyone** is responsible for both success and failure.

A process adopted by some UK firms is that of the 'learning organisation'. The concept of empowerment shapes the way the business operates, in all areas of activity. The contrast with the traditional organisation is shown in Table 5.1.

The benefits of empowering employees can be seen though tangible improvements in customer services, particularly within retail/service businesses.

A successful growing business must always put the customer first. By empowering the workforce, management need not concern itself with having complex systems of supervision and control. Instead, decision-making is aligned to responsibility, and this reduces overall costs and improves bottom line profitability and customer retention.

Table 5.1 The learning organisation

Function	Traditional organisation	'Learning' organisation
Where are we going? (Beginning)	The vision is provided by the owner(s) or top management.	There is a shared vision that can emerge from within the business. The owner(s) or top management are charged with pushing this vision forward.
The ideas are formulated and implemented. (Where do we want to be?)	The owner(s) or top management decides what is to be done and the rest of the organisation acts on these ideas.	The ideas are put forward and agreed at all levels of the business. The ideas become 'owned' by all.
The job process is assessed and undertaken. (The means)	Each person is responsible for their own job responsibilities, and the focus is seen to be an individual one.	Tasks can be shared and the outcomes can interrelate with those of others thus improving efficiency.
Problems and conflicts are resolved. (Evaluation)	The problems are resolved by pressure and/or influence from above.	Conflict is reduced by negotiation and collaboration.
Leadership and motivation. (The ends)	The outcomes are the responsibility of a chosen few.	The shared approach through empowered staff and inspired commitment rules.

Source: Adapted from Peter Senge, 'Transforming the Practice of Management' in Fred Luthans, *Organizational Behavior*.

So why is every organisation not applying the principles of empowerment and the learning organisation? Because for many it requires a fundamental change in the way the organisation is managed and operated. Culture values and 'the way we have always done it' can get in the way of introducing new approaches to running the business. Mature businesses in particular will find it difficult to adapt to new ways of thinking and doing.

The challenge for the mature business is to question accepted ways of doing business and be ready to face change. This issue will be explored in more detail in Chapter 7, where we explain the overhauling stage of the DIAMOND model.

An example of empowerment in practice is provided by Mason's Coatings.

MASON'S COATINGS – EMPOWERMENT OF EMPLOYEES

The arrival of Chris Steel as Managing Director in August 1997 ushered in the advent of a new concept of team involvement and change within Mason's Coatings, which came into effect a year later. Steel lays this element of job involvement and eventual empowerment, as follows.

> We must release the untapped potential of everybody to solve problems and continuously improve on all aspects of the jobs we do. The continual improvement process should provide us with a system and skills to ensure that we are able to solve problems together.

The recognition of the importance of empowerment resulted in a number of employees undergoing special training within areas of production, where a range of problems appeared to occur the most often. These team leaders were, as a result, able to log and track the source of these problems and stem any potential faults well in advance. As the Quality Manager, John McDermott, explains further:

> The mechanism allows employees to identify areas for improvement and provides assistance, and involves them in achieving their improvement goals.

Employees recognising faults can contact a special team that addresses these faults. The team of four facilitators can take action either at departmental level or through a rapid yet more formal approach through management. Feedback, either to the team or the individual, is also supported by an analysis of any resulting saving or benefit. This drive for employee empowerment manifests into direct contact between production staff and the customers themselves.

Source: Chris Ward 'World Class is Aim of New Scheme', *Derby Evening Telegraph*.

When working together as empowered teams, individuals will have even more impact than as an independent business unit. Managers as leaders have to appreciate that expectations within any business must focus on teamwork, team leadership and employee participation. This will lead to the development of teams which, after consistent and sustained effort, will evolve into 'high performance' or 'self-directed' work teams.

Empowerment has to be acknowledged as a process of freeing up and enlightening employees and teams, in order for them to have access to, and operate successfully within, an unpredictable and global business environment.

The importance of teams

Some organisations can be depicted as operating like machines, with rules and control systems which define the precise way the business is run and managed. It is not hard to find examples of organisations which are managed in this way – McDonalds, the fast food chain, has a clear way of delivering service to its customers. Tasks are clearly defined and guidelines identify the parameters within which employees can operate. In some environments, this type of approach may be appropriate. For example, certain defence-related activities follow a clear path and chain of command which must be followed.

Most organisations do not operate like machines – they are populated by people not robots! Businesses that operate solely by rules find very quickly that situations arise which have not been anticipated by those rules. Rules can breed inflexibility and make a business less responsive to change. Furthermore, working as individuals, rather than together, may result in not pulling in the same direction and, therefore, not making the maximum contribution for a given level of effort. A response to the potential weaknesses of working as individuals, within tightly defined rules, has been the emergence of the importance of teams and teamworking.

It is widely acknowledged that teams outperform individuals acting alone or in larger organisational groupings, especially where the task requires a wide combination of skills, judgements and experience. Most people see commonsense benefits in working together as a team. However, typically, they do not know how teams form and how to harness the most positive impact from teamworking. In this section we look at these issues and assess their importance for the growing business.

Teambuilding

Many books have been written about the subject of teams and teambuilding. It is not the purpose of this book to provide the reader with a comprehensive review of the subject, but rather to provide growing businesses with an insight into what makes teams perform and what conditions need to be met for this to happen.

Some very important insights into teams are provided by Katzenbach and Smith in *The Wisdom of Teams*.

(a) A stretching performance target or challenge provides the basis for creating a team. Teams tend to form around these challenges, whether it is working on specific projects with deadlines or working to achieve a defined performance target.

(b) Organisations often overlook the 'team basics' – that is, the conditions which are necessary for effective team performance. These include the size of the team, its objective and purpose, the balance of skills and approach. Taking a disciplined view of these issues provides the foundations for team success.

(c) Team opportunities exist throughout a business – not just in certain areas like sales or management. The challenge is to identify the common purpose and build a team around this.

(d) Creating the top team is the greatest challenge of all. Senior executives can be very individualistic, which sometimes works against team ethics. Also, the focus for senior management is typically more long-term, and this often does not provide a clear purpose to aim for.

(e) Most performance and reward systems are focused around the individual and not teams. This naturally emphasises individual accountability rather than team accountability. To facilitate a team environment, the emphasis of reward structures in organisations may need to be revisited.

(f) Businesses which have strong performance standards tend to generate more 'real teams' than those organisations which promote teams as an end in themselves. Teams simply do not become teams because someone calls a group of individuals a team. Real teams emerge when given tough performance challenges.

(g) High performing teams are extremely rare. These are teams which produce exceptional results and outperform other teams. A high degree of personal commitment is required to make this happen.

(h) Teams are increasingly becoming everyday primary vehicles for delivering performance in organisations.

The first major hurdle that presents itself is the resistance of the group which is going to work together, either all of the time or for a short period. This can be based on three sources of individual concern:

- lack of conviction – the belief that teams will not work or perform better than individuals, unless the circumstances are unusual or unpredictable;
- personal discomfort or element of risk – that the team approach is too time-consuming and risky;
- insecurity – the fear of opening up to a team and perhaps showing failure.

There are several conditions which need to be met to allow teams to form effectively. Essentially, teams become teams through the following:

(a) a disciplined and shaped common purpose. This refers to the need to ensure that the team is clear about the performance target it is seeking to achieve. Without this, the team has no common purpose around which to form.

(b) a clear and defined working approach. The team needs to establish a common framework, which sets out the parameters for working together towards the objectives set. In the absence of this, the team risks approaching the project from different perspectives and not pulling together in the same direction.

(c) an acknowledgment of complementary skills at a high level. For a team to work, the skills of that team need to complement each other rather than be duplicated. Using a sporting analogy, there is little point in having a football team full of attacking players with no-one in defence and in goal.

(d) a sense of mutual accountability for success and failure. Each member of the team needs to feel that they are equally responsible for achieving the stated goals.

In Business Reservations provides an example of team building and working in practice.

TEAM BUILDING AT IN BUSINESS RESERVATIONS

Founded in 1988 by Hayley Phillips-Moul, In Business Reservations (IBR) is a specialist conference-venue-finding agency. Dean Vitellozzi, Operations Manager, explains the competitive edge that IBR has:

Due to the specific requirements and product knowledge required by our clients, it was much easier for a specialist conference agent such as IBR to become a 'one stop shop' and also offer an accommodation booking service, than it was for a travel agent to branch out into the field of venue finding. Growth and reputation has now given us the buying power to negotiate added value and preferential rates for our customers.

The move into the global market has been made in tandem with the trend for customers to seek wider and more exotic locations for their conference venues.

No organisation can operate without a committed and empowered workforce, and Vitellozzi endorses this fervently. This cultural harmony that IBR nurtures, even through rapid growth and expansion, can be identified by all. This growth has increased staffing levels from 33 to 53 over the past year and forced a move to larger and more appropriate premises. The induction process for all new staff plays to potential strengths and develops areas of weakness. As Vitellozzi explains:

What we look for when we interview and employ staff is the right attitude, dedication and attention to detail. The pure foundations of empowerment.

New members of staff follow a recognised induction programme; this is to give them a full awareness of IBR's activities and their role. Within their first week they are given a blanket grounding into the functions of the other departments, before starting in their own team. They are issued with a comprehensive training pack that indicates yardsticks of attainment and methods of achievement. The use of a 'traffic light' training progression for everyone is not only recorded in this pack but also by posters and charts pinned up around the main office. This progression is checked by their team leader and follows three key stages:

- at the red stage there has been no training, only an insight at induction;

- at the amber stage sufficient knowledge is gained to carry out team skills competently;

- at the green stage, full training has been given, the employee is assessed and able to train others.

Each head of department and any team member can feed into and support business plans within the organisation in a climate of mutual empowerment. As Hayley Phillips-Moul explains:

A three year business programme has been drawn up for each department. Heads and team members have had an influential role in the shaping of these plans. These plans spell out a programme that will increase by 40 per cent our input of business into the hotel industry.

Monthly briefings are attended by all, the structure and format is decided and organised by a different team each month, and they are responsible in turn for the supply of target and progress data. These teams will then lay out performance and variance analysis at these meetings, and are required to explain any deviations.

Team activity results in the business being able to react quickly to changing business needs – a key attribute in moving from the maturing phase to the overhauling phase within the DIAMOND model.

What makes high performance teams different?

As empowered units within a business, these teams can be defined by a number of characteristics:

- committed to each other – a philosophy of 'if one fails, we all fail';

- rare! – because these teams can sometimes set themselves artificial regimes of pressure to achieve sustained and consistent growth;

- where you find them, not where you want them to be;

- committed to a philosophy of 'extended team effort' – they are 'super-empowered' in that at every stage ideas and initiatives are double-checked by the team;

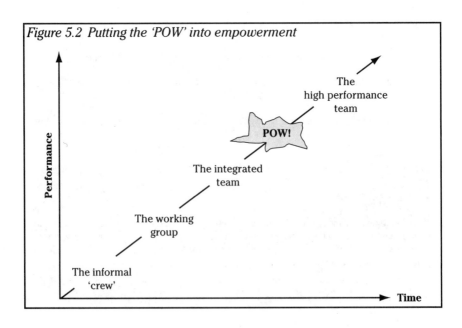

Figure 5.2 Putting the 'POW' into empowerment

- flexible – as skills the team possesses can be interchangeable for the benefit of the team as a whole;

- prepared to accept a shared leadership role – even though there may be a 'figurehead' leader for organisational purposes.

A sense of purpose and challenge, combined with an empowered team, provides the right conditions to develop a high performing team, which can contribute significantly to business performance.

The positive consequences of team working

The impact of positive team working can be summarised as:

- reduced overheads and costs;

- increased productivity;

- closer customer focus;

- fewer layers of management bureaucracy;

- increased speed to market for products and services;

- increased motivation and employee commitment;

- improved self-esteem for employees.

What happens when they get stuck?

If one accepts that teams are a valuable way of improving performance then, given the right conditions, it makes sound business sense to encourage team-working. But what stops this from happening?

What happens when a team really gets stuck? Should the team be abandoned or should something be done to get the team back on track again? Sometimes, it can be better to call proceedings to a halt and adopt a different approach. However, Katzenbach and Smith advocate a number of techniques which can help get the team unstuck:

(a) *Revisit the basics* – rethink the team approach, ask what the original objective for the team was. Effectively, start from scratch to try to identify what issues have blocked the success of the team.

(b) *Go for small wins* – winning brings teams together. Setting realistic goals allows the team to focus on performance, rather than inter-personal conflicts which may hinder team performance.

(c) *Introduce new information and approaches* – fresh ideas and additional information can re-invigorate the development of a team. New information can be used to challenge the team's thinking and open up new ways to move forward. For example, a team looking at improving sales performance may find it useful to look at benchmarked data from competitors or use customer feedback to shape their thinking.

(d) *Take advantage of facilitators* – facilitators can act as catalysts to get things moving. They can create focus for team activities and bring valuable team-working skills, which may be lacking in the team that is stuck.

(e) *Change the composition of the team* – sometimes, the team dynamics simply do not work and a change is needed in team members or team leader. If the leader is the block to good performance, he needs to be removed by management.

These techniques can emerge from an intervention by management or from the team itself. Action taken by the team is likely to prove more successful, particularly as management intervention is sometimes viewed as interference. Notwithstanding this, management must be aware of when it is appropriate for them to intervene.

Conclusion

In this chapter we considered the issues surrounding the maturing stage of the DIAMOND model. Businesses can remain at this stage for a number of years.

People issues are paramount at the maturing stage. The challenge for businesses is to ensure that people and teams are appropriately motivated, so that their contribution to business success is maximised. The use of appropriate incentivisation techniques is an important part of this.

The concept of empowerment and innovation plays an important part in bringing the best out of teams within a business. The case studies illustrate this and provide good examples of how to apply some of the team concepts in practice.

As part of the transition from the maturing to the overhauling stage of business growth, it may be necessary to seek finance to achieve new business strategies. The next chapter considers how the growing business can be financed.

6

Financing the growing business

Introduction

'Money makes the world go round' is a well known phrase. It could easily be adapted to 'Money makes a business sound', because there is little doubt that cash is the lifeblood of any business. If the finances are not properly structured then there is every chance that the business will fail, particularly during rapid growth when the spectre of 'over-trading' (where the rate of expansion outstrips the financial resources of the business) is everpresent.

The importance of managing cash flow is well recognised by most business people. However, the route to an optimal funding structure is not so clear, largely because of the wide range of financing products that are actually available and the many different sources from which these can be obtained. This is illustrated in Table 6.1.

Not all financing sources will prove to be appropriate or accessible for a business at the various stages of growth and development. The purpose of this chapter is to examine the key financing options in more detail, highlight the main characteristics and identify when they may be most appropriate to use.

Equity

Equity finance is generated when a business issues share capital to outside investors. In its purest form, equity represents true risk capital for the investor because normally the shareholders are not contractually entitled to an income stream from their investment and are the first people to lose financially if the company does not perform. The

Table 6.1 Types and sources of finance	
Financing product	*Source*
Equity (seedcorn, development, growth)	Financial markets Venture capitalists Business angels Personal wealth
Loan capital (bonds, debentures)	Financial markets
Overdraft	Bank
Start-up/small company loans	Banks Government
Traditional debt	Banks
Mezzanine debt	Banks
Asset finance	Banks Leasing companies
Invoice discounting/debt factoring	Finance companies – bank affiliated
Grants	National and local government European Union
Working capital management	Own debtors, creditors and stock

potential return generated for the equity shareholder must, therefore, be higher than for other financing products in order to compensate for the risk.

The return is generated through a combination of dividend income and the growth in the capital value of the business to which, as a part owner of the business, the investor is entitled, and which can be crystallised at the point of sale of the shares. The extent of the capital value of the business attributable to the shareholder will depend on the proportion of the business owned. To get a greater return you must own more of the business.

Because of the high return aspirations that exist within equity, it is inherently an expensive source of finance for the business. Therefore, the temptation is to rely on cheaper sources of finance such as debt. The required compound return to a venture capitalist equity provider may be 25 per cent to 35 per cent per annum, compared to 9 per cent interest per annum charged on a loan provided by a bank.

However, as we will see later, the payments on debt finance must be

114

met. Indeed, the fact that the business is not obliged to make any payment to equity shareholders, in contrast to scheduled loan repayments, means that it is advisable to have a strong equity base, encompassing share capital and reserves, to sustain the business.

Sources of equity

Financial markets

The most high profile method of obtaining equity finance is by issuing shares on the financial markets, such as the London Stock Exchange. Traditionally, this source of finance has been restricted to businesses that have already gone through the early stage of the growth cycle and can demonstrate some level of maturity reflected by:

- a three-year track record;
- sustainable profitability;
- minimum net worth;
- market strength;
- strong management;
- robust systems.

Whilst the above criteria would certainly still apply to a full listing on the London Stock Exchange, other financial markets have been established to accommodate the requirements of less mature, high growth and more speculative enterprises. Such markets include the Alternative Investment Market (AIM) and OFEX in the UK, EASDAQ for Europe and NASDAQ in the USA.

AIM in particular has now become an established source of finance. In March 1999, the following statistics applied:

- over £1 billion raised;
- total market value £6 billion;
- over 260 companies listed.

The flexibility inherent in markets such as AIM has allowed many small businesses access to equity capital. In extreme cases, particularly in relation to software or biotech businesses, equity capital has been raised for companies with an idea that has yet to manifest itself in a product or a sale!

It would appear, therefore, that the financial markets do represent a viable source of equity funding for both established businesses looking to finance the next stage of expansion and young, entrepreneurially driven businesses in the early stages of growth. There are other tangible benefits of achieving a listing on a recognised stock exchange, including:

- *making acquisitions* – issuing new shares as consideration for acquisitions instead of using cash resources or borrowings;
- *prestige* – enhanced status can lead to improved buying power and an increased market perception of the company;
- *motivation* – more attractive and measurable share option schemes can be introduced for management and ;
- *operating efficiency* – the rigour imposed in the lead up to flotation in respect of systems, structure and production processes can result in improved performance;
- realisation of value – the market provides a mechanism for existing shareholders to extract value by the sale of shares on, or sub-sequent to, flotation.

However, many growing businesses shy away from the financial markets as a source of funds and, in many cases, quite rightly so. The drawbacks include:

- *costs* – at the time of writing in early 1999, the cost of floating on AIM can range from £300,000 to £500,000. In addition, the internal cost incurred through the absorption of management time is substantial;
- *accountability* – management must abide by the regulations imposed by the market and must report to and, where necessary, accept criticism from the new shareholders;
- *loss of control* – if a substantial fundraising exercise is undertaken, the existing shareholders may lose voting control;
- *illiquidity* – a ready market may not always exist, particularly in the case of small companies, where only a small proportion of the share capital has been made available to outside shareholders. This means that you may obtain a quoted price for your shares but be quite unable to sell them.

COMPUTERLAND

ComputerLand UK PLC is a quoted company on the Alternative Investment Market providing IT services in remote support, outsourcing, training, systems integration and other services including related IT products to mid-corporate users.

The business was founded in 1989 by Graham Gilbert, a young entrepreneur who had recently graduated from university. The company traded as a franchisee until 1997 when the rights to the name and trade mark were acquired from its USA-based parent.

A fast growing company reporting turnover of £6.7 million in 1995, increasing to £18 million in 1997 (operating profit 1995 – £185,000; 1997 – £699,000), ComputerLand successfully achieved a listing on AIM in 1997 raising £1.5 million of new money in the process. The principal reasons for choosing to float were stated to be:

* to fund growth of the high margin/high potential service side of the business through the recruitment of IT personnel and improved marketing;

* to provide access to secondary funding for growth by acquisition; and;

* to provide powerful staff incentivisation through liquid and measurable share option and SAYE schemes.

Although ComputerLand successfully achieved a flotation, it required very focused management involvement. In particular, Graham Gilbert and his top team needed to spend what, to them, seemed to be a substantial amount of time addressing the procedural matters associated with the flotation to the possible detriment of the actual business they were trying to run!

However, the advantages of an AIM listing were realised very quickly as within six months ComputerLand returned to the market to raise a further £3 million of new money to fund two acquisitions and to satisfy additional working capital requirements.

Graham Gilbert commented: 'We have been very pleased with our experience, the balance sheet is strengthened, our profile enhanced, acquisitions have been made possible and our people have a much greater sense of involvement.'

Once a successful listing has been achieved the required return for investors must be satisfied. The annual average returns on the FT All Share Index can be analysed as shown in Table 6.2.

Table 6.2 FT All Share Index annual average returns	
Period	Real returns
1918–1993	7.9%
1980–1993	13.1%
1990–1993	17.8%
Source: BZW Equity & Gilt Study	

The returns enjoyed by investors in listed shares can be compared to the relatively risk-free returns on government bonds, which have averaged 1.5 per cent to 3 per cent over the same period. The additional return for the additional risk is clear to see. To meet this requirement, the business is under constant pressure to increase dividends and achieve growth in capital value.

Venture capitalists

Venture capital is a source of equity funding that is specifically designed for growing companies. The provision of venture capital is normally undertaken by a range of specialist fund managers who have been entrusted with a proportion of a larger fund (typically a pension fund) to invest.

A venture capital investment can range from a few hundred thousand to many millions of pounds and can be applied in a variety of situations, most commonly:

- start-up 'seedcorn' capital – to support a new concept, product or company;
- development capital – to support expansion;
- buyouts and buy-ins – to support the acquisition of the company by its own, or an outside, management team;
- acquisitions – to support the purchase of another company.

In 1997 £4.2 billion was invested in 1,200 companies by British Venture Capital Association members. Of this £2.8 billion was invested in the UK of which 80 per cent went into 'first time' investments in companies, with the remainder being follow-on financing to companies already in receipt of venture capital.

In all situations, the venture capitalist is looking for businesses that have the capacity to grow. This is not to say that investment will be restricted to the small number of high growth markets that are apparent at the time. The venture capitalist will view a niche player in a mature market with equal favour as long as there is the potential to expand in that niche.

In tandem with the capacity to grow, any business in which a venture capitalist invests must be able to demonstrate that there is an excellent management team in place. Remember, the venture capitalist is investing in a company with growth prospects that are yet unproven and must rely on the management to deliver and execute its planned growth strategies.

A robust case must be presented to the venture capitalist in the form of a detailed business plan (see Chapter 3 and Appendix 5 for what is included in a business plan). The well worn statistic that 'out of 100 proposals, only one will be successful' emphasises the importance of this issue, and also tends to confirm the view that venture capitalists are less likely to entertain highly speculative start-up ventures.

It is interesting to note that James Dyson, inventor of the world famous Dyson vacuum cleaner, had to go to East Asia to find financial backing for his idea. UK funding, from whatever source, for such an innovative start-up was conspicuous by its absence.

Despite this, venture capital is a source of funding that appears to be ideal for the growing business. A source of funding that is prepared to back entrepreneurial management teams of young, possibly unproven businesses – so where is the downside?

The downside quite clearly manifests itself in the cost of the investment. The venture capitalist will be targeting a compound annual rate of return of between 25 per cent and 35 per cent. The reason for such high returns is that every investment made by the venture capitalist will, to a large extent, relate to an enterprise or an opportunity that is unproven. Some will undoubtedly fail. The ones that succeed must make an exceptional return in order to compensate for those failures.

A return of this magnitude is achieved by the way in which the investment made is structured by the venture capitalist. The venture capitalist will certainly take a significant stake in the business (typically between 20 per cent and 50 per cent) in return for an investment in ordinary shares. As the business grows in line with the plan, the value of the ordinary shares will increase and the venture capitalist will look to crystallise that value by exiting from the business within a defined time frame, usually four to seven years. This exit is engineered by a trade sale, flotation or secondary buyout (see Chapter 9 for information on exits).

In addition to the capital return generated on ordinary shares, it is likely that the venture capitalist will be entitled to a share of the annual profits of the business through a receipt of an ordinary dividend based upon a fixed percentage of the profits made.

Although the capital return on ordinary shares is the main route to high returns for the venture capitalist, it sometimes comes as a surprise to business that, in monetary terms, the greatest proportion of the initial investment will be in the form of redeemable shares or unsecured loan stock. In both cases, the key characteristics are that the investment is repayable in the medium term, and that a fixed coupon or interest rate is charged. The emphasis here is that this portion of the investment is lower risk and attempts to provide some guarantee of return to the venture capitalist.

To see how this basket of investments generates the return, a hypothetical example is detailed below.

EXAMPLE

ABC Venture Capitalists invest £1 million for 30 per cent of the equity in a business with profit after tax of £300,000. The investment is split £200,000 into ordinary shares and £800,000 into redeemable preference shares. The ordinary shares are entitled to a dividend equal to 5 per cent of profit after tax. The preference shares have a coupon (interest rate) of 10 per cent, and are redeemed over five years.

The venture capitalist exits after five years when the business is sold at a multiple of 10 times profit after tax.

The rate of return to the venture capitalist is calculated on the basis of cash flow received, and is illustrated in Table 6.3.

Although the time frame attributed to a venture capital investment is typically considered to be less than five years, a venture capitalist may stay in for a longer run, making additional investments as the business develops.

120

Table 6.3 Rate of return to ABC Venture Capitalists

	Year 0 £000	Year 1 £000	Year 2 £000	Year 3 £000	Year 4 £000	Year 5 £000
Profit after tax		350	400	450	500	550
Venture capitalist's cash flows						
Investment	(1,000)					
Ord dividend		17	20	22	25	27
Pref. dividend		72	56	40	24	8
Pref. redemption		160	160	160	160	160
Exit						1,650
Net cash	(1,000)	249	236	222	209	1,845
Return to VC	30%					

COMPASS CLEANING

Compass Cleaning is an established contract cleaning company focused on the food retail sector. The business has demonstrated steady growth since 1995, with turnover increasing from £4.1 million in 1995 to £8.2 million in 1998, and this growth has been generated both organically and through acquisition.

Throughout this period Compass Cleaning has benefited from venture capital support with an initial investment in 1994 of £250,000 by 3i Plc, the leading venture capitalist. This allowed Compass Cleaning to grasp an opportunity to increase its trade with a major supermarket retailer. In return for this investment, the venture capitalist secured a minority stake in the business.

Towards the end of 1998, Compass Cleaning was ready for the next step change in the growth plans. This involved the acquisition of West Riding Cleaning Company, which enabled Compass Cleaning to double its turnover, expanding into a new and significant client base, including Sainsbury's and Boots, across a wider geographic spread.

The acquisition required a second stage venture capital investment. The well established relationship meant that 3i understood and were comfortable with the management's plans and were able to act quickly to provide an injection of £650,000 which, when combined with bank funding, allowed the transaction to complete in August 1998.

To reflect the increased level of investment in Compass Cleaning, the shareholding attributable to 3i increased by 15 per cent, but remained a minority stake.

In summary, venture capital is undoubtedly a key source of funding. Key characteristics include:

- being specifically designed for high growth businesses;
- focusing on excellent management with a sound business case;
- requiring a high rate of return generated by an exit in the short to medium term;
- resulting in significant equity dilution for the existing shareholders.

Business angel/private investor

The venture capitalist may claim to be the natural choice for risk capital to finance all young and rapidly growing companies, however, there is a view that start-up and very early stage growth companies are relatively unattractive to the venture capitalist. This is due to the very high risk nature of the investment and the small sums that can be involved – in some cases less than £100,000.

If there is a funding gap at the start-up or early growth stage, it may well be filled by the business angel. The concept of the business angel has developed from the increasing pool of successful entrepreneurs that have generated significant personal wealth and are looking to invest some of that wealth and experience in young growing businesses. The differences between a business angel and a venture capitalist, in terms of approach and size of investment, are demonstrated in Tables 6.4 and 6.5.

The benefit of a business angel to the growing business is clear. Firstly, and most obviously, a funding requirement is satisfied. Thereafter, the lack of complexity involved in the transaction, lower returns and the ability of a business angel to get directly involved in the running of the business make the business angel an attractive prospect.

A variation on the business angel theme is the situation where a wealthy individual or group is prepared to invest in a business on the basis of the opportunity presented, without getting actively involved in the running of the business.

Table 6.4 Differences in approach

Characteristic	Business angels	Venture capitalists
Investor	Entrepreneurs	Institutions
Firms funded	Small, early stage	Track record, more mature
Due diligence done	Minimal	Extensive
Location	Important	Not important
Legal contracts	Simple	Comprehensive
Involvement/monitoring	Active 'hands-on'	Strategic
Exit	Of lesser concern	Highly important
Rates of return	Of lesser concern	Highly important

Table 6.5 Size of investment

	Business angels	Venture capitalists
Average value of business funded	£288,000	£3,254,000
Average amount invested	£55,000	£945,000

In both cases the extent of the investment does not always have to be small.

TRANSLINC

TransLinc, formally the vehicle contract hire and transport services division of Lincoln-shire County Council, was acquired by its management and employees in March 1998 for a consideration in excess of £7 million. One would expect such a transaction to be funded in part by venture capital. In this case, however, it was a prominent local businessman who provided the risk capital, investing approximately £3 million.

It was not only competitive pricing which won the day for the local businessman against the venture capital competition, but his ability to apply direct experience of succeeding in the commercial world was considered hugely valuable to a business coming out of local authority control.

Whilst raising finance through a business angel is becoming more popular, there are obvious problems including:

- identifying appropriate individuals – they are not as immediately accessible as venture capitalists;

- the level of hands-on involvement and control required by the business angel;

- potential for personality clashes – you are dealing with individuals not corporations;

- inability to provide second stage funding – resources may be limited.

Personal wealth

Last but not least, equity capital can be raised from the personal resources of the existing shareholders, and this can range from savings accounts to the use of personal loans. This will certainly be the case in a start-up situation and will apply in early stage companies.

A study found that only 23 per cent of small high growth companies heavily utilise outside funding in their earliest stages, whilst 27 per cent use a mix of self and outside funding, and the remaining 50 per cent are primarily self-funded (see M. Van Osnabrugge, *Comparison of Business Angels and Venture Capitalists*).

When outside funding is sourced, shareholders may well be obliged to make further investments alongside venture capitalists as a demonstration of serious commitment.

Whilst investment of significant personal wealth will certainly put the risk factors into sharp focus, it should be remembered that the more you can fund yourself, the less equity dilution you will suffer, and the greater the share of the gain you will enjoy when ultimate success is achieved.

Debt finance

The key characteristics of debt finance are that:

(a) interest on borrowings have to be paid promptly when they are due, unlike dividends on shares; and

(b) most borrowings have to be repaid by a certain date, following an agreed repayment profile, unlike ordinary share capital which is only repaid on sale or liquidation.

In addition, many forms of borrowings are secured on the assets of the business. Therefore, if interest or capital repayments are not met, the lender can revert to the security value held in the particular asset in exactly the same way as a mortgage is secured on the value of the home.

The commitment to pay interest and meet capital repayments, combined with the added asset security, means that the risk to a lender is much less than the risk to an equity investor. As a result, the cost of debt finance is considerably cheaper than equity finance and therefore should, theoretically, always be a preferable source of funding for all businesses.

This argument is valid up to a point. The business must be able to meet interest and repayment commitments every year, and this can put a business under severe pressure in a bad year. This can be demonstrated by way of an example.

EXAMPLE

Company Y is funded wholly by equity and Company Z is financed half by equity and half by debt.

The implications of the alternative funding structures, using a variety of financial performance criteria are examined in the table below:

Company Y

| Equity (£1 shares) | £1,000,000 | | |
| Debt (10% interest) | Nil | | |

	Good year £000	Average year £000	Poor year £000
Operating profit	250	150	50
Interest	–	–	–
Profit before tax	250	150	50
Taxation @ 30%	(75)	(45)	(15)
Profit after tax	175	105	35
Earnings per share	17.5p	10.5p	3.5p

Company Z

| Equity (£1 shares) | £500,000 |
| Debt (10% interest) | £500,000 |

	Good year £000	Average year £000	Poor year £000
Operating profit	250	150	50
Interest	(50)	(50)	(50)
Profit before tax	200	100	0
Taxation @ 30%	(60)	(30)	0
Profit after tax	140	70	0
Earnings per share	28p	14p	0p

In good and average years, the funding structure of Company Z results in an increase in the earnings per share for shareholders. However, in a poor year, when the interest commitments still have to be met, it cannot make a profit. By contrast, Company Y can still make a return for shareholders even in a poor year.

The extent of reliance on debt is a key measure when considering the financial stability of a company. There are a number of methods of measuring a company's overall borrowing position. The principal measure is 'gearing', which is most commonly defined as loan capital plus bank and other borrowings, expressed as a ratio of shareholders' funds. This relationship is illustrated in Table 6.6.

Table 6.6 Gearing

Debt	£000
Loan capital	1,000
Bank overdraft	200
	1,200
Shareholders' funds	
Ordinary shares	100
Reserves	1,100
	1,200
Gearing	1:1 or 100%

In most businesses a gearing percentage of 50 per cent would be considered attractive, although combined with steady profits and sustainable cash flows, businesses can manage comfortably at a much higher level. By contrast, companies in highly cyclical markets would be well advised to keep gearing levels low.

The lessons from this analysis are that debt finance can, and should, form an important part of the funding package for any business, including a growing business. However, a balance should be maintained to ensure that the commitments associated with debt do not place too great a burden on the business.

There are a whole range of debt-based products available. Some, such as bonds and debentures issued on financial markets, are more appropriate for long-established companies, but there are still plenty of other options to consider.

Sources of debt finance

Overdraft

For many, the most obvious and apparently the most accessible form of debt finance is an overdraft. Whilst an overdraft certainly has a place in the overall funding structure of a business, its use should be restricted to dealing with the short-term cash requirements (working capital) that are a normal part of ongoing trading. An overdraft should not be used as a basis for funding the long-term growth of a business. This is because:

(a) it can be expensive – a company is charged for an overdraft facility even when it is not used;

(b) it can be withdrawn – the facility is repayable on demand and can be withdrawn at short notice.

Start-up/small company loans

Whilst most debt financiers would acknowledge the pressing need for well structured funding to be allocated to start-up and small companies, the lack of security and absence of track record makes this difficult. One way around this has been the establishment of the government guaranteed loan scheme.

Arranged by the DTI, through most of the major clearing banks and other financial institutions, the key characteristics of the government guaranteed loan scheme are as follows:

- general purpose finance for businesses lacking security or track record;

127

- the Government guarantees a proportion of each loan made under the scheme (70 per cent to 80 per cent);
- available for capital projects or as working capital;
- minimum £5,000 – maximum £250,000;
- loan period 2 to 20 years;
- certain categories of businesses excluded.

The scheme is recognised as a useful and practical source of finance for the young business. However, its continued existence depends entirely on the ongoing support of central government.

Traditional debt

Traditional debt provided by banks can be the cornerstone of the funding requirements for a growing business. By clearly defining the size, interest charge and repayment profile, traditional debt provides the framework around which the rest of the funding structure can be designed.

The starting point for banks is that they want to ensure, as far as possible, that the business can afford to pay back the borrowing. In consideration of this fundamental point, the bank will first assess the quality of the security that lies within the assets that underpin the business. A business with a strong balance sheet that incorporates unencumbered (i.e., no loans secured against) property assets, plant and machinery, stock, trade debtors, etc. will present a very attractive prospect for bank lending. The terms issued will reflect this.

COMMER GROUP

Commer Group, a leading independent pub operator with an aggressive growth strategy, acquired pubs with a value of £2.89 million, obtaining debt finance of approximately 75 per cent of this value repayable over a 12-year period. The strong security inherent in the pubs acquired allowed debt financiers to be generous in terms of the size and term of the loan.

In most situations, banks will formalise the security they have over a business by creating fixed and floating charges over the assets of the business.

- *A fixed charge*, similar to the mortgage on a house, provides the lender with a legal interest in a specific asset. If the company defaults in repayment of the loan, the lender can, for example, appoint a receiver to take possession and sell the asset.

- *A floating charge* provides more general rights over all the remaining assets of the business, which again can be invoked on the default of a loan.

For many businesses, and particularly young businesses or businesses in the service sector, the asset back-up or underpin may be minimal. However, this does not necessarily preclude them from debt finance. In certain circumstances, it is possible to raise debt on the back of a steady and predictable cash flow, albeit at a higher cost, lower quantum and for a shorter term, with five to seven year periods not being uncommon.

Banks will look at a variety of measures in order to identify the true 'debt capacity' of a business. These will then be translated into a schedule of covenants made up of ratios and measurements, within which the business must operate, if it is not to default on the terms of the loan. A typical covenant schedule could read as in Table 6.7.

Table 6.7 Typical covenant schedule

Covenant	Measure
1 Loan to asset value ratio	60%
2 Interest cover ratio	3:1
3 Cash flow cover	2:1
4 Total gearing	70%

Notes:
1 The total loan outstanding must not exceed 60 per cent of the value of the identified assets.
2 The annual interest charge must be three times covered by profit before interest and tax (PBIT).
3 Interest and capital repayments made to the bank must be twice covered by free cash flow.
4 Total debt cannot exceed 70 per cent of shareholders' funds.

Covenants provide the bank with a measure of control over the business. They will be monitored closely and regularly and, if breached, the bank can invoke certain rights, such as an investigation into the business by independent accountants. However, when there has been a fundamental deterioration in the performance of the business, protection provided through covenants may prove inadequate. In such a situation, the bank will revert to the security, and the fixed and floating charges it has over the assets of the business.

Whilst traditional debt provides the bedrock of funding for businesses, there is often a gap between the funding requirement, and the level of traditional debt available. This gap is often filled by equity providers.

Acknowledging the wishes of businesses to reduce the cost of equity, in terms of return and dilution, banks have designed more sophisticated debt-based products to fill the funding gap. Such a product is mezzanine debt.

Mezzanine debt

Mezzanine debt, as its name suggests, provides a layer of debt on top of traditional debt. Ranking after traditional debt in terms of security, mezzanine debt is usually repaid in one total payment (known as a bullet repayment) between five and ten years after being taken out. This is clearly a higher risk for the bank, and a greater return commensurate with that risk is earned by the bank through:

- high interest rates;
- premium on the bullet repayment;
- potential conversion into a small equity stake on flotation or sale of the company.

Based on current market conditions, total returns to the mezzanine provider may be in the region of 20 per cent, compared to 9 per cent to the provider of traditional debt, and 25 per cent to 35 per cent to the venture capital equity provider.

The example below illustrates the use of mezzanine debt.

EXAMPLE

Baris UK Limited, a specialist sub-contractor, was acquired from its parent company in a management buyout, using the following financial structure, to meet the consideration and to fund ongoing growth:

	£000
Traditional debt	700
Mezzanine debt	250
Equity	300
Total funds raised	1,250

The mezzanine debt attracted an annual interest rate of 4 per cent above bank base rate and was repayable in full at the end of five years. The strong projected cash flows of the business demonstrated that the higher cost debt could be serviced and repaid. If mezzanine debt had not been utilised, the funding gap would have been filled by venture capital involving the release of 10 per cent to 20 per cent of equity by the management team.

Mezzanine debt is an attractive and realistic option for the growing business, particularly as it minimises the requirement to release valuable equity. However, it is absolutely fundamental that the business has strong and sustainable cash flow from which to meet the premium, interest and the full repayment. Mezzanine finance is still a debt that must be repaid. Over-reliance, particularly during economic downturns, can place severe pressure on the business.

Asset-based debt

In contrast to traditional senior debt and mezzanine debt which are secured on the back of stated business performance supported by the asset underpin, asset-based finance focuses on specific assets or group of assets. Asset-based finance can be applied to fixed assets such as plant and machinery, equipment or motor vehicles and current assets such as stock and trade debtors.

Asset-based finance can be very relevant for the growing business. Lease or hire purchase, for example, can be used to provide the machinery required for production. Instead of having to pay a large lump sum out of cash resources, a lease or hire purchase agreement allows the business to spread the payments over a period of time. This enables the business to match future revenues received from the utilisation of the extra productive capacity against the lease or hire purchase payments.

Invoice discounting and debt factoring

Invoice discounting and debt factoring have developed to become very important financing tools for the growing business. Very often, cash is locked up in trade debtors and may not be realised for some months. An invoice discounting facility may allow a company to draw down cash to a greater extent than would be available via an overdraft facility, sometimes up to 85 per cent of the value of the debtors. But how can this be done?

This type of facility is granted through a close examination of the debtor profile of the business and identification of specific attributes including:

- good debt collection record;
- no over-reliance on key customers;
- robust customer profile including blue chip clients;
- low levels of returns or credit notes;
- normal trade debts, not contract debtors, for example;
- good accounting systems.

The invoice discounting firm will satisfy itself in respect of these matters through an audit, and by maintaining a close ongoing relationship with the client. In certain circumstances they may take over the running of the debtors ledger by providing a factoring service.

As the business grows, the level of trade debtors will also grow. The cash available from an invoice discounting facility will increase proportionally, providing automatic support for growth. This is the key attraction of this type of facility. On the downside, there is a perception that once into an invoice discounting arrangement it is very difficult to get out of it, and an awareness that if there is a downturn in business, the facility will shrink at a time when stable funding support may be required. Nevertheless, with careful management invoice discounting provides a very useful option for the growing business.

Working capital management

All the methods of finance described above are provided by external bodies.

Whilst third parties will almost certainly contribute to the funding structure of the growing business, there is much that the company can achieve itself through pro-active working capital management. This is discussed within Chapter 4. However, the following simple example demonstrates how working capital can be manipulated to generate additional cash.

Table 6.8 represents a high growth start-up business with standard working capital ratios:

- stock – 60 days of gross sales (60/365 × turnover)
- debtors – 90 days of gross sales (90/365 × turnover)
- creditors – 90 days of gross costs (90/365 × costs)

Table 6.8 Standard working capital ratios			
P&L	Year 1 £000	Year 2 £000	Year 3 £000
Sales	2,000	3,000	4,000
Costs	(1,500)	(2,250)	(3,000)
Profit	500	750	1,000
Balance sheet			
Stock	333	500	666
Debtors	493	739	986
Cash	43	565	1,337
Creditors	(369)	(554)	(739)
	500	1,250	2,250
P&L reserves	500	1,250	2,250

Table 6.8 demonstrates quite clearly that cash growth can trail profitability by a considerable extent. The cash impact of growth is 'locked up' in stock and debtors. By improving the working capital relationships, reducing stock levels, reducing debtor payment cycles, extending creditor payment cycles, etc., cash resources can be released for use elsewhere in the business.

On applying the following working capital ratios, the improvement in cash is immediately apparent in Table 6.9:

- stock – 30 days of gross sales;
- debtors – 60 days of gross sales;
- creditors – 95 days of gross sales.

Table 6.9 Improving working capital ratios

P&L	Year 1 £000	Year 2 £000	Year 3 £000
Sales	2,000	3,000	4,000
Costs	(1,500)	(2,250)	(3,000)
Profit	500	750	1,000
Balance sheet			
Stock	166	250	333
Debtors	328	493	657
Cash	396	1,092	2,040
Creditors	(390)	(585)	(780)
	500	1,250	2,250
P&L reserves	500	1,250	2,250

Pro-active working capital strategies that can increase cash generation include those shown in Table 6.10.

Table 6.10   Pro-active working capital strategies

Asset/(liability)	Target	Strategy
Stock	Decrease	• 'Just in Time' management • Improved production systems • Improved buying patterns
Trade debtors	Decrease	• Establish formal credit control • Credit check new customers • Improve terms of trade • Discount for early payment
(Trade creditors)	Increase	• Lengthen payment cycle • Negotiate instalment payment • Improve terms of trade

---

Whilst all the above are legitimate and recommended policies for a cash-conscious company, they should not be taken so far as to harm commercial relationships with customers and suppliers. Otherwise, time will be absorbed managing disputes, with an associated cost that may negate any cash flow improvement achieved.

Conclusion

There is no standard formula to apply for financing a growing business. Much depends on the type of business, the stage of development, and the products that are available at the time. Figure 6.1 provides a broad summary.

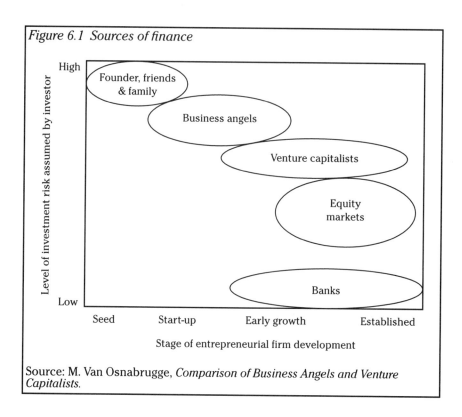

Figure 6.1 Sources of finance

Source: M. Van Osnabrugge, *Comparison of Business Angels and Venture Capitalists*.

What is fundamental is to ensure that time is taken to put together a funding structure that is appropriate, and that this is reviewed on a regular basis. You cannot afford to think 'let the business run and the finance will look after itself'.

Another important watchword is 'balance'. Do not place over-reliance on one particular type of funding – ensure you have a good mix, particularly between equity and debt.

7

Seeing around corners

Introduction

By now you and your business managers will be aware of working in an environment that can sometimes appear full of pitfalls, traps and regulations. The sense of walking a tightrope between success and failure is not uncommon as the business grows, and unforeseen risks or diversions can be unwelcome visitors as you try to negotiate a clear course for the business.

At the same time, you will be aware that risk forms an integral part of business life, indeed, it is the risks that you take that generate the rewards. The way you identify, assess and respond to those risks is therefore important to the success of your business, and this is why businesses are increasingly devoting more time to risk management.

In this chapter we examine risk in its many forms, whether it is regulatory, failure of business systems or the loss of a key person.

We will discuss later in the chapter a methodology for defining the key risks in your business, by identifying a broad range of risks, assessing the potential impact on the business, and developing a response which will help you manage those risks. As well as covering a broad spectrum of risks, we look in detail at specific areas of general risk which will impact on businesses, such as the introduction of the euro and the year 2000 issue.

We also consider the dynamic nature of risk management and the constant need to reassess risk because of the changes to your risk profile as the business passes through the various stages of growth. More specifically, we explore the stage in a company's growth at which an understanding of the company's risk profile will allow it to successfully overhaul the business and regain the focus to achieve further growth.

The overhauling stage

The business has passed through the early stages of growth and has matured, with emphasis now being placed on control and professionalism, to cope with the increasing size and complexity of its operations. Size and control dampen the entrepreneurial spirit, the business begins to lose touch with its market and there is a mismatch between the market objectives of the business and its management.

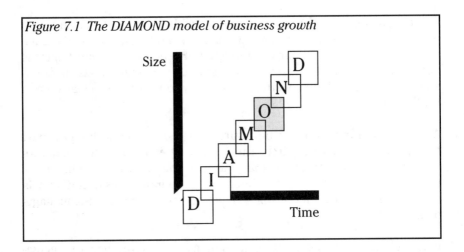

Figure 7.1 The DIAMOND model of business growth

The overhauling stage recognises these features as risks going to the heart of the business. The demise may be slow, but once a business loses market focus and fails to motivate or incentivise its management, it can begin to drift.

Characteristics

The characteristics of businesses at the overhauling stage of growth are summarised below:

- teams/individuals held accountable for results

- incentive offered for good performance

- improved customer/marketing focus

- influx of high quality people

At the overhauling stage the business regains its direction through reorientation and a clear focus on objectives and accountability. This can re-energise the business. The example of JSC illustrates this.

JSC

JSC started life as a family farm. The opportunities for processing rather than growing produce were identified by the founder in the 1970s, who saw the possibilities in taking other farmers' produce and adding value by cleaning and sorting vegetables. Close relationships with the supplier base and good distribution channels allowed the company to grow rapidly, increasing its throughput in the 1980s and developing a strong distribution network servicing wholesale markets.

The company grew its business largely on the back of volumes – expanding its processing capacity several times. At the end of the 1980s the founder retired, passing on a well established business to his sons. The market, however, was increasingly showing signs of strain, the product essentially being a commodity, and the cleaning and sorting process adding little value. Moreover, the main customers for the basic product were supermarkets, who were also looking at low margins on high volumes and were increasing their stranglehold on the supply base.

In a traditionally low cost, low profit sector, the second generation management recognised the strength of the business they had inherited, but also some market-place weaknesses. The founder's elder son, a business graduate, set about refocusing the business. Recognising the risk of staying in the volume end of the market, the management set about identifying where value could be added to the product. What type of customers would pay a higher price for the same raw material and why?

Over the next few years the emphasis was changed away from the traditional sorting and cleaning to pre-prepared vegetables for the catering industry. Management had focused on the life cycle of their product and where the waste was incurred in the business. They identified an end-user who was not price-sensitive – what they would

pay for was a product that saved them time. In addition, the business could use produce which would have been waste in the traditional process.

Management's conviction was supported by investment in bespoke machinery. They
also looked carefully at business operations and the true cost of servicing a customer.
How would they ensure the retention of their workforce and management? There
followed a clear set of principles by which the business was run. The team was
strengthened, particularly in financial management. Business performance was monitored on a daily basis and clear focus was put on customer quality. Perhaps most
importantly, the added-value concept was spread to other products and is now deeply
embedded in the culture of the business.

Throughout the 1990s the business grew in terms of both turnover and profits, turning
over £5 million in 1998 with profits of over £500,000. The overhaul has given the
business even greater prospects. A strong asset base, excellent distribution channels
and good supplier relationships are the building blocks to further profitable growth,
while other sectors in their market suffer from profit erosion

Transitional issues

The transitional issues confronting organisations at this stage include:

- business could run away with its own success

- overpromise – underdeliver

- burnout (people and concept)

Regaining energy and direction in the business starts with understanding where the business is by analysing your position. The ability
to assess and respond to your risk profile is an important part of
this process. It will give you the depth of analysis to restructure
your business and develop its opportunities, whilst controlling the
risk.

Maintaining growth – the risk of stagnation

There are numerous examples of companies which have not been able
to move with the times and have suffered as the economy, their

competitors, the market, etc. has moved on around them. This can be a 'creeping death', as the impact is not felt suddenly but over a period of time, as competitors' businesses and products improve, whilst the business relies on the 'tried and trusted' and slowly loses market share. As Victor Kiam said, 'procrastination is opportunity's natural assassin'. A business might find itself in this position after years of successful growth for a number of reasons.

(a) Management and key shareholders are content with the living that the business is providing and are not prepared to take the risk of further development. The age profile may mean that income is more important than investment, and time scales are short-term for the key influencers of the business.

(b) 'Success breeds contempt'. A successful business may not have recognised the signs of maturing, and investment in future growth is secondary to short-term profitability. Some complacency has crept into the business.

(c) The business has lost its driver. For instance, a second generation family business may no longer have the skills or the drive to re-create the original growth.

(d) Younger members of the management team who are capable of generating the growth may lack the decision-making powers because of the shareholding structure.

(e) The team is capable of running the existing business, but does not have the acumen to take the business through the next cycle of growth.

(f) The products are getting tired and falling behind the competitor's products because of lack of investment or innovation.

A more mature business is likely to have established controls and systems for managing the business, a management team supporting all the key functions and a formal approach to communication, for instance through board meetings and structured management meetings. Planning will be forming an increasingly important part of the business and will probably be formalised into strategy and detailed forward forecasting.

Whilst all these features give a business structure, and in theory the ability to react more quickly to customers' demands, creeping bureaucracy and the dilution of the entrepreneurial aspects of the business present management with a number of issues, if they are to continue to grow the business.

In order to grow further, therefore, the business must address these underlying issues to guard against maturity becoming stagnation.

The response to the circumstances will depend on management's ability to recognise the need to overhaul the business. What worked before cannot be assumed to work in the future. The business must focus on its objectives and revisit every aspect of the business. For example, does the business have the right management skills? Are executives motivated and incentivised to grow the business? Do we have the right focus on the market and the customer? Do we have to revise our product or market offering?

THE DENBY GROUP PLC

In the late 1980s Denby Potteries had run into hard times. It was one part of a group, with four other businesses, in the glass and tableware industry which shared combined central head office functions. Coloroll acquired the business in 1987 and took the decision to decentralise the head offices, such that each of the individual businesses, including Denby, had its own design, accountancy and management teams. This was a crucial decision in turning around the fortunes of Denby.

At the time of the takeover by Coloroll, Denby was overstocked and so were its retailers due to over-production. The new local management team cut the product range from 3,500 lines down to only 850, leading to increased efficiency in production processes. Additionally, the design function now set about redesigning and replacing the existing products.

Such an overhaul of strategic direction and aspirations takes time. In Denby's case, this process took 18 months from the start of the redesign process through to evidence of success through sales growth.

Following Coloroll's receivership in 1990, the management team of Denby undertook an MBO from the receiver and, based around a number of the overhauling strategies that had initially been made possible by Coloroll's decision to decentralise head office functions, started to grow the business again.

The post-MBO team implemented a number of strategies to take the business forward into the future.

Firstly, there was a refocus on market sectors. The management team decided to target a real growth market sector, and to create significant competitive advantage.

They reduced the product range even further, through a process of examining consumer trends and consumer dynamics, and were able to identify a number of potential growing markets in what historically had been a relatively mature industry.

The principal consumer trend was a move to more eating and living in the kitchen, where previously families had used dining rooms. There was now a trend to having an attractive kitchen environment. Having observed this, Denby decided that the optimum strategy would be to focus on attractive, practical design-led kitchen products rather than formal dining products and giftware. The design team then refocused its efforts to this strategy, and a review of internal systems took place. This reduced the time lag from design through to production, thereby allowing the business to be more flexible and responsive to consumer demands.

The second issue that was addressed was that of heavy discounting of the product. This had occurred during difficult trading conditions in the late 1980s. The management team were of the opinion that the depth of discounting did not significantly benefit the retail proposition for their target customers, and reducing the discounts would not significantly reduce their sales. In order to prove this, there was a gradual and hard fought battle to reduce, in three stages, the level of discounts provided to retailers in the UK. This was essential in order to maintain the brand positioning that was sought by the management team, that of a high quality, well perceived but practical kitchenware brand.

A further issue that had to be tackled by the management team was the actual retail outlets through which the company's products where sold. During the late 1980s, there had been almost a 'stack them high sell them cheap' approach. With the new focus on a high quality brand for Denby, there was effort made to focus on quality stores to ensure consistency with the brand image. Products were sold through the John Lewis Partnership, Debenhams and other well known and reputable high street stores. This had a significant effect in that brand loyalty and brand quality significantly increased, and had substantial positive effects on turnover and margins.

The turnaround for Denby has been significant. In 1998, sales turnover had risen to £35 million with profit before tax on the continuing business of £6.9 million.

Understanding your risk profile

As a business you face a range of risks and your ability to identify which are specific to your business is important. In the following pages, we take you through a process of distilling risks, so that you can focus your resources on those areas which will have the greatest impact on your business.

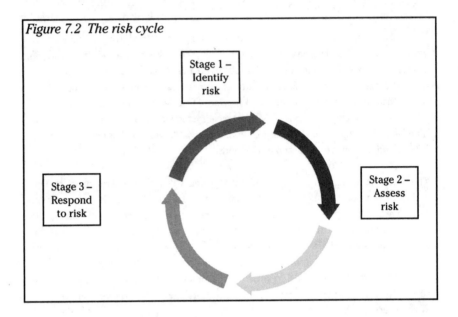

Figure 7.2 The risk cycle

In the simple model shown at Figure 7.2, three distinct stages of the process are represented:

- risk identification – an understanding of both your internal and external risks

- risk assessment – having identified your risks, what is the potential impact on the business?

- risk response – 'close the circle' by developing responses which will control or minimise the impact of your risks

Identification

Businesses need to understand the difference between internal and external risks. Naturally, you will be able to influence internal factors more readily. The business has little control over external risk, but understanding the issues will help manage those risks more effectively.

Assessment

Deciding on how you might respond to a risk will depend on your assessment of the impact of an event occurring. Is it likely to happen? If so, what will be its impact? Do not spend much time developing responses to possible events if, in the worst case, the cost is one that could easily be borne by the business.

Response

Your response should fit the risk. There are many ways of insuring against specific circumstances which, although unlikely, would be disastrous if they occurred. You may refocus resources; for instance, you may concentrate on debt collection in recessionary times, or in extreme circumstances you may withdraw from a particular market. For example, a number of businesses left the Russian marketplace during 1998 following the collapse of the rouble.

Importantly, the process depicted in Figure 7.2 is shown as cyclical, demonstrating the need to reassess your risk profile on a regular and systematic basis. For instance, moving towards an economic slowdown, e.g., falling sales, or supplier failure are being identified more regularly as risks. Also, millennium compliance risks, whilst significant for any business, are transitionary.

Identifying risks

When you make a business decision, focusing on the risk of making the wrong move is a natural response. For instance, when a business considers making an acquisition or buying new plant it may draw up detailed plans, forecasts, etc. and fully assess its decision. A business faces many less obvious day-to-day risks, for example:

(a) The general regulatory environment – that is, what is expected from the business by laws and regulations, such as those relating to reporting, health and safety and the environment. Does the business operate in a particularly sensitive regulatory environment, and would non-compliance restrict its ability to operate?

(b) The implications of economic or political change or more specific issues such as the 'millennium bug' or the introduction of the euro.

145

(c) Specific risks relating to the business and its internal management structure. Is it strong enough or flexible enough to survive a significant change in the marketplace?

(d) Do the dynamics of the management team or the age profile bring its own risks? Has management succession been considered, for instance?

(e) What would happen if a key business manager were to leave, become disabled or die?

In order to start to narrow down these risks, we shall examine some generic risk sources. We start with the process of defining internal and external risk.

Table 7.1 Internal and external risk	
Internal	*External*
Products People Business infrastructure, processes and systems	The economy Social factors Political and regulatory framework The environment

Internal risk factors

Products

There will be risks associated with your product or service. These will vary and could range from the product not being marketable to the risk that the product could damage a third party.

Competition – your competitors will be working to produce better products at cheaper prices and, unless you enjoy a very specialised or protected niche, a competitor launching a better or cheaper product will be a significant risk to your business.

UK textiles manufacturers began to suffer in the 1970s and 1980s as cheaper imports from the Far East eroded their profitability. The motor industry and others suffered a similar fate. This was a significant change in the marketplace, and many UK manufacturers responded by looking for cheaper sources of supply in low cost locations themselves.

Customers and market changes – markets and customer requirements, perceptions and expectations change. If your product has a high fashion content, you will be aware how fickle markets and customers can be. An example of this is seen in the holiday industry in the last 30 years, with the growth of cheap holidays overseas.

Quality – poor quality is generally associated with loss of customers, but what about product returns or, even worse, damage to a third party? Some highly regulated businesses have very defined quality standards. Nike, the sportswear group, had to recall a sports shoe in 1998 because of a series of customer complaints.

Technological change – technology is relevant to many products and services, either directly, or because of its use in the production process. Recent advances in technology have changed many areas of business, including infrastructure, production processes and communication. Products such as the typewriter have become almost obsolete as businesses invest to gain competitive advantage. This is an example of a device which has been superseded by faster, better devices. Similarly, products in technologically dynamic environments, such as telecommunications or information systems, have been superseded with increasing rapidity.

Suppliers – your customer will not be interested in supplier failure, and suppliers can fail you in quality, delivery or service. They also go out of business. How good is your supply chain management?

People

Skills and experience – people are assets. Could you succeed without the skills and experience of your management and workforce? Lack of appropriate skills or experience is a significant risk and this applies just as much to shop floor skills as to the senior management team.

Fraud and error – people make mistakes or can be dishonest. These can present significant risks if there are not mechanisms to identify and control them. Do not be 'blinkered' in this – it is much wider than the 'hand in the till'. What about theft of your product ideas and intellectual property? In reality, the full impact of fraud is significantly under-reported because of the desire not to publicise control failings.

Beware also of the 'Peter principle': 'In a hierarchy, any employee tends to rise to his position of incompetence' (Dr Lawrence J. Peter). Barings

Bank was brought to its knees by a 'rogue trader' after many years of successful trading. Whether this was the outcome of incompetence, dishonesty or the impact of giving authority without control is unclear.

Industrial action – disrupted production will probably mean loss of business, not just for the period of the action but possibly for the longer term. A disaffected workforce can also frustrate management's objectives.

Business infrastructure, processes and systems

Planning – to put it simply, a lack of planning will greatly enhance the risk of failure.

Control – a series of strong focused controls will reduce risk, because it enables the business to take action early enough for the response to be effective. Inadequate control will lead the business into areas of risk that it may have been possible to avoid. Give yourself a 'bird's eye view' or have a 'look-out'.

Systems breakdown – increasingly, businesses rely on complex systems which can fail. If there is no action plan or contingency arrangement then breakdown of a system can have a catastrophic impact on the business. This issue has heightened relevance as we approach the millennium.

External risk factors

The economy

Peaks and troughs in economic activity are familiar, and a reliable crystal ball would be useful if it were available. Unfortunately, it is not, and much is left to our ability to predict future economic trends from limited information. Whether it is the recessionary conditions at the beginning of the 1990s, the strengthening of sterling in 1996 or the collapse of the Japanese economy in 1997, these events will impact on businesses.

Although predicting economic trends is notoriously difficult – as is evidenced by the range of forecasts from authoritative sources – there is an increasing amount of detailed research available. In particular, the number of independent surveys that are now being undertaken means that a consensus view can be formed. By regularly reviewing published information, and possibly more specific market research, you should be able to form a view of the economy and the implications of change for your business. Two examples which highlight the impact of structural change follow.

EXAMPLE

Company A specialised in point of sale advertising moving into the recession of the early 1990s. Despite being profitable since incorporation, the business had failed to diversify out of a sector which was highly susceptible to economic downturn. Advertising and marketing budgets were cut as companies sought to impose cost restraint and business in this sector simply dried up.

EXAMPLE

Company B exported over 70 per cent of its products into Benelux countries, invoicing in sterling. After a highly successful period in the mid-1990s, profits and cash flow were decimated as sterling strengthened against other European currencies.

Social factors

Society changes in its views of fashion and its buying patterns. Moreover, demographic changes such as the impact of the 1960s baby boom influence buying patterns. We have also seen changes in mobility, working patterns and family structures in recent years.

Political and regulatory framework

There is an impact of political action on your business which is distinct from economic policy, interest rate changes or tax legislation. Your business may be highly regulated – insurance brokers for instance – or may suffer directly from government action or comment. Examples of this include the impact on food products (beef and eggs), and there are also more general risks such as failure to comply with the law, for instance environmental or employment laws.

149

EXAMPLE

Company C is a supplier of specialist educational products to schools. The directors have an awareness of political change because of its impact on the education sector. The focus on literacy and numeracy introduced by the Labour Government diverted buying power from their traditional products. Flexibility in design and supply has enabled the company to respond to a significant change in their marketplace.

Increasingly, it is not just the environment that is impacting businesses, but social attitudes towards environmental control. Environmentally unfriendly businesses face increasing costs (tipping and disposal), whilst recycling businesses have identified opportunities in the hardening social and regulatory attitude towards environmentally damaging actions.

The environment

Is your business affected by the environment? Your business may be dependent on weather (e.g., farming, the holiday industry) – sales of soft drinks, ice creams, leisurewear and sun protection products depend to a large extent on people being outside in the sun.

Using the example of a UK-based manufacturing business producing products for large warehousing installations, the following risk areas have been identified in Table 7.2. This provides a useful illustration of the application of risk assessment techniques to an organisation.

Having identified the internal risk factors, we need to identify those areas of the business which are 'at risk', i.e., which assets could be damaged. We use the term 'assets' loosely to cover any facet of the business that might be affected, for instance:

- your product or service;
- your people;
- other tangible assets;
- your business infrastructure;
- your funding;
- the intangible worth of the business.

Table 7.2 Internal and external risk factors – UK manufacturing business	
Internal risk factors	*External risk factors*
Products • Patent design infringements • Safety products • Competitor move towards customisation **People** • Lack of skilled shop floor workers • Inflationary pressure due to other local employers • Three key managers due to retire in the next five years • Pressure on IT salaries due to demand in the market **Business infrastructure, processes and systems** • Year 2000 compliance • Lack of business-specific information to identify reasons for margin erosion • Process efficiency • Reliable supplier base • Disaster recovery	**The economy** • Recessionary conditions • EMU • Strength of sterling favouring competition in continental Europe **Social factors** • Attitudes to health and safety at work **Political and regulatory framework** • Reduced capital spending • Health and safety at work **The environment** • Waste disposal costs

Your product – your product may be impacted by poor quality or may be produced at a high cost because of poor buying or inefficient processes, supply failure, etc. In addition, your product could be copied if it is unprotected.

Your people – the impacts range from poor morale to actual physical injury. Your workforce is sensitive, liable to leave you and constantly seeking to increase its cost. Poor performance can reflect how your workforce feels, how it is treated and whether it is properly trained and has the relevant experience.

Other tangible assets – most businesses will have a range of other assets, from capital assets to debtors and cash. All these can be vulnerable, for instance through a bad debt or obsolescence of equipment.

Your business infrastructure – we refer here to the whole range of

151

processes, policies and systems which underpin your business. Your business may work very efficiently because of this infrastructure. Its failure or disruption may be damaging.

Your funding – many growth businesses could not survive without the support of a funder and his or her commitment to the business. This relationship is important and needs managing, particularly if performance is not meeting expectations.

The intangible worth of the business – the value of your business may be vested in its ability to generate profit or its reputation, rather than tangible assets. The value of the goodwill will grow where the business has a reputation for high quality products, timely delivery, etc. If these features deteriorate or there is adverse publicity, the value of the business can be damaged.

We have expressed the risks taken from our example in the matrix shown in Table 7.3. The next step is to consider the potential impact of the risk profile on the business.

Impact assessment – inherent and control risk

Having identified your specific risks, the business needs to consider the nature of the risk, for instance, whether it is inherent in your business environment or associated with your ability to control the risk. The concepts of inherent and control risk are widely used to understand the source of risk. We have defined them as:

> * **inherent risk** – a risk that exists in your business environment irrespective of the control procedures established to detect that risk or prevent a detrimental impact on the business.
>
> * **control risk** – the risk that your internal procedures or other controls do not detect the risk or prevent it having a detrimental impact on your business.

An everyday example is a busy airport. With several aeroplanes taking off and landing every minute there is an inherent risk that there will be a collision. In an uncontrolled environment, it would simply be a matter of time before there was a collision.

A highly controlled environment is the response, not only because of

Table 7.3 Risk identification matrix

Business assets	Internal factors			External factors			
	Business infrastructure	Products and services	People	The economy	Social factors	Political and Government	The environment
Your product	Technological change	Development Product safety	Skill shortages		Fashion	Legislation	Weather
Your people	Training incentivisation		Retirement of key management	Inflationary cost pressures	Demographics	Minimum wage	
Other assets			Fraud	Financial markets			
Your business Infrastructure	Planning reliable supplier base			Recessionary impact on suppliers			Natural disasters
Your funding	Credit control Forecasting			Interest rate increases Institutional constraint		Investment incentives	
The intangible worth of the business	Year 2000 compliance Lack of information	Competition	Loss of key employee	Falling profits		Taxation regime	Waste disposal costs

the level of risk but also because of the potential impact. Because of the need to maintain tight take-off and landing schedules, the inherent risk is accepted and does not change. Instead, the focus is on the control risk, i.e., the risk that the established systems will fail.

This is also relevant to other businesses because of the relationship between risk and reward. Simply by going into business, you are accepting risk and, generally, high risks are associated with higher rewards. It follows therefore that, whilst you may avoid certain high risk situations because of insufficient reward, you may actively pursue other high risk projects. Table 7.4 indicates how some inherent risk conditions could be responded to.

Table 7.4 Responses to inherent risk		
Examples	*Inherent risk*	*Response*
International trade	Currency fluctuations lead to losses	Foreign currency hedging
Few customers	Customer failure could have significant impact	Seek wider customer base. Vet and monitor customers closely
Retail	Theft	Security

The business can use inherent and control risks to assess the impact on its operations as follows (see Figure 7.3).

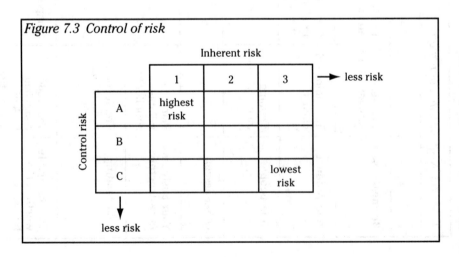

Figure 7.3 Control of risk

Firstly, assess the inherent risks you have identified into categories 1, 2 and 3, with 1 being the highest risk.

Now review the control procedures that you have in place to prevent that risk having an adverse impact. Grade the specific risks according to the strength of the control environment, with A being the highest risk (i.e., a poor control environment). You will now be able to refine your risk analysis, for instance:

A1 A high risk area in need of careful control and management. You have identified a high level inherent risk with little control in place to identify or negate the impact.

C3 A low risk area, it is considered a low level inherent risk and in any event there are controls to deal with it.

This process should help to define where resource is most effectively used. A C3 risk is not one you would normally focus significant resource on, whilst an A1 risk is an 'accident waiting to happen'. To be effective in the assessment, you will need to be clear what makes a risk a high risk.

This can be done by looking at:

• the likelihood of a risk condition having an impact on the business.

• the size of the impact.

This can be illustrated by a simple example familiar to most businesses – the risk of not being paid a debt that is due.

A business with a few large 'blue chip' customers may assess the inherent risk of not being paid as low. However, because the size of the individual debt is significant, management may consider that, although the inherent risk is low, (i.e., the event is unlikely) the impact of the event (i.e., the failure to pay) would be so significant as to merit taking further action to control the risk.

Commercially, a business with a spread debtor book of small companies with variable credit ratings may take the view that, although bad debts are likely to occur from time to time, the impact of a specific debt going bad would not be significant. Accordingly, management may accept this as a normal business risk and not respond further.

In the same way as we used control/inherent risk to grade risk earlier, we can use the incidence/impact method to assess a business's high and low level risks (see Figure 7.4).

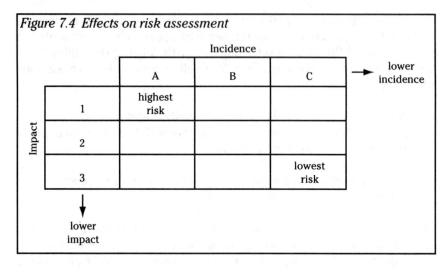

Figure 7.4 Effects on risk assessment

The analysis will help to define the high level risks so that they can be controlled or avoided. An A1 risk for instance should be avoided or highly controlled, and may also alter your assessment of the level of reward you require for operating in this area. In the example used above, a large debt with a customer with a poor credit rating would represent an A1 risk.

Risk is generated in not complying with certain regulations. For example, health and safety and environmental legislation applies to many businesses, and might be avoided until such time as an inspection is made. The consequences of failing to comply range from a small fine to the closure of the business. In most circumstances, the risk can be controlled by identifying what steps need to be taken to comply.

These risks are 'time bombs', i.e., circumstances which exist and which have an adverse impact, but which are uncertain in terms of timing. Either a business is alert to these factors and has planned ahead, or it simply buries its head in the sand and waits for the impact to happen.

At the other end of the risk profile are rather remote or unlikely events which, should they occur, would be potentially devastating to the business. Examples can include loss of a key manager, which could be particularly harmful in a smaller business, or a direct attack by a competitor on the business's key product.

Developing a risk response

A thorough risk review will equip a business with the knowledge to understand its risk profile and, in particular, the likelihood and consequence of certain events occurring. To be effective, this needs to be followed up by **actions** which respond to the risks.

You have several options:

(a) *Avoid* – you can choose to avoid the risk. This may be where you have identified a project as having both high risk incidence and impact as in our earlier example.

(b) *Acceptance and control* – understanding the nature of the risks allows you to develop specific central mechanisms to prevent, be forewarned of or reduce the impact. Good examples are disaster recovery plans. Remember, it is not just detection and prevention that are important but an effective response if an event does occur.

(c) *Accept and leave uncontrolled* – you may choose to leave the risk uncontrolled on the basis that the incidence and the impact is low. You take the view that the event is unlikely to occur and if it did the cost would not be significant.

By identifying and assessing your risks, the business is in a position to develop an effective response. For instance, consider the following examples.

EXAMPLE: KEY PERSONNEL

For key employees such as your operations or marketing manager, you might consider how a key individual would be replaced. Your assessment of the loss may range from minor inconvenience to almost irreplaceable and your response will naturally vary depending on this assessment. There is some merit in developing 'what if' scenarios, i.e., who would replace the individual and how that would be transitioned. You may conclude that a replacement could be recruited quickly, but in other circumstances there could be a strong need to ensure that succession plans are in place.

The loss of the key person will have a financial impact on the business and it is important not to underestimate what this impact could be, particularly in a smaller business where many of the functions and contacts are held by this person. An appropriate response may be to insure against the risk of loss through key man insurance. The same thought process may be followed for all 'assets' of the business. For instance, your

---

property, your IT system, etc., the loss of or damage to which would have a significant impact on the business. However, the risk of insuring against potential loss can be expensive particularly for a small business and should be weighed against the level of risk.

EXAMPLE: INTELLECTUAL PROPERTY

A risk common to businesses involved in product development is the effective loss of the product to a competitor, where the ownership of the product is inadequately protected. The initial investment and marketing costs are rarely shown on the balance sheet, but the ideas, drawings, etc., may be the most valuable asset of the business. In the formative days of the business, however, the expense of registering your ideas may appear to outweigh the benefits. This may be a source of some regret later. The value of intellectual property may outweigh anything else on the balance sheet, but if the rights are unprotected then the value may fall through your fingers.

We will examine two areas of risk, IT systems and the euro, which are pertinent to most businesses in more detail later in this chapter.

A changing risk environment

Perhaps the most important feature of risk assessment is recognising the dynamic nature of the business environment, the business and you, the individual. All these are changeable – a risk you might take in the initiating stage of growth, you may not consider taking at the maturing phase. Why is this? Let us consider those three elements:

- the business environment;
- the business;
- the individual.

The business environment

There are so many influences in this environment and most of them are generating change. Your competitors are working on new products, your people are considering their next career move, the Government is approving new legislation, etc.

158

The business

Elsewhere in the book we have discussed the stages of growth defined by the DIAMOND model of business growth. Although we have focused on the overhauling phase in this chapter, each stage will bring different sets of risks, and some of these risks are summarised in Figure 7.5.

During the initiating phase, for instance, the level of risk you take reflects the *need* to gain business, the *need* to raise finance without the benefit of your track record. It may also reflect what is at stake. The business's perspective may have changed by the maturing phase. There is probably more choice, you are no longer 'risking the business' every time you consider a major transaction. You may have more flexibility to back away from high risk situations and, indeed, you may be able to take the same actions as you did at the initiating phase, but because the business now has the resource to withstand some failures, the perceived risk is lower.

The individual

Your perceptions of individual risk will also change. In the initiating stage you may have taken high personal risks – stretching yourself to make a financial commitment to the business. However, the risks you take are likely to be greater initially because you take certain actions out of necessity (e.g., to get business). As the business and your wealth grows, you may find yourself more reluctant to take risks with your 'retirement fund' than you did when you were starting out. In simplistic terms, as your wealth grows your opportunity to rectify a failure diminishes and, therefore, you may become more risk-averse.

Figure 7.6 shows the possible relationship between risk-taking and wealth/age, where an entrepreneur becomes increasingly more risk-averse, through a personally driven motivation to protect wealth. This can represent a risk to the business because personal and business risk profiles may start to conflict. There are, of course, examples where the entrepreneurial and risk-taking spirit override other considerations.

It is important that you as an individual understand your own risk profile and how to achieve your objectives:

(a) how you secure an adequate income in retirement;

(b) how you protect your interests in the business by insuring others;

Figure 7.5 Risks at different stages of growth

Dreaming	Failure to finance business
	Personal financial risk
	Risk of giving up alternative career
	Your planning assumptions are wrong
	Failure to protect intellectual property
Initiating	Personal finance commitments
	Dependence on few key people
	Need to take greater risks to succeed
	Profits are confused with cash which runs out
	Dependence on few customers
	Product requires further development
	Little scope for withstanding the unforeseen
	Very susceptible to change in market, loss of key employee or supplier failure
Attacking	Systems established but not settled, increasingly under pressure
	Increasing pressure on resources – financial and human
	Human resources are challenged and frustrated
	Administrative overload
	Business lacks strength to withhold market change
	Overtrading as sales expand faster than resources or systems
Maturing	Business stagnates
	Management are losing touch with the marketplace
	Innovation and entrepreneurial spirit is being dampened
	Business fails to attract new people
Overhauling	Increasing cost base with new quality people
	Over-promising – under-delivering
	Burnout as the pace of change increases
	People skills not readily available or very expensive
Networking	Business is in the public eye – corporate image is susceptible to attacks
	Loss of strategic perspective as focus on day-to-day operational basis
	Opportunities are missed
	Business lacks flexibility to be responsive
Diversifying	Business fails to understand risks of diversification
	Resources strained by assimilation of acquired businesses
	Increasing gap between headquarters and front line
	Image becomes strained

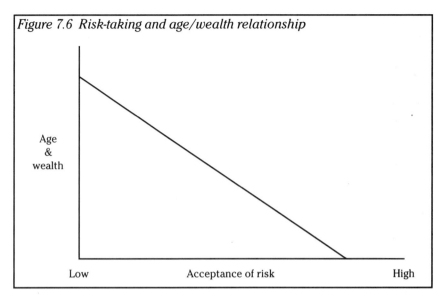

Figure 7.6 Risk-taking and age/wealth relationship

Age & wealth — vertical axis

Low — Acceptance of risk — High

(c) how you balance your wealth effectively between the business and your personal investment;

(d) are your family protected if you could no longer work, or is your wealth 'trapped' in a business to which you are the key?

Products are available to protect your personal interest, but what is appropriate and when? We explore how you respond to personal risks through financial services products in Appendix 9, and look at the types of products which are relevant at various stages of the DIAMOND model.

Two specific risks which are faced by many businesses today are:

• the introduction of the euro – an external inherent risk?

• IT systems – the focus of your internal control systems?

We shall examine each of these areas in some detail before concluding this chapter.

European monetary union – why does it matter?

European monetary union (EMU) has an immediate effect for many UK businesses. The introduction of the euro means the creation of the world's second largest trading bloc. This rich marketplace is certain to be an attractive market for UK exporters to exploit. However, every other business in Europe, if not the world, will be thinking the same.

Any growing business needs to carefully consider its current or future export strategy in the light of the low interest rate, fixed exchange rate and price-transparent marketplace which will be found in Europe.

Many other non-export businesses may also be able to benefit from the impacts of EMU as:

(a) exchange rates are likely to be significantly lower in Europe than in the UK in the short to medium term;

(b) imports may become cheaper as cross-border competition is expected to intensify;

(c) new product opportunities arise for euro-compliant or euro-based services.

Other businesses are likely to be under threat from increased competition. The desire of many companies, both UK and European to use the euro as the principal currency of transaction may force businesses to modify their business systems to be able to deal in euros or manage using a foreign currency for the first time.

Consequently, it is essential that UK businesses plan for the euro in order to exploit all the opportunities it creates and to mitigate the risks.

Background

From 1 January 1999 the 11 'first wave' European Union (EU) Member States had their exchange rates irrevocably fixed against each other as part of the process of EMU. The monetary policies of these 11 countries are now controlled by the European Central Bank (ECB).

The euro was born as a major international currency on 1 January 1999. The national banks of the 11 Member States (known as the 'Euroland' countries) remain in existence providing operational support to the ECB, but have adopted the euro as their official unit of account. The former national currency units (FNCs) remain in existence as sub-units of the euro.

There is at present a transition period running from 1 January 1999 to

1 January 2002 during which time payments can be, but do not have to be, made in euros. This general principle of 'no compulsion, no prohibition' means that it is up to the parties to a transaction to decide whether to complete the transaction in euros or in the FNC.

The euro will be an electronic and paper currency until 1 January 2002, when euro notes and coins will come into circulation and will fully replace the domestic currencies of the participant States by 1 July 2002.

The practical implications of EMU on businesses in the UK and in Euroland can be viewed on direct and indirect bases.

Direct implications

The main direct implication of EMU is the need to transact in euros. For many businesses this means that they will have to change their internal systems and review their IT processes to ensure that they are euro-compliant – i.e., they can work effectively in both the euro and the FNC.

Furthermore, the EMU regulations have specific rules on how rounding of exchange rates between the euro and FNCs should be carried out. This can have significant impacts on exchange gains and losses for businesses.

The EMU rules provide for 'Lex Monite' which loosely translates as 'money is money', such that contracts in EU countries will continue over the transition period to the euro, and cannot be avoided simply due to the change in currency.

Indirect implications

There are many indirect implications which need to be considered by the successful growing business. They include:

• *Price transparency.*

  In many markets, prices throughout Euroland will be quoted in euros. Thus, price comparison between countries will be much easier and a considerable amount of pressure may come to bear on some industries which pursue discriminatory pricing policies throughout the Euroland region.

• *Price point selection.*

  Many goods and services are set at psychologically attractive 'price points', £1.99, £4.99, etc. On translation to the euro these will evidently not be such attractive psychological prices and consequently there may be cause to increase or decrease prices to the nearest price point, with implications on profit margins.

- *Packaging/product size.*

  Changing packaging or product size may be one way around the issue of price point selection.

- *Dual pricing.*

  UK businesses using price lists based in sterling for export sales will have to decide whether to stand the foreign exchange risk of quoting prices in euros (or FNCs). Furthermore, retail operations will need to decide whether to show both the euro and FNC equivalent on products, invoices, etc.

- *Market opportunities.*

  The Euroland area is the second largest trading bloc in the world in terms of Gross Domestic Product (GDP). It is therefore a large and wealthy area for UK businesses to sell their products to and many businesses may decide to expand existing export operations from into one or two EU countries, into the whole 11, or even to consider exporting for the first time.

  Also, the fact that all the Euroland countries operate in the same currency may mean that where previously it was uneconomic to try to sell into individual countries, the larger scale may mean that this is now possible.

- *New product opportunities and competitive advantage.*

  The introduction of the euro means that some businesses may be able to develop new products (such as IT or export services) in order to assist companies doing business with and in Euroland.

- *Euro creep.*

  A number of UK-based multinational companies will expect their suppliers to be able to invoice them in euros for entirely UK-based transactions. Over a period of time it is anticipated that these suppliers will in turn try to pass on some of their exchange risk to their suppliers. This process has become known as euro creep.

- *Acquisitions and mergers.*

  The larger single currency marketplace is expected to see a significant increase in national and international merger and acquisition activity as businesses seek to penetrate new markets and achieve economies of scale in the wider marketplace.

- *Distribution strategies.*

The advent of the euro means that many businesses will now be looking at the whole of Euroland as their domestic marketplace. Consequently, there is likely to be a large amount of reviewing of distribution strategies as businesses attempt to penetrate new regions of Euroland.

Furthermore, the anticipated growth in Internet shopping means that distribution of many goods will need to be achieved from one central sales function.

- *Input cost reduction.*

The increased competition across Euroland is expected to lead to real falls in the value of business inputs in many markets. Thus, increased focus on active and effective purchasing strategies is required to ensure the best deals are sourced from Euroland.

- *Reduced banking fees.*

With the anticipated merger and acquisition activity in the banking market it is expected that there will be a competitive squeeze on banking fees across Euroland and the UK.

- *Reduction in cost of borrowing.*

Lower interest rates in Euroland mean that the Euro is an attractive market currency to borrow in. There is also likely to be an abundance of capital available throughout the 11 Member States and, with reduced banking fees, this all adds up to a strong capital market.

Any business which obtains financing in euros will have to be capable of making repayments in euros. As such, the business opens itself up to foreign exchange risk from UK–euro currency movements, unless there is a steady euro income stream to offset the risk.

- *Simplified hedging and foreign exchange risk management.*

If a business previously bought from France and sold to Germany, it would have had to cover its foreign exchange risk against both currencies separately. With the advent of the euro, the French purchases and German sales will both be at fixed rates in euros, thus creating a natural hedge.

Furthermore, if a business sells to all 11 countries, only one hedging mechanism is now required, rather than the 11 which would previously have been necessary.

- *Groups.*

  Any business which has subsidiaries in Euroland will need to consider how the subsidiary is going to compete in euros, how they will handle accounting for the subsidiary in consolidations and in what currency money will be repatriated to the UK.

  Any business which is a subsidiary of a Euroland business may come under pressure to convert fully to euros or be required to submit accounts, information and management charges in euros.

- *Euro accounting and taxation.*

  It will be possible for UK companies to file their accounts in euros from 1 January 1999. Further, they will be able to pay their taxes (corporation tax, PAYE, NI and VAT) in euros if they so choose.

IT systems

As a business grows, the computer systems necessary to process transactions and provide the necessary systems infrastructure will become more complex. The IT systems and their continued availability often become a critical component to the successful running of the business. There are not many businesses that can afford to be without their computer systems for even a day. The risk that a business runs if it loses access to data or suffers from fraud in relation to its IT systems has been shown in a number of recent surveys.

An Audit Commission report, *Ghost in the Machine: An Analysis of IT Fraud and Abuse* (*update*), disclosed that 45 per cent of public and private sector organisations suffer from computer fraud and abuse problems.

A surprisingly large number of these frauds are not discussed publicly for many reasons including undermining credibility in the eyes of customers, embarrassment, potential effect on share price.

The principal risks identified by the Audit Commission were considered to be:

- computer viruses;

- attacks by external people (hackers);

- general fraud by members of staff.

The Internet was viewed as representing the security challenge of the millennium.

The virus

The computer virus has been with the IT industry for many years now and virus writers seem to have no problem in releasing new versions in response to software developments. Viruses come in many forms and can even infect data files such as Word documents and spreadsheets. As the functionality inherent within software increases, so does the scope for the virus writer. A rigorous policy for virus protection incorporating memory-resident virus-scanner programs and controls over loading files that originate outside the company is an essential feature in reducing the risk from virus attack.

The hacker

The external hacker has been a systems bogeyman for a long time. With the recent explosion in Internet usage and companies connecting the office systems to it, the hacker has been reborn. Many companies have implemented Windows 95 and Windows NT servers which are both comparatively new operating systems. A new generation of hackers has grown up specialising in these operating systems and in identifying and exploiting security weaknesses.

Often, the company implementing the system does not have the time and money resource to properly implement the software in a way to reduce the exposure to hackers. Many businesses do not have anyone present that understands the systems at the level necessary to prevent unauthorised access. This can result in external and internal hackers getting into the company's systems.

The growing business should ensure it understands the business risk in all new technologies that it adopts. In cases where knowledge is not held within the company, an external review by a competent expert should be undertaken to assess the risks inherent in the system. It is often the case that some inexpensive and simple measures can deal with the majority of the risk and reduce it to acceptable levels.

Fraud

General fraud by members of staff forms an insidious threat that pervades throughout a company. The best defence to this type of threat is ensuring that sound controls are present. These should cover both the functions that staff carry out as well as general system controls. Through an effective combination of preventative and detective controls, most risks can be reduced down to an affordable and insurable level. These controls should deal with both prevention and detection of fraud and unauthorised access.

Where a company is dependent on the continual running of its system, any risk to these systems is a risk to the business itself.

Threats to the system can be considered from four perspectives and in respect of each the value of the asset to the company should be evaluated along with the likelihood of each risk. The possibility of the system breaking down may be compared to the hull of a ship – one good hole and you're sunk! The four areas are:

- the physical equipment;
- the people using it;
- the software that is used;
- the data that is stored.

Physical equipment

The main risks to physical equipment come from theft, unauthorised use and destruction. To prevent the theft of equipment a variety of actions can be taken, such as:

(a) siting critical equipment such as servers, confidential printers, modems and communications equipment in secure areas;

(b) using anchoring devices or electronic tags for less valuable items of equipment.

With the proliferation of PCs within most companies unauthorised use can be difficult to deter and detect. However, there are software programs that can control what uses a PC can be put to and even log the activity.

The risk of destruction can arise from a variety of sources, including:

(a) electrical problems – regular testing of appliances as well as uninterruptible power supplies can help users;

(b) fire and flood – sensible siting of equipment as well as fire and smoke detectors are essential steps.

An item of physical equipment that is often overlooked is the company back-ups. These contain valuable data, and yet are not always properly secured. For example, data that was considered secure on the office system can be rendered insecure when re-stored on another system elsewhere.

People

People are a key feature in avoiding any systems breakdown and in considering system security. System security is very definitely a people issue. There has not yet been a single fraud committed within a company that did not have a person behind it!

The people issue begins with sound recruitment procedures. The company should always take up references. This is particularly relevant where people are in key IT positions. Further areas to consider are the division and rotation of duties for key staff. Effective people management can go a long way to ensuring that the risk is minimised. An effective deterrent in any organisation is simply having employees whose morale and job satisfaction are at a high level.

Software

Software covers all programs and includes:

- operating systems such as Windows 95, NT, Novel Netware, Unix;

- packages such as Excel and Lotus Notes;

- accounts programs;

- bespoke programs;

- utilities such as Norton;

- database management systems such as SQL, server and Oracle.

Businesses depend on one or more programs from several of these categories. Reliance is placed on the software being properly installed, operating correctly and licences being obtained. Associated risks include:

(a) *licensing* – the company may not have the requisite number of software licences and thus be exposed to legal action and attendant bad publicity;

(b) *obsolescence* – software may become obsolete through either the market having moved on or other issues such as year 2000 compliance and the introduction of European monetary union;

(c) *virus infection* – all software is open to the risk of virus infection. This can be reduced through the use of proprietary virus detection and elimination programs and through having proper procedures for dealing with externally originated files;

(d) *adequacy* – as a business grows there is the possibility that the original software choice is no longer adequate. Periodically, a review should be carried out to determine whether the software in use is adding value to the business and helping it to grow or whether it is an impediment to growth.

Data

The most important asset in any system is the data and access to the data. Business data will include the usual historical accounting information as well as more critical 'real time' information such as:

- outstanding orders;
- financial projections;
- strategic plans;
- marketing information and databases;
- supplier information and sources of supply.

This data is useful both to your business and to your competitors. Maintaining the integrity, availability and security of the company's data is a very important function. The availability of data is best ensured by taking a daily back-up of all data and storing this in a secure offsite location.

The security of data is more complex and is achieved through a mix of password operating system restrictions that will vary from system to system. It is important to realise that there are many routes to a data file and they must all be controlled. It is relatively easy to take a copy of a data file from a company's system and then explore at leisure the task of getting into it. If the operating system is set up correctly in the first place then unauthorised copying of the data file becomes more difficult.

One aspect which is often overlooked is the Data Protection Act. Briefly, this requires that personal data be registered for the purposes for which it will be used and that it be kept secure. As the use of databases proliferates throughout a business, it is easy to get behind on this requirement.

Even though the systems in use grow in complexity and size the business can control the main risks through the use of controls and good management. These will contribute towards ensuring that the system is secure and that the underlying data remains available and that integrity is maintained.

Conclusion

We have presented a methodology in this chapter to help you identify, assess and respond to specific risks associated with your business. We have also highlighted the dynamic nature of risk and how the relationship between business risk and personal risk might impact on the business.

Our aim is not to remove risk from your business – this would never be possible nor desirable. Risk comes with opportunity and will therefore always be a natural partner in any business. It is how you manage the risk that matters, remember that:

> If you don't risk anything, you risk even more.

> Erica Yong

8

Building value

Introduction

We now reach the final stages of the DIAMOND model – the networking and diversifying stages. The business has started out, grown, matured and overhauled its operations. The final stages of the DIAMOND model are characterised by the business seeking to build value, by developing its brands and entering into strategic alliances to extend its market reach.

The networking stage

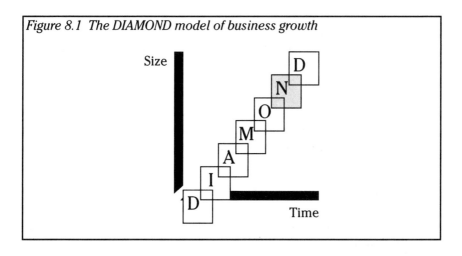

Figure 8.1 The DIAMOND model of business growth

Effective networks are crucial to business success because they increase the span of control of the business; economise on time and other resources, and possibly help to control an unstable business environment. The

173

challenge is to find ways of more systematic planning, monitoring and pruning network information.

Aldrich and Brickman, *Mastering Enterprise.*

Characteristics

The characteristics of the business at the networking stage are as follows:

- the business is the focus of external scrutiny

- earnings are managed for a diverse shareholder group

- the maintenance of the corporate image becomes an important issue if the business becomes decentralised

- the structure of the working environment focuses on 'roles' rather than 'jobs'

- the strategic business processes are just as important as the tactical ones

The business is capable of external scrutiny

At the networking stage, the business is likely to be fairly large, probably operating within a group structure. Whilst not necessarily being publicly quoted, the business is likely to attract the attention of interested parties, whether they are suppliers, media or financial institutions, to name but a few.

Because of this attention, and perhaps as a consequence of its size, the business is able to withstand external scrutiny, in the form of questions relating to financial performance, employment practices, customer relations and so on.

Earnings are managed for a diverse shareholder group

To fuel its growth, the business is likely to have grown though acquisition and additional investment. Resources for this may have been provided by venture capitalists, banks, employees and other financial institutions. The company may have floated on one of the UK markets – the Stock Exchange or the Alternative Investment Market.

All these factors, over time, will have broadened the shareholder base of the business, and the business will be accountable to a number of individuals and institutions for its performance.

In decentralised businesses in particular, the importance of maintaining the corporate image is paramount. Otherwise, the business may become an amalgam of very distinct and separate businesses or operational units which do not share a common identity.

Corporate image is as important for those working within the business as it is for customers and other parties in the external environment. The right corporate identity can present the image of a reliable and professional organisation, which provides quality and good value. A positive corporate identity can extend to building a brand or image for a business. This brand needs to be maintained constantly, and not just given the occasional lick of corporate paint. This element is perhaps the most important, as it is the shop window of the organisation. The strength of brand and the way in which the business can stretch and utilise its good name is a key competitive advantage. Examples can be seen with Coca Cola, McDonald's, Mont Blanc, etc.

Roles in preference to jobs

The 'role' a person has within a business can be seen to be a series of patterns of behaviour that is expected of them. The 'job' element focuses on the tasks within any business activity; which permits the employee to complete a piece of work.

As the business grows and becomes more complex in structure, employee responsibilities get broader and become less clearly defined. Employees, particularly at the more senior levels, start to develop roles which reflect multiple responsibilities in the organisation. Job descriptions to a large degree became obsolete, and employee roles are defined with reference to the complex and changing requirements of the business.

Strategic processes and tactical processes

As the business becomes larger and more diverse in its activities, management can be burdened with dealing with lots of routine operational issues. This diverts management focus away from the wider and more strategic issues facing the business. In order to combat this, businesses at the networking stage need to ensure a formal planning framework exists which allows management to consider strategic issues on a

175

regular basis. This could simply include putting strategic issues on the management agenda, on a monthly or bi-monthly basis. Alternatively, it may be more appropriate to establish a new forum to consider strategic issues, which enables operational and functional managers to work together in developing growth strategies for the business.

Transitional issues

At the same time, and in common with the other parts of the DIAMOND model, the business can find itself confronted with a number of transitional issues:

- the business is too inflexible to react quickly to market forces
- the business hierarchy is cumbersome and rigid
- the business operates in a global market
- staff turnover of quality personnel can be high in key areas

The business is too rigid to be responsive

The problem may hinge upon three basic dilemmas:

(a) the business cannot match or adapt its basic skills to a rapidly changing external environment;

(b) the business cannot accept that new skills are required; and

(c) the business is unable to transform these skills into new and more competitive products and services.

A combination of complex business structures, skills which have not been updated and a rapidly changing environment can result in paralysis for the business at the networking stage.

Tackling the rigidities in the business, whether in the form of organisation structures, or individual skills, is of paramount importance if the business is to move to the final stage of the DIAMOND model.

One of the major choices that a diversified or networked business may need to make concerns whether the business should remain privately owned or become a publicly quoted company. As we discussed in Chapter 6, the need for finance may drive this decision. An important factor to consider is the impact of this on the role of existing owner-managers. The business will became accountable to a far wider group of stakeholders and City institutions who represent shareholder interests. In addition, the business will be required to maintain high standards of corporate governance and comply with financial reporting rules. The stakeholders will influence the shape of the future strategy of the business, and this could act as a constraint to future development.

There are many examples of businesses which have moved into public ownership. A more recent trend has seen some businesses moving from being public to private. For example, Richard Branson took Virgin Group (Music, Publishing and Retail) public in 1986. However, over time Branson became frustrated with the reporting requirements of being a listed company and the need to make regular presentations to City institutions who were interested in short-term profitability. Accordingly, he took the Group back to private ownership.

Operating in a global market

National borders are no longer a barrier to competition. In Europe, the introduction of the euro and its implications for price transparency will increase competition between the businesses in the 'euro zone'.

Global opportunities mean that product investment will speed up as competitors try to be first to get to the global market. The rewards are high, but so is the price of failure.

Businesses which operate across many different countries have to adapt systems and processes which cater for the specific requirements of the locality. This can result in difficulties in sharing information across different parts of the business – an issue which will be dealt with at the end of this chapter.

The strategic alliance or partner agreement between British Midland and airlines such as Virgin is a good example of a reaction to the needs of the global marketplace.

Retaining key employees

As the business becomes more complex and bureaucratic, some key employees may start to become concerned about the hierarchies and rules that have developed in the organisation. This may restrict their ability to be flexible in their roles. Coupled with this, good quality staff will be highly sought after by other businesses. At this level, the pool of talented staff is restricted, and businesses need to fight hard to get the 'best and brightest'.

With this in mind, it is essential that working environment, roles and responsibilities and financial incentives are sufficiently attractive for key employees to remain with the business. Chapter 5 examined the issue of incentivisation in detail.

The diversifying stage

The diversifying stage is characterised by a business which is driving growth through strategic alliances and commercial relationships, which enables a rapid response to a fast-moving marketplace. The culture of businesses at this stage is highly focused, the means by which they operate – and the markets in which they do so – are highly flexible. The final stage of the DIAMOND model enables the business to spread its wings and expand into new and more lucrative markets.

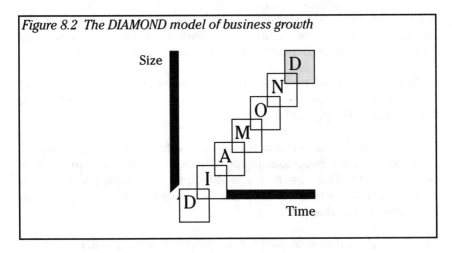

Figure 8.2 The DIAMOND model of business growth

Context

This diversification of the business may have been achieved by adopting a number of transformation strategies, for example:

(a) *vertical integration* – this may be the formation of distinct businesses within one company, but having component parts useful to it. For instance, a computer company has businesses that supply computer sub-systems to its main computer production function.

(b) *related diversification* – this creates growth by building upon the basic business function but expanding it into similar core areas. For example, Canon not only produces cameras, but also photo reproduction systems and other business information systems.

(c) *horizontal integration* – this is where businesses are able to merge when they are seen to be at the same stage in the 'supply chain'. For instance, mergers between banks and building societies. In this area, the benefit of cost reduction through shared resources is a key benefit.

(d) *unrelated diversification* – this element needs tight control and is a high-risk process. Grand Metropolitan can be seen to be a classic example of unrelated diversification, with a wide range of products and services from hotels, drinks and leisure activities.

As the business continues to develop and grow within the diversifying stage, a number of issues should be considered.

(a) Re-assessment of product brands should be carried out regularly. This will allow products that are not performing to be abandoned or sold off. This assessment must be objective with results that are rapid and decisive. A great deal of money can be lost by trying to revive a dying product, especially within a business that attaches elements of sentiment to it.

(b) Core management skills are adaptable and flexible enough to support diversification into other activities.

(c) The business may be able to generate reserves of cash to help fund projects by smaller firms and act as a form of banker to permit these smaller firms to initiate product and brand development within niche markets. This should reduce in-house and long-term development costs. For example, the pharmaceutical giants rely on small pharmaceutical companies to carry out some of their development activities.

This market awareness also permits the business to capitalise on the strength of its brands in the marketplace. These brands may be varied and may form an 'umbrella' of brands, which are delivered through individual business. The large confectionery and pharmaceutical companies provide illustrations of such businesses.

With these points in mind, it is worth now looking separately at the

179

characteristics of a business at the diversifying stage of the DIAMOND model.

Characteristics

These businesses will now possess the following visible characteristics:

- flexible and market-responsive

- their customer focus is one of customer satisfaction

- able to form strategic empowered alliances through integration

- their brand image is alive and focused

The business is flexible and market-responsive

By the time the business has reached the diversifying phase, it is able to respond quickly and effectively to changes in market conditions. The business has the resources, local market presence and market knowledge to do this. The business guards its competitive position very closely and is able to react to competitive pressures with great speed and effect.

The focus is on the customer

John Thompson in *Strategy in Action* sets out four key elements that a firm must acknowledge as fundamental to achieving a strong customer focus. The business must:

(a) recognise that the customer is the most important contributor to the long-term success of the company;

(b) involve all employees in meeting customer requirements;

(c) see that every activity is part of an overall process that is designed to satisfy customers' needs and wants; and

(d) seek continuous improvement.

These factors must be seen to underpin and form the basis for any interaction between the business and its customers.

The business is able to form strategic alliances

The business is able to enter into alliances with other organisations that are based on tangible outcome for all. These alliances deliver real customer benefits and strengthen the competitive position of the business.

The brand is alive

Brand is typically associated with a product. For example, Burger King, the high street fast food outlet is a well-known brand which is owned by Grand Metropolitan. However, some brands are associated with the company itself – Coca Cola provides an example here.

The power of the brand cannot be understated. It represents 'super-profits' for those businesses which get it right. Simply associating a well known name with a product can increase the value and marketability of that product. A firm advocate of this approach is the Virgin Group, which has used the Virgin brand in a number of diverse businesses, from music, publishing, financial services, soft and alcoholic drinks to air and rail travel.

Customers associate a set of values and qualities with a brand. A business needs to continually invest in maintaining the brand image. An infamous example of destroying a brand was provided by Gerald Ratner, who criticised his own jewellery products at a well publicised business conference. Ratner's comments precipitated his demise and that of his business.

Business structures

The increasing size and complexity of the business calls into question the role of the corporate centre. In the earlier stages of growth, a functional structure, reflecting the main tasks of production, marketing, finance and personnel may have been appropriate. As the business grows, more complex structures are required to reflect geographic territories, diverse product ranges and unrelated commercial interests.

Simple functional structures can prove very problematic in coping with a diversified business, because of the differing needs of individual components of the business. One of the ways of tackling this weakness is through improved co-ordination between functions. For example, product or regional sub-groups can include representatives for each functional area, i.e., marketing, finance, production, etc. and can act as a forum for developing fresh approaches and resolving problem areas.

Where a divisional structure is called for, one of the common problems which is encountered is the basis of the structure. Should the business be organised on the basis of products, markets, geographical location, function or expertise? The decision will have significant impact on the way the business is managed and the strategies the organisation employs in specific markets. In addition, for larger businesses, it is not a decision that can be easily reversed and a re-organisation can prove to be very expensive.

Whatever the basis of organisation, the business will need to decide the extent to which activities and responsibilities should be devolved within the structure.

A number of models exist which identify the management styles of businesses (see Figure 8.3).

- Strategic planning

   This is the most centralised of the three approaches. Here, the centre acts as the corporate planner, setting the agenda and roles and responsibilities for the business. The divisions act merely as operational units which deliver the requirements of the centre. This has all the hallmarks of the classic large-scale bureaucracy. Whilst central control is exercised, divisional managers do not have the flexibility to react to local conditions. The potential costs are both in expensive bureaucratic controls and lost opportunities.

- Financial control

   This reflects the most devolved of the management styles. The centre acts as a 'banker' for the divisions, providing funds to pursue local strategies, which are not directly influenced by the centre. Having said that, the centre will intervene where poor performance is identified. This is a fairly extreme form of devolution of control – most large companies prefer some say in the strategies and even tactics of their operating subsidiaries or group companies.

- Strategic control

   This lies between strategic and financial control and reflects the typical structure adopted by many divisionalised or decentralised businesses. It is characterised by the centre:

182

Figure 8.3 Business management styles				
Approach	*Features*	*Advantages*	*Dangers*	*Examples*
Strategic planning	Top-down. Prescribed approach supported by strong controls	Strong co-ordination of activities	Centre out of touch. Divisions behave tactically	Lex
Financial control	Financial targets. Controls over investment. Bottom-up reporting	Responsive	Lack of direction. Centre adds limited value	BTR Hanson
Strategic control	Strategic and financial targets. Bottom-up reporting. Less detailed controls	Co-ordination is good. Divisional management motivated	Culture of negotiation. New bureaucracies emerge	ICI Courtaulds

Source: Adapted from Johnson and Scholes, *Exploring Corporate Strategy.* Originally taken from Gould and Campbell, *Strategies and Styles.*

- defining and shaping overall strategy;
- deciding on the balance of activities and role of each subsidiary or group company;
- defining and controlling organisational policies on recruitment, holiday entitlementand so on;
- assessing performance and acting where poor performance is identified.

The role of senior management at the networking and diversifying phase is to select an organisational structure which complements the activities of the business. Whichever management style is adopted, the business should be conscious of the dangers of that particular style, and its implications for the business.

Strategies for growth

At the networking and diversifying stages of the DIAMOND model, the business is faced with multiple strategic choices, combined with several alternative mechanisms for executing its intended strategies.

The choices reflect the scale and development of the business to date and are summarised in Table 8.1.

Table 8.1 Strategies and methods of execution	
Strategic choices	*Alternative methods*
Protect existing position Market penetration Product development Market development Diversification	Organic growth Acquisition Strategic or joint alliance

Below we will examine each of the strategic choices available to the business and the differing methods of achieving them. The choice will largely depend on the circumstances of the business and the market segment the business wishes to address.

Strategic choices

We looked at the opportunities for strategy development using the Ansoff Matrix in Chapter 4. This model is even more relevant at the networking and diversifying phases, where the business is faced with a larger number of potential choices.

Protect and build upon existing position

Most strategic activities in business involve developing or building from current activities, rather than starting in completely new areas. Accordingly, businesses seek to 'stretch' their product/service offerings to improve the competitive position in existing markets.

A protective strategy may require consolidation in the marketplace – this does not mean standing still, but taking a critical look at the activities of the business and its fit with market needs. This may result in withdrawal from specific market segments, because of a recognition that the resources required to maintain a competitive position are too high.

Market penetration

This involves exploiting opportunities to gain market share. The success of such a strategy will be dependent on a number of factors including the skills and resources of the business, the nature of the competition, and whether the market is growing, static or in decline. The business will need to judge the likely success of such a strategy in the light of these conditions.

Product development

There is good reason to engage in new product development. It may be to meet new market needs, or service existing needs not currently provided for by the market – Pfizer's Viagra is the fastest selling drug ever recorded.

The pharmaceutical industry provides a good example of the downsides of product development as well – research and development cost can be high and there is no guarantee that a product will ever reach the marketplace.

Market development

Opportunities may exist to expand into geographical areas with current products. Larger businesses are more likely to adopt global strategies, where geographic market development is high on the strategic agenda. Other strategies include the development of new uses for existing products. For example, stainless steel, which was originally produced to make cutlery but is now used to make car exhausts, beer barrels, etc. as well.

Diversification

This is a strategy which takes the business into new markets with new products. This can be a very risky strategy to adopt if it is not carefully thought out. For businesses entering the final stage of the DIAMOND model, growth constraints in other areas of the business may mean that a diversification strategy is the only one which offers a serious prospect of continued and sustainable growth. Diversification can take various forms. Related diversification involves remaining within the broad confines of the 'industry' that the business operates in. For example,

Direct Line, who started out by providing cheap motor insurance, has diversified into home loans, mortgages and other aspects of insurance.

Unrelated diversification is by its very nature a riskier prospect, as it involves entering a market which is not well known to the business. In many instances, market entry is typically achieved through acquisitions, which enables the business to purchase skills and knowledge not currently possessed by the business itself.

There are a number of possible advantages in adopting a strategy of diversification. These are summarised in Figure 8.4.

Figure 8.4 Advantage of diversification strategies	
Possible advantages	*Examples/comments*
Related diversification	
Control of suppliers	Price advantage in bringing function in house, i.e., printing
Control of markets	UK shoe manufacturer owns retail outlets to get guaranteed distribution
Cost savings	Fully integrated steel plants save cost on reheating and transport
Building on technology skills	Precision engineering equipment manufacturer in one market entering into another with similar technical requirements
Spreading risk	Avoids over-reliance on one product/market, but builds on related experience
Unrelated diversification	
Need to use excess cash	Better return achieved on assets
Even out cyclical effects in a given sector	Toy manufacturers make subcontract plastic moulded products for industry
Exploiting under-utilised resources and skills	Placing good management skills into poor performing business
Source: Adapted from Johnson and Scholes, *Exploring Corporate Strategy*.	

Much research has been conducted on the impact of diversification on performance. The evidence is inconclusive, although it is noted that successful diversification is difficult to achieve in practice. Profitability can increase as a business becomes more diversified, however, this relationship goes into reverse if the business becomes too complex. Profitability suffers and the business may split up as a result. An example of this was the split of Hanson Plc into four separate companies, specialising in energy, tobacco, chemicals and building materials.

Making choices

In the face of so many competing choices, the business must establish a basis for selecting those strategies which will achieve the overall objectives of the business and contribute to sustained and profitable growth. Strategy selection will be driven by a range of factors, including the nature of the market opportunity, the skills and resources of the business and the potential for growth and profitability. These factors, amongst others, can be used to rank the alternative choices.

Once the strategic choices have been made, the methodology for achieving the strategy needs to be considered. Before moving on, it should be noted that on many occasions, the opportunity to enter into a joint alliance or make an acquisition can be a key driver in selecting strategy for the business.

Alternative methods

Organic growth

Many businesses rely on internal development as the means to achieving growth – particularly in relation to new product development. This is an approach which allows the business to grow at its own pace. Risk is reduced, although opportunities may be missed.

In the earlier stages of growth, limited access to capital may have meant that this was the only growth route available to the business. As the business grows, and has a more substantial trading record and balance sheet, the opportunities for 'short-cuts' to growth may be possible.

Mergers and acquisitions

Mergers and acquisitions are commonplace – we hear about them on the news every day. For example, in the telecommunications sector, Vodafone, the UK mobile phone operator merged with Airtouch, a US mobile phone operator to gain a greater presence in the global tele-communications market. Granada's hostile acquisition of Forte was based on the premise that the Granada Group, a business with interests in television, roadside service stations, etc., could operate the Forte chain of Little Chefs and hotels more profitably than Forte and improve shareholder value. The City institutions were convinced by this argument and supported the successful Granada bid.

A compelling reason to grow by acquisition is the speed at which a company can enter a new market segment, and capture market share. This may be a more cost-effective way of achieving market share in a target market, rather than starting from scratch. Handled properly, this can prove to be a very successful methodology for growth.

As one would expect, there are potential problems associated with acquisitions. Primarily, they revolve around the ability to integrate the new business into the activities of the existing business. This can be particularly complex where a strong culture exists in the acquired company.

Strategic/joint alliances

Strategic alliances in one form or another have come about because of the increasing pressures and complexities of the global market. In the airline industry, a number of national carriers have co-operated to provide a global network of routes around the world. This allows any one carrier to offer a route which includes flights involving other national airlines, thereby offering the customer the opportunity to purchase a single ticket for what may include several long-haul and short-haul destinations.

In the aerospace industry, British Aerospace's investment collaboration with its French and German counterparts to build the 'Eurofighter' provides another example of a strategic alliance.

Whilst alliances may seem very attractive, in many cases they simply do not work. There must be a shared and equal commitment to the alliance, otherwise the seeds of failure are already present. Alliances should be handled with care. Each business should be very clear about what it expects from the joint collaboration. If it is not working, it is better to call things to a halt – a lot of time and money can be spent in brokering alliances which end without achieving the desired results.

The use of technology, in the form of the Internet, and the introduction of the euro, both increase the prospects of operating a more global marketplace. For large UK-based or multinational businesses, global strategies offer bigger market opportunities and can bring cost reduction, as activities are carried out in the most cost-effective location. For example, a number of large companies are taking advantage of the large pool of IT-literate graduates in India to carry out routine programming and data correction tasks at rates which are highly competitive – in fact as much as two or three times cheaper, in some cases.

Managing knowledge and information

There is an increasing recognition that the 'intellectual assets' of a business are the strongest part of the business balance sheet. These intellectual assets represent the knowledge contained within the organisation, vested in individuals, about the system processes, customers, and the ways of 'doing things' in the business.

The purpose of managing knowledge and information in an organisation, particularly a diverse organisation, is the benefits that arise from:

- not continually re-inventing the wheel;
- gaining a competitive advantage;
- reduced costs and improved profitability from selling information to clients.

Businesses, particularly those located across many sites or in different countries, have sought to develop 'Intranets', as the IT vehicle through which information can be shared. A number of global businesses, including large international banks, have sought to develop 'Intranets' as a way of gaining a competitive advantage in the marketplace.

The investment required for the development of Intranets to facilitate knowledge sharing is high, and the success rate of knowledge management projects is yet to be effectively measured. A word of caution – knowledge- or information-sharing requires a willingness on the part of people to share information and to place a value on that information. Without these two facets, the investment in technology will not produce the desired result.

As the saying goes, 'knowledge is power'. People may be unwilling to share knowledge on the basis that it erodes their position as an expert. Dispelling this view requires a change in the culture and attitudes of an organisation. This is not something that is easy to attain. Also, information must have a value placed upon it before employees are willing to record and share that information. Some businesses have linked information-sharing to their appraisal systems, so that employees are positively encouraged to share information and load information on to an Intranet.

Whilst one might argue that knowledge management is a fad, as business process re-engineering was in late 1980s/early 1990s, it is clear that capturing and sharing the intellectual capital of the business is immensely valuable. The key issue to recognise is that knowledge-sharing is not simply achieved by introducing the relevant technology – it requires the willingness of members of the business to share and use that knowledge in a way that positively benefits the business.

Conclusion

We have considered the final stages of the DIAMOND model within this chapter. Reaching these stages of growth has enabled the business to build value, typically by developing its brands and extending market coverage through strategic alliances.

Key to these final stages of growth is the organisational structure and management style adopted by the business. We concluded that whatever structure is selected, it is important to decide on the extent to which activities and responsibilities are devolved, and to be aware of the dangers of each management style.

We also considered a number of growth strategies to apply within these final stages and the various methods of implementing them.

Finally, we explored the concept of knowledge management and its importance to all businesses.

At any of the seven stages of business growth, as depicted by the DIAMOND model, there may be an opportunity or requirement by the owners to exit from the business. The next chapter considers a number of ways in which this can be achieved.

9

The exit

Introduction

The DIAMOND model identifies the various phases of growth that businesses typically pass through during the business life cycle. At any stage in this life cycle, the business can fail, plateau or sell up. This chapter examines the means by which companies sell up or exit from the business

Having successfully developed and grown the business, issues can emerge which focus shareholder and management strategic planning towards an exit. Reasons to exit from the business include:

(a) the incumbent shareholders wanting to realise a return on their investment (internal);

(b) changes in the characteristics of the company's marketplace, such as over-capacity and the need to develop products more quickly (external).

There may also be factors relating to the business's funding structure, which may require management to restructure the finances or sell the business. For example, funds introduced at the attacking stage by a venture capitalist may now be due for repayment. This could relate to the repayment of preference shares or mezzanine loans and/or participating dividends (which might ramp up over time) to the venture capitalist. A sale of the business may be necessary to fund these repayments.

Several methods exist which enable shareholders to realise a return on their business investment and sell all or part of the business. These include mechanisms such as a management buyout, management buy-in, flotation or a trade sale. A summary of each of these methods is covered in this chapter.

Valuation

Before the disposal process begins, an assessment of the company's market value needs to be completed. But the question is what is the business worth? Unfortunately, there is no simple answer to this, except to say that you will know when you have sold it! As with the price of anything, the basic economic theory of supply and demand will drive the outcome.

As a way of putting the 'first peg' in the ground, however, a number of methods do exist. Whilst there are a number of different methods, the most common valuation method of profitable companies involves applying an appropriate earnings multiple to the company's future net maintainable earnings (FNME).

The FNME, as the first part of the name indicates, relates to the future, which immediately introduces a degree of subjectivity to the whole process. In practice, the FNME of a company is based on both its recent trading performance and an assessment of where the company and its industry are in their relative business cycles. The FNME should eliminate non-recurring income and expenses, e.g., unusual or exceptional bad debts, profit or loss on the disposal of fixed assets, etc. Accordingly, costs associated with a venture capitalist, such as monitoring fees and non-executive fees, should be excluded.

Having established the company's FNME, the next stage is to calculate an appropriate earnings multiple. The principal source of earnings multiples, or price–earnings (P/E) ratios as they are commonly known, are from companies quoted on the Stock Exchange (main market or AIM). Ideally, the quoted companies selected should operate in similar markets to that of the private company, produce similar profit margins and operate with similar levels of gearing. The more quoted companies matching these characteristics, the better the estimate of an appropriate earnings multiple.

In order to allow for the differences between private and public companies, the earnings multiple derived from the above process should be discounted, with 25 per cent to 50 per cent being the normal range of any discount. The rationale for this reduction is that public companies tend to be larger and therefore more robust, and they have a ready market for their shares. The larger the private company and the longer it has sustained good levels of profitable trading, the lower the discount factor will be.

Once a relevant P/E ratio, which is a measure of post-tax earnings, has been established, all that remains is to adjust the company's FNME (a pre-tax measure) by applying a notional tax charge. The notional rate used should reflect the size of the company and the industry it operates in.

Therefore, the final formula for the valuation is:

$$\text{Adjusted P/E ratio} \times \text{FNME} \times (1 - \text{notional tax rate})$$

EXAMPLE OF A VALUATION CALCULATION

	£000
Profit before tax	1,500
Add back:	
exceptional loss on disposal of fixed assets	250
excess directors' emoluments (ownership costs)	150
bad debts written off	50
Adjusted profit before tax	1,950
Average P/E multiple of similar public companies	15
Appropriate discount range (say)	25% to 40%
Notional tax charge	31%

Upper valuation (£000):

$$15 \times (1 - 0.25) \times £1,950 \times (1 - 0.31) = £15,137$$

Lower valuation (£000):

$$15 \times (1 - 0.40) \times £1,950 \times (1 - 0.31) = £12,110$$

To recognise the subjectivity of the valuation process, a range of values should be calculated. The bottom of that range indicates a conservative price – the upper a more bullish price.

Timing

Whilst external or internal issues may force the disposal timetable, it is important that the timing of the company's sale is right. Ideally, the business needs to be on the upward part of its growth cycle. Attempting to sell a business on the back of poor results will reduce the chances of successfully negotiating a satisfactory price. Similarly, if the company's market is viewed as being in a period of growth, buyer confidence will be high with a resulting positive effect on the price of the business.

One should also remember that having assessed the company's current trading position and the state of its market, the correct decision might be to delay the disposal for the short term at least.

Grooming the business for sale

As with selling anything, the more time and effort spent on improving its appearance the better the price achieved. Take, for example, selling a car. Before attempting to sell a vehicle, we would ensure the car was clean inside and out, any minor damage was repaired and that it had been recently serviced.

During the period leading up to the disposal, the key objective for the directors (who are probably also shareholders) is to maximise overall shareholder returns. This will be achieved by maximising profits through, *inter alia*, controlling overhead expenditure and extracting non-trade assets and unused assets. The rationale for removing non-trade (e.g., directors' cars, etc.) and unused assets lies in the basis of how the company is valued, which in this scenario is a profit-based methodology. Therefore, the only assets needed are the ones required to generate the profit stream.

Which exit route?

Management buyout (MBO)

In circumstances where the management of a business is not its share-holders, an opportunity exists for the management to 'buy out' those shareholders.

If a strong management team is running a business, because they 'own' the company's goodwill through the customer relationships they have, their technical ability or even the entrepreneurial drive, they may be the only people to whom the business could be sold. However, as well as needing a strong management team, the business should be in a growing industry, have products which are recognised as some of the best (brand recognition), have low levels of gearing and be cash-generative.

These characteristics permit a business to heavily 'gear up' (financing primarily through debt) its funding structure at the buyout stage. The subsequent repayment of this debt helps towards the venture capitalist achieving his required annual return.

The price an MBO team can pay for the business is dictated by the business's ability to raise new funding. If only limited debt funding is available, the MBO team may not be able to pay an adequate price for the business. In such cases, the seller or vendor may be asked to fund the transaction in the short to medium term by deferring the receipt of their consideration.

In practice, it can be difficult for an MBO team to compete against a trade buyer, not only because of the funding limitations highlighted above, but also because of the beneficial synergies a trade buyer can potentially bring to the target business. To counter this, an MBO offers non-quantitative factors such as retaining the business's identity as well as maintaining employee security. In addition, because management is on the 'inside', they can better assess the true potential of the business, allowing them to pay what appears to be a better price. The buyout process also has the advantage of being far more discreet than is often the case with obtaining a trade buyer, and provides existing shareholders with a relatively quick exit.

The MBO of Company A provides a good illustration of some of the issues discussed.

COMPANY A

Company A started life back in 1988 as a venture led by its current managing director and technical director together with some US partners to import apples from North America to the UK market. They had both learned their trade working within the industry in Lincolnshire, from where they decided that they wanted to run their own business. Ten years on they have remained with the company, and along with the other directors have seen the business grow from strength to strength to become one of the largest fresh produce suppliers to the UK's supermarkets.

You may ask yourself, therefore, how this business can exemplify a successful management buy-out when its management already owned it from day one? Well, after only nine months of trading, an offer to purchase the business was received from a major UK-based fruit importer and processor. The offer came at a time when, although the business was only in its infancy, a sale made good business sense for the following reasons:

(a) the 1989 harvest from the company's main supplier was forecast to be significantly reduced;

(b) a food scare broke out (which was subsequently disproved) linked to a chemical applied to apple trees;

(c) friction had developed between the other US shareholders;

(d) clear strategic benefits existed for the potential buyer to acquire an apple and pear specialist who traded extensively with the leading supermarket chains.

The new owners provided limited additional capital investment during the company's development, as its people were and always will be its key resource. The directors had built and maintained excellent relationships with their key customers, as well as its suppliers from all over the world.

Throughout the early 1990s, the business grew strongly and by 1996 had expanded to an annual turnover in excess of £30 million. In spite of this, the directors became increasingly frustrated with their owners' lack of input in formulating strategy and the breakdown in relations concerning relocation of staff from Lincolnshire to the South of England.

This breakdown in relations, combined with consistent year-on-year performance improvements crystallised the decision to pursue the possibility of completing a management buyout. The business displayed many of the classic components of a successful MBO:

- highly skilled and motivated management team;

- sound historical financial performance;

- excellent growth potential;

- owner with limited control or ability to replace the company's existing skill base.

The directors approached BDO Stoy Hayward in October 1996 for help in putting their plans into action. This involved assisting in the preparation of a business plan for circulation to potential funders for the acquisition, whilst at the same time negotiating with the owner to agree the price and other key terms of the potential sale. The quality of the people is almost always the primary consideration for external funders such as venture capitalists and banks, but the owner also realised that the ongoing support of the management team was vital to ensure the long-term viability of the company. This fact was invaluable in closing the deal with the owner at a very favourable price, and the directors regained control when the buyout completed in March 1997.

Since the buyout completed, the company has continued to build on its solid base, with the profits now accruing directly to those who generate the business – the directors who are now also the majority shareholders. Turnover is forecast to be £50 million and relationships remain excellent with all customers. As a measure of their success, the company opened a new purpose-built facility for both storing and packing the fruit in December 1998. The directors now firmly believe that the operational efficiencies to be gained from trading from a prestigious stand-alone building will give them the springboard to move into new product areas and grow the business even further.

Almost two years on, the company is a great example of how the management buyout process can truly reward those whose hard work in the early days can be instrumental in ensuring the business's long-term success.

Management buy-in (MBI)

MBIs are a fairly new phenomenon, created from the abundance of institutional funding seeking out acquisition opportunities and the availability of high calibre individuals, usually from large companies, who would now rather be owners than managers. MBIs are, however, potentially susceptible to the weaknesses of both MBOs and trade buyers, as they suffer the same funding restrictions as an MBO and, as with a trade buyer, they are coming in from the 'outside'.

Consequently, only exceptional (or lucky!) MBI candidates successfully end up completing a transaction. In reality, pure MBIs (i.e., the company's management is completely replaced) rarely happen. Normally, management from the target company forms part of the new management team and in some cases invests alongside the MBI candidate.

Flotation

The flotation of shares provides a means of both realising an investment and raising additional finance. The flotation process was considered in Chapter 6.

Trade sale

The most traditional route for selling a business is through a trade sale. Like any sale, this involves identifying a willing buyer for what you have to offer, which in this case is a business. To help maximise the proceeds from a trade sale, a well defined process can be followed.

Identifying trade buyers

The objective is to identify a 'star buyer', that is, a buyer who has a strategic reason for buying the company. The benefit of finding a star buyer could be a sale price above market value. Spending time on this part of the sale process can therefore be very beneficial.

Selecting inappropriate buyers may result in the company remaining unsold or, perhaps, being sold at below the maximum value. Identifying the correct buyers is therefore critical. A selection of the methods used for identifying likely buyers includes:

(a) utilising the company's own contacts (i.e., suppliers, customers, local competitors, etc.);

(b) using business directories and the financial and trade press to locate companies in the same or similar industries;

(c) placing an advert;

(d) utilising the company's advisers, who can use their contacts and networks.

Normally, a mixture of each of the methods outlined is adopted, resulting in what should be a fairly extensive list of potential buyers. This list should then be reviewed to filter out unsuitable buyers by applying a simple checklist, such as:

(a) is the potential buyer financially capable of acquiring the company – i.e., are they financially sound or do they have access to sufficient resources?

(b) is the buyer significantly larger than the target (while a large company has the financial muscle, it may not be interested in a relatively small acquisition)?

(c) do potential synergies exist – overhead savings, higher raw material volume rebates, etc.?

(d) do the product ranges fit well with the buyer's products?

(e) will the buyer gain access to markets/customers to which they currently have no access?

Having filtered the initial list, the company can then justifiably dedicate time and resources to the remaining list of potential buyers.

Sale memorandum

To sell the company, a full and descriptive document covering the key aspects of the business will need to be prepared. Sufficient information must be provided to potential buyers to enable them to make an assessment of the business. At the same time, certain salient pieces of information should be withheld until the later stages of the sale process, to avoid sensitive details falling into the hands of potential competitors who have no intention of buying.

As a guide, the sale memorandum should be written under the following headings:

- history and ownership;
- financial information;
- nature of operations – facilities, plant, IT systems, etc.;
- details of suppliers, customers and competitors;
- management structure;
- future developments;
- reasons for sale.

The sale memorandum should be written in an enthusiastic style, highlighting the company's achievements and its future potential. It is important, however, that the document has balance and is not too one-sided. The result of being too economical with the truth at this stage will lead to erosion of the price later in the disposal process, and a potential waste of time and money.

Contacting buyers

Contact can be made either by the company or, as is more commonly the case, by the company's advisers. The benefit of the adviser making the first contact is that it ensures the identity of the company remains unknown. Ideally, before even the name of the company is released, all buyers should have agreed to and signed an appropriate confidentiality agreement. This legally binding agreement provides the company with an enforceable contract with the recipients of confidential information and a mechanism by which the vendor can in the last resort sue for damages, should information released under the agreement be abused.

With a confidentiality agreement in place, the sales memorandum can now be released.

Price negotiations

The vendors must have a clear idea of the kind of deal they want and should have established the price below which the business will not be sold. This ensures the sale process does not continue longer than is necessary.

Although a theoretical valuation will have been completed, the level of actual interest, and hence an indication of the true market value of the company, will not be known until the first offers are received. The greater the number of interested parties submitting offers, the more intense the competition, and the better the chances of achieving a high sale price.

The skill of the negotiator at this stage is playing on this competitive environment, to ensure the buyers submit their best offers. If the number of interested parties is low, the ability to create a competitive environment is greatly restricted and the buyer has the upper hand.

Structuring the transaction

The simplest structure for any transaction is a cash offer at completion. However, bridging the gap between the vendor's price expectations and the buyer's willingness to meet that figure can lead to elements of the consideration being deferred and paid at a later date.

The obvious thing to consider with deferred payments is the risk of actually receiving the payment at all! This is important when comparing offers which include a large deferred consideration against a cash sum up front. As the saying goes, 'a bird in the hand is worth two in the bush'.

Having said that, deferred consideration in the form of bank guaranteed loan notes, with an appropriate coupon rate (i.e., vendor receives interest on the deferred amount until it is paid) is very safe and can assist with the seller's personal tax planning. If the consideration also includes shares of the acquiring company, the seller should satisfy themselves as to the potential 'strength' of those shares and the ability they have to sell those shares in turn to realise their value. Therefore, it is more attractive normally to receive shares in a public company where a ready market exists than a private company.

Tax considerations

This is always a significant issue for owners of businesses who are shortly to realise significant capital gains. The purpose of the disposal process is to maximise the net proceeds from the sale. Therefore, whilst the issue of taxation has been raised only towards the end of this chapter, it is something that should be considered at a very early stage. Tax considerations of the shareholders can dictate not only the structure of the transaction but also the timing of when the business is sold, reaffirming the importance of involving advisers as soon as possible.

DISPOSAL OF AN OUTDOOR GARDEN FURNITURE MANUFACTURER

Although only started early in 1995, the company, a garden furniture manufacturer, grew quickly and by 1997 had sales of £1 million, producing an adjusted trading profit before tax of £300,000.

The vendor, who had not expected the rate of growth to be that rapid, realised that the company's premises and management resources were going to be insufficient to maintain the level of growth previously experienced.

As the vendor was nearing retirement age, and in order to allow the company to realise its full potential, the timing seemed to be right to sell the company.

Working closely with BDO Stoy Hayward, an initial list of 25 potential acquirers was identified. Each of these companies was then approached to establish what interest (if any) they had in acquiring the company. From these approaches, 12 companies expressed an interest, and after signing and returning an appropriate confidentiality agreement, they each received a copy of the company's sale memorandum.

Over the next four to five weeks the process involved responding to any queries raised and an additional information release. The decision was taken to put back the deadline for offers by one week to accommodate additional information requests. Indicative offers were received from four potential buyers five weeks after the release of the sale memorandum.

The initial view from the vendor and advisers was that the offers received were too low in view of the company's strong trading performance at that time. The companies which had made offers were contacted again and, following a further two weeks of negotiation, the offer that was eventually accepted had improved by 30 per cent.

Following a successful due diligence exercise and satisfactory tax clearances, the transaction completed eight weeks later.

From start to finish the whole process took 15 weeks.

Conclusion

We finish with a few hints and tips on what to watch out for in the selling process.

- get the timing right

- spend time in identifying potential buyers and weed out the inappropriate ones

- use suitably qualified advisers at an early stage

- prepare a detailed sales memorandum covering all the key aspects of your business

- ensure a confidentiality agreement is in place before the sales memorandum is released

- be clear about the price below which you will not sell

- if deferred consideration forms part of the deal, ensure it is secure and relatively risk-free

- where shares are offered, assess your ability to trade those shares

- take tax advice early on in the selling process

10

Managing through recession

Introduction

Throughout this book we have discussed the issues faced by businesses as they pass through various stages of growth. When considering growth using the DIAMOND model framework, it is important to recognise that not every business will grow through each of the seven stages. At any time during its existence a business can:

- plateau at a certain stage of growth;

- be sold (see Chapter 9);

- fail.

In this chapter we will consider the extent of, and reasons for, business failure in the UK, and the strategies and tactics that can be employed by business to manage successfully during a recessionary period or economic slowdown.

In many cases business failure results from simply not following good business practice. The purpose of this book has been to highlight many aspects of good practice and how these aspects relate to the various stages of growth a business may pass through. This chapter focuses on how a recession or economic slowdown can impact upon the business environment and increase the rate of business failure.

Reasons for business failure

Like death and taxes, in a competitive market economy, business failure will always be with us. In 1997, a relatively prosperous year for the UK economy, 14,447 companies went into receivership or insolvent liquidation (according to Department of Trade and Industry statistics).

Although liquidations and receiverships in 1997 were only 51 per cent and 20 per cent respectively of their 1992 levels, which was the peak of the last UK recession, it is too simplistic to view recession as the sole cause of business failure. There are many other factors that cause some companies to prosper while others fail.

Society of Practitioners of Insolvency (SPI) survey

The SPI undertake an annual survey, which includes a review of the reasons for business failure. Their seventh annual survey covers the period from 1 July 1996 to 30 June 1997, and some of the key findings are set out below.

(a) A loss of market was cited as the primary reason for corporate failure in 27 per cent of cases. This was a particularly serious factor in the retailing and manufacturing sectors.

(b) A loss of long-term finance and lack of working capital was cited in 25 per cent of cases as the primary cause of failure.

(c) Management-related reasons, including fraud, over-optimistic business planning, erosion of margin, product obsolescence, and over-gearing were considered the principal reasons for failure in 22 per cent of cases.

Factors causing business failure

There are many reasons why businesses fail and, although some businesses fail for unique reasons, there are many whose failures can be categorised, as shown in Figure 10.1.

Figure 10.2 sets out the number of corporate insolvencies since 1992.

Corporate insolvencies for the third quarter of 1998 represent 1 per cent of the total limited companies in England and Wales (third quarter of 1992 was 2.2 per cent), according to DTI statistics.

This illustrates the fact that corporate insolvencies have fallen significantly since the peak of the recession in the early 1990s. Nonetheless, this should not encourage complacency amongst the business

---

Figure 10.1 Reasons for business failure

Adverse market changes

- Changes in demand for the product – particularly relevant to fashion and technology business
- Location – common in retail business, for example, where retail parks are opened near market towns
- Changes in regulation – for example, family-owned butchers unable to meet the cost of refrigerated counters imposed by the EU
- Contraction due to recession
- Over-capacity caused by no barriers to market entry

Personal characteristics and circumstances management

- Weak or unskilled management unable to make difficult decisions effectively
- Breakdown in the relationship between the owners, typically where two or more owners/directors
- Personal problems of the managing director/owner affecting his ability to manage the company
- Inappropriate succession planning
- Self-delusion concerning specific asset values

Costing, accounting and profitability

- Inability to cost products correctly
- Ignorance of the market and under-pricing goods
- Imprudent accounting which hides problems of the business, i.e., not recognising stock obsolescence
- Failure to produce timely accounts – meaning a time delay in becoming aware of issues
- Over-optimism in budgets leading to poor financial planning, and concern from lenders
- Poor working capital management
- Excessive overheads
- Erosion of margins for key products
- Over-reliance on one product or customer
- Over-reliance on a few key suppliers
- Over-reliance on key personnel, e.g., sales director

Marketing and sales

- Poor targeting of marketing effort, leading to high cost but low returns
- Lack of effective incentives for sales staff
- Lack of competitor analysis and understanding

Product quality
- Poor quality and finish of product leading to customer dissatisfaction and ultimately loss of customer
- Shortage of technological knowledge
- Late delivery leading to deterioration in customer relations
- Shortage of skilled staff
- Over-engineering a product leading to irrecoverable costs

Strategy
- Lack of clear direction for management team
- Lack of analysis of how the market has changed/will change
- Lack of communication and control over implementation of the strategy
- Assuming inappropriate level of risk

Bad debts
- Poor screening of new customers
- Poor monitoring of existing credit limits
- Ineffective chasing procedures

Finance
- Lack of long-term finance
- Lack of equity
- Long-term assets out of balance with short-term liabilities
- Poor management of working capital (especially stock)
- Failure to manage exchange rate
- Inability of management to invest their own funds in the business

Figure 10.2 Number of corporate insolvencies

	1992	1993	1994	1995	1996	1997
Liquidations	24,425	20,708	16,728	14,536	13,461	12,610
Bankruptcy	32,106	31,016	25,634	21,933	21,803	19,892
Administrative receivership	9,319	5,362	3,877	3,226	2,701	1,837
CVA	76	134	264	372	459	629
Administration orders	179	112	159	163	210	196
IVA	4,686	5,679	5,103	4,384	4,466	4,545
	70,791	63,011	51,765	44,614	43,100	39,709

community, and the next section looks at the steps a business can take to ensure it is well placed to survive and grow through a recession.

Business strategies during a recession

A recession is normally defined as two consecutive quarters of negative growth in the UK economy.

At the time of writing in early 1999 we keep hearing and reading that there is now the danger that the UK economy will not only slow down but may move into a formal recession. The more we hear and read this, it is natural that our optimism falls, with a resultant risk that we talk ourselves into a recession and turn pundits' philosophies into grim reality.

The BDO Stoy Hayward Business Trends Report – Quarterly Review (published November 1998) pulls together the results of all the main business surveys, and this points to falling business confidence from small firms right up to the largest in the country.

It would be fatal for a business to just wait until an economic downturn impacts on it. Prior to economic downturn, the business should take a critical look at all aspects of its activities and should devise plans for making sure the business is in the best possible condition to face the uncertainties to come. This is in fact an essential management procedure whether or not a recession does arrive. Recessions, it has to be remembered, also provide good commercial opportunities for those that survive.

By adopting a critical review of procedures, any business will improve both its financial performance and stewardship of its assets and provide better protection for the owners and employees of their business. The points that are set out in this section are basic good management housekeeping points which no business should overlook.

Each part of the business should be critically reviewed and key strategic issues should be identified and tackled in order to make the business leaner and fitter, either to enhance competitive advantage in the future or to guard against the financial impact of a recession.

Cash flow

Cash is king

It cannot be stressed strongly enough that 'cash is king'. If a company is unprofitable but has cash resources, then it has time to change the business and make it profitable once more or organise a structured exit thereby providing the owners with some return on their investment. Conversely, even a profitable company will fail if it runs out of cash. In reality, good businesses can get support if they act as soon as a problem is identified.

During the last recession there were many cases familiar to business advisers where good businesses were lost purely because their capital resources dried up and were not capable of being replaced. At this particular time, the focus of all management must be very heavily weighted into conserving cash at all costs and reducing cash outgoings to an absolute minimum commensurate with the essential running of the business. It is vital that all non-performing assets are recognised and converted into cash.

Short-term forecasts

It is essential that short-term cash flow forecasts are drawn up which literally examine the cash requirements to operate the business on a daily basis. This does not have to be a particularly sophisticated document, but every business owner should be clear what the present cash position is and how it is likely to change over the next week or so. Having drawn up short-term forecasts using realistic assumptions, management needs to act.

Longer-term cash forecasts

As well as keeping a close eye on the short-term cash position it is important that the longer-term issues are not overlooked. Trends need to be identified to make sure that a business will continue to operate within the facilities agreed between it and its banker. Surviving for the next week or so is one thing, but it is important to keep the wider picture clearly in mind. If danger signals are spotted, it is time to turn your attention to eliminating this problem before it becomes serious.

Adjusting longer-term cash flow plans

Because of what is happening in the short-term cash flow forecast, it may be necessary to adjust the longer-term cash flow plans of the business to reflect more accurately the direction in which the business is going. This could lead to early discussions with a bank to see whether increased facilities could be negotiated to accommodate the longer-term requirement. If the application for increased facilities is declined, a business needs as much time as possible before the event actually arrives in which to re-engineer its circumstances and avoid breaching agreed facilities.

Keeping communication open

When a business owner recognises that difficulties are looming, it is vital they do not retreat into their shell, because it is at that time that communication is at its most important. It is important not to overlook the necessity of taking advice wherever possible. The business owner should be talking constantly to his accountant and banker. Because of the effects of the last recession, many businesses are still suspicious of the reception they will get from their banker when discussing business problems, but the alternative is no communication at all. The one thing that bankers hate most is nasty surprises.

Breaching bank covenants

Bank covenants are requirements to operate within agreed financial parameters, for example, keeping a minimum amount of good trade debtors. In looking at a business's usage of cash, it is important to watch the bank covenants which will have been agreed the last time the facility was reviewed. If the cash flow forecast shows that the bank covenants are going to be breached, the business should warn the bank immediately rather than wait until the event happens, by which time options to help the business may have been reduced or eliminated.

Negotiating bank facilities

If a business identifies that a temporary addition to the negotiated bank facility is required, it is important that it does not ignore the current overdraft limit and go on issuing cheques. The business should contact the bank and get permission to issue the cheques before it breaches its limit. It is at such times that individuals need to consider carefully their exposure to personal liability as directors or shadow directors.

Chasing trade debts

In a business the most obvious source of cash is from trade debts. Producing the goods or service and invoicing them to a customer does not mean that the transaction is complete. It is only a good transaction, even if on paper it is profitable, once cash has been paid into the bank account.

We will examine good credit control procedures later in this chapter, but for now it is important that a business realises that it needs to chase the collection of trade debts on a daily basis. It is true to say that a debtor which has only finite cash resources is likely to pay the creditor which harasses them most. Remember that in the past many good businesses have failed purely because they have been over-reliant on the collection of a large trade debt which failed to materialise.

Caution with new customers

Ironically, many businesses find that in difficult economic climates it is somewhat easier to attract potential new customers. Initially, this may seem a good thing but extreme caution must be used. Is the business sure that it wants to attract this type of new business? Does the new business come with unacceptable degrees of credit risk? Is this new 'business' a customer that has been turned away from its traditional sources?

Using working capital

It is always important to recognise that a working capital facility such as a bank overdraft should not be used to support the purchase of fixed assets or investments. It should be used for working capital purposes, i.e., the resource which enables a business to trade. Any part of working capital which is hard-core or non-moving should more properly be dealt with on a term-loan rather than an overdraft basis.

Management information

Keeping up to date

It is essential for a business to generate sufficient information so that its management can be constantly appraised of the current position and how it is changing. In other words, good management information acts as a highly effective early warning system. This management

210

information need not always be full management accounts – many managers develop their own key indicators.

Detecting trends

The timely production of monthly management accounts is an obvious essential. When actual performance is compared with budgeted expectations, it is possible to see what trends are forming, in order that action can be taken immediately where necessary.

Spotting danger signals

An examination of the key operating ratios and balance sheet relationships should be carried out by the business in order to spot danger signals. These could include a deteriorating gross margin, extended debtor days or stock obsolescence.

Using experience

A good accountant will have observed in many businesses how problems have arisen and, most importantly, how they have been solved. Businesses can benefit from this experience by using a good adviser who can potentially save the business a lot of time and trouble.

Drawing comparisons

It can be a very lonely position owning and running a business and so it is important that a comparison is made from time to time between a specific business and other operators within the same market sector or niche. Unless this is done, it can be difficult for a business to gauge its profitability, usage of working capital, production efficiency or a whole host of other management issues against the performance of its competitors.

This comparison or benchmarking exercise will throw up many interesting action points which a good manager will implement to maximise operating performance. There are many sources of information available in order to carry out a benchmarking exercise. Businesses can search Companies House files for a specific competitor and compare the filed financial information with its own performance. However, this is likely to be of limited use and, in any event, historic. Financial information on competitors can be found in trade journals and commercially accessible databases. A word of warning though – when comparing accounts remember that companies do not have consistent accounting policies and this will necessitate adjustments if meaningful comparisons are to be made.

Also, a large amount of benchmarking work is being carried out by the DTI, and this is available to businesses through local Business Links.

Action points

The results of benchmarking and a review of the management accounts will enable the business to draw up a list of action points. Time and resources will then need to be allocated to put them into place.

Measuring the changes

The next set of management accounts will enable you to measure the improvements or even deterioration in the position since the action plan was implemented. This review will then throw up a further series of points which must be addressed.

Sales and marketing

Profit over turnover

Businesses should not just chase increased turnover. Increased turnover does nothing for a business unless it is demonstrably profitable. If it is not profitable, increased turnover can just increase financial strain. Stocks and debtors rise and so too does the risk of bad debts.

Best information for managers

The information systems within a business have to be capable of informing managers which products, branches or customers are the most profitable. Without this information, it is impossible for management to concentrate on those areas of business which will produce the best returns.

Observe competitors and markets

In order to make the business as competitive as possible, it should constantly be aware of what prices competitors are charging and what developments are taking place within its market sector. Once management is armed with this information it must act to improve its own competitive position.

A successful business should be able to anticipate and plan for market changes. The techniques a business can use are, for example:

- tracking sales by product;

- keeping up to date with industry developments through trade journals;

- customer surveys.

Building payment incentives

If the business is trying to increase sales it is important that those people who are generating sales for the business are as motivated as possible. It may be important to revisit the way the business rewards these people and increase the weighting of their remuneration structure towards commission and away from basic rates. Also, commission should not be paid to staff until the business has been paid by its customers.

Reviewing marketing

All businesses in the period leading up to an economic downturn should examine their marketing plans very carefully. It is obviously not sensible to eliminate all marketing expenditure, as this short-term conservation of cash will lead to ultimate deterioration in the levels of business obtained. Action should be taken, however, to concentrate marketing resource on those individual initiatives which promise to give the quickest payback in terms of new business.

Reviewing staff

When economic conditions are tough and the rest of your workforce is dependent upon sales performance to guarantee their own jobs, keeping on a poor salesman is likely to be extremely bad for morale.

Talking to customers

No business is perfect and it is still amazing so see how many businesses do not take the time and trouble to actually go and talk to their customers. It may occasionally be a hard discussion to have, but it is an absolutely essential one. The business needs to know

213

from its customers how satisfied they are with its service and, most importantly, how they would recommend improvements to that service.

Unless the business is providing customers with product or service at the right quality, time and price, then the business is vulnerable to losing those customers, particularly when the economic environment hardens.

Marketing audits

Either with the help of external advisers or on its own, a business should subject itself to a marketing audit. This will review where the business is within its marketplace, where its unique selling points exist and how it can optimise competitive advantage. With the help of a full SWOT analysis, it can identify how to maximise the usage of its strengths and opportunities and pay attention to potential weaknesses and threats.

Timing invoices

Businesses should time the actual despatch of sales invoices to customers to minimise the credit period during which the debt is outstanding. Even delaying the despatch of a sales invoice by a few days could mean that the customer can legally take another 30 days' credit, and this is an unnecessary waste of working capital. In cases where long-term contracts are involved, regular invoices on account are essential to maintain cash flow.

Learning from customers

In order to attract additional quality customers, businesses need to face up to their failures. For instance, it can be useful to talk to those ex-customers who no longer trade with you to find out precisely why they left. Was it the service, the attitude of some of your company personnel, the price, the quality? The business needs to establish what turned off the old customer, and then make sure that the chances of it happening again are minimised.

Getting the right customers

Whilst all businesses like to have large important customers, it is important to make sure there is a reasonable spread across the customer base. Concentration of sales on one customer does make a business vulnerable to the potential failure of that customer or subject to unfair pressure from that customer.

Dealing with complaints

Every business should formally record customer complaints. Management should, from time to time, examine this record and take action in order to minimise the chances of similar complaints being raised in the future.

Reviewing marketing materials

Businesses often continue just using the same marketing materials year after year. However, due to printing and technological changes, it can be relatively inexpensive to refresh materials or bring in major changes to the design and look of the literature and documentation.

Getting the most from customers

When concentrating on boosting sales performance, a business has to be conscious of trying to increase the number of times a customer comes back for the product or service, and of increasing the average value of each sales order.

Ensuring payment

If possible, businesses should negotiate payment by their customers through the BACS system or by direct debit to increase the chances of being paid on the negotiated date.

Timing payments, discounts and VAT claims

It may be possible for a business to negotiate early settlement of debts in return for reasonable levels of discount, and there may be cases where it is more important to get that cash into the bank than it is to receive 100 per cent of the invoice price. Also, it is important not to forget to lodge timely VAT bad debt relief claims if a customer fails to pay. It just makes the cash position worse for the business by paying over the VAT when there is no need to do this.

Cost of sales

Cut out overtime

It may be stating the obvious, but businesses should seek to eliminate the use of all non-essential overtime. Overtime at premium rates in times of economic difficulties is crazy.

Honesty with employees

If the business is in difficulties, it is important to be truthful with the employees. In particular, if the economic situation does decline, the business is going to need its employees firmly on its side. By taking them into its confidence, the business will win the respect of its employees and, more importantly, will have a stronger and more cohesive team to fight the future economic conditions.

Review production routines

For an enterprise to be successful it must have a sustainable, profitable flow of work. One key element of profitability is obtaining maximum efficiency and minimum available cost.

One of the main factors producing inefficiency and cost overruns is inertia within an organisation. Procedures and systems that exist simply because 'that's the way they have always been done' can be dangerous in a changing market.

Management should periodically conduct reviews of its systems as though it was starting the business from a greenfield site, considering the best methods of production, costing, accounting and management. In short, management should always be prepared to 'think the unthinkable' (even if this cannot be implemented for practical reasons). Incidentally, thinking the unthinkable includes closing the business if it becomes unviable in the long term.

Sourcing materials

The business should ensure that it does not become over-reliant on one source of critical material. Difficulties within that supplier could seriously put your own business performance in peril. Always dual- or triple-source critical materials.

Just in time techniques

Many large companies have radically changed the way they have materials delivered into their factories. The purpose of this is to reduce the length of time that material is held within a factory before despatch to a customer. These JIT (just in time) techniques are equally applicable to small and medium-sized businesses and can significantly improve the use of working capital.

Minimising stock levels

JIT techniques can minimise stock levels and this can once again have a great impact on the amount of cash the business needs to use. But do remember if your business is supplying customers who use JIT, your own stock levels could rise unless you amend your own manufacturing procedures accordingly.

Forming connections

In an attempt to improve the price at which materials are sourced, it is often possible for several businesses to form a loose association – almost an informal co-operative – to increase their joint buying power. This is best done on a national or at least wide geographical basis to avoid competitive difficulties within a local marketplace.

Wages and recruitment

Needless to say, in difficult economic times there must be a freeze on wage increases and almost a total block on recruitment.

Contracting out

In certain instances it may be possible for a part of a business's production requirements to be contracted out more efficiently. Businesses should have an open mind and examine whether this is feasible.

Generating contracts

Conversely, perhaps the business can attract other businesses to out-source part of their production requirements on a cost-effective basis. Obviously, a similar cost/benefit exercise would need to be completed before the business should invest in conducting a marketing campaign to attract this type of business.

Bonus incentives

The business should consider paying its production management team bonuses related to improvements in production efficiency and reduction in output prices.

Pay incentives

The business should consider paying everybody in the business a degree of their remuneration directly linked to improvements in efficiency or profitability.

Review standards

It is important that standard costs and process times are constantly reviewed to make sure that they continue to represent actual circumstances. To do otherwise would be to mislead management, and render them incapable of effectively negotiating good and accurate selling prices or knowing what products to stop making and selling if price is the main determinant.

Capitalising on success

Any business which is manufacturing or producing a number of different product lines must be able to assess which are the most profitable in order to capitalise on the limited number of opportunities. Management can then concentrate on producing and selling those products which generate the greatest return.

Negotiate hard

In negotiating with suppliers, a business needs to be as tough with them as customers are likely to be with the business. In harsh economic times sales are difficult to get, so the business should negotiate discounts with its suppliers or, alternatively, extended credit periods. Both of these have actual cash values for the business. Be on guard though – this works both ways and your suppliers may read this book.

Cut your losses

If the business identifies production lines which are not generating acceptable levels of margin or contribution to overheads, it should stop producing those goods. This may impact on the number of employees required, but the overall performance of the business should improve.

Review staffing

Sadly, it is during an economic slowdown that businesses need to take a long hard look at both direct and indirect employees and justify whether their continuing employment contributes to the efficient operation of the business. If a business finds that it is 'carrying' any employees then difficult decisions may have to be taken for the benefit of the business as a whole. However, an assessment will need to be made of any redundancy costs and how these are to be funded.

Review working patterns

If the business is operating on multi-shift working patterns, consider whether these can be changed in order to reduce payroll and overhead costs.

Planning redundancies

Whilst one hopes that no business has to embark on a programme of redundancies, there is one piece of advice that should be considered. It is not sensible to deal with a redundancy programme in a piecemeal fashion. Such a policy has a very corrosive effect on the morale of those people remaining in the business, as they are constantly worrying when the next round of redundancies is going to be made. If a business does have to embark on a programme of redundancies, assess the situation carefully and deal with it completely and at once.

Overheads

Reviewing suppliers

It is amazing to find that many businesses still have procedures for buying goods and services which are frankly inadequate. These businesses do not take the time or trouble to check whether they are buying efficiently or whether there are significant savings to be made by changing suppliers or negotiating better deals with current suppliers. There are considerable savings in overheads to be made if businesses look critically at how they currently buy and find out whether better deals can be made.

Economic ordering

In order to minimise cash outlays, a business should look at how frequently it buy things such as consumables. By ordering more frequently but in smaller quantities, the business will be able to keep lower stocks and improve its pattern of cash outlays.

Justifying expenditure

As far as expenditure such as subscriptions, seminars, conferences, training, etc. are concerned, a business should start from a zero base and justify all expenditure it makes on such items. It may well be that the majority can be cancelled until business conditions improve. It is also wise to eliminate all entertaining.

Development programmes

Every business should take a close look at its research and development programmes and isolate essentials from luxuries. Only expenditure on R&D items which are essential for the continuing and effective operation of the business should be authorised. It is highly likely that long-term development programmes will need to be deferred.

Revenue possibilities

Premises utilisation should be reviewed in order to identify whether a business can sub-let in order to generate revenue or instigate a sale and leaseback.

Check expense claims

A small matter perhaps, but depending upon the number of people a business employs, it is important that a business only reimburses expenses which are essential and business-related.

Justify expenditure

Expenditure on repairs should be fully justified before being authorised, but be aware of potential problems in the long term if repairs are repeatedly postponed.

Advertising priority

If there is a measurable relationship between sales and advertising in a business, then it is sensible to maintain this expenditure. If there is no such correlation, advertising is probably more of a profile-raising exercise in which case it should be deferred.

Considering marketing

Most businesses at a time of economic slowdown will be taking a long hard look at their marketing budgets. In difficult economic times, it becomes even more important to have a continuous and sensibly financed marketing programme. However, due consideration should be made as to the costs of financing such a programme.

Calling in consultants

There is a whole range of consultants who can review a business's telephone and communication systems and its use of utilities such as gas and electricity. They can often come up with plans which will radically change the amount of money a business spends in these areas, and their reward is normally only tied to cost savings, so the business does not have much to lose in letting consultants perform their audits.

Fixed assets

Fixed assets to cash

Businesses should seek to identify any fixed assets which can be turned into cash. In most businesses, there will be pieces of plant, equipment, fittings, etc. that are no longer essential.

Negotiating terms

If the business is mid-way through purchasing fixed assets, with facilities provided through a hire purchase company or leasing company, they should be approached to determine whether the business can extend the agreement and reduce the monthly outgoings or, alternatively, negotiate a capital holiday. There is a certain ironic truth to the fact that the bigger the debt the easier it is to get part of it cancelled. Also, watch out for the effect on any personal guarantees that have been given.

Prudent purchases

One simple rule in difficult economic times – do not buy any fixed assets unless absolutely essential. The exception to this rule would be where expenditure leads to rapid cost reduction and a swift return to profitability, but such cases will be rare.

Stock

Looking at stock

Many businesses believe that they have old stock items which will at some point in the future be turned into profitable business. However, examples exist of builders and developers who have become insolvent by hanging on to their land banks, when it would have been more justifiable to turn this asset into much needed cash to reduce bank pressures.

With this in mind, businesses should similarly examine all old stock to identify items which can be turned into much needed cash. The mere act of holding stock is a financial drain on a business, and one simple rule is do not hoard stock. The only stock that should be on the business's premises is that which is essential for feeding into your production routines in the very short term.

Question supplier changes

A business should not simply accept price increases which suppliers try to impose but should question their validity and, more importantly, check other sources to see if it can buy in cheaper elsewhere.

Reviewing purchases

Businesses should take a radical view of their purchasing routines, if necessary, by utilising external consultants in order to reduce to a minimum the actual time the stock remains in business premises.

Negotiating payments

In taking on board new financial commitments, it should be borne in mind that there are many ways in which a business can negotiate payment for the commitment. The purchase of a motor vehicle provides an ideal example. It may be beneficial to the business's cash flow to pay a small deposit, followed by 24 or 36 minimum monthly payments and a large final balloon rental which is funded from the disposal proceeds.

Debtors

Checking terms and conditions

In the first instance, a business should get a good commercial solicitor to examine its current terms and conditions of trade, including the use of retention of title clauses. The business should make sure that it is obtaining sensible protection against potential bad debts. Also, it should check that there are no loopholes which can result in its customers withholding payment or returning goods which they claim are faulty but which are really surplus to their requirements.

Credit control systems

It is absolutely essential that the business has an excellent credit control system. It is important that goods and services are invoiced as soon as possible and that this invoice is followed by a properly prepared statement of account. Once the credit period has expired, there should be a system for the timely production of reminders building up into verbal contact on a daily basis.

Insuring against bad debts

It is important, where possible, to insure against bad debts.

Make comparisons

As part of the benchmarking exercise referred to earlier, it is important for the business to assess how effective it is at debt collection by comparing its performance with that of its competitors.

Allocating credit limits

Every customer should be allocated a sensible credit limit and this should not be exceeded.

Credit checks

All potential customers should be subjected to rigorous external credit checks.

Factoring

It is true that in recent years many more companies are willing to enter factoring/invoice discounting arrangements in efforts to free up cash from debtors. This source of finance can be expensive, but does have the benefit of generating funds from sales invoices much more quickly than a business can normally persuade its customers to pay.

Incorporating maximum protection

Although not always successful, the business should make sure that its solicitor incorporates within the business's terms and conditions the maximum protection flowing from retention of title clauses. This means that title to the goods does not actually pass to the customer until they have been paid for.

Checking customers

The business should review its customer base and drop those that are bad payers and those whose nuisance value outweighs their benefit.

Widening the customer platform

The business should make real attempts to widen the customer platform rather than concentrating on just a few.

Creditors

Paying creditors

The first reaction in difficult times is to delay paying, and at first glance this seems an entirely natural reaction. A word of caution, however. If the business can afford to pay its creditors on time this should be done, as to over-extend a credit period unnecessarily means that your creditors are highly unlikely to help you should you ever need a favour.

Communicating with creditors

If the business cannot pay its creditors, consider how the other party feels. If the position were reversed, the business would be worrying about whether a debtor was intending to pay you. It is always far better to discuss payment difficulties, as a creditor would at least welcome being kept up to date. Also, in the vast majority of cases, the creditor will bend over backwards to help a fellow business through this difficult time. One thing which is certainly the case – the creditor does not want you as a bad debt.

Having looked at a large number of issues that need to be reviewed within a business if it is to be as lean and fit as it can be, it is also worth considering two further areas.

Opportunities

One person's disaster is often another person's opportunity. In any recession insolvencies inevitably increase, and whether a business is buying from a receiver or a liquidator, it should be able to negotiate an extremely good price for individual assets. This could apply to items such as stock or plant and equipment, or indeed the whole of the business.

During the last recession, for example, there was a large shake-out within the hotel industry which enabled purchasers to reduce significantly their capital and overhead base. This enabled the new businesses to be operated profitably, whereas previously their over-burdened debt structures just produced heavier and heavier trading losses.

Options available

Turnaround

Early identification of the warning signs for a troubled business are essential for a turnaround to be undertaken. The business should not have an immediate cash crisis and there should be time for a detailed analysis of the problems of the business, so that an action plan can be put in place together with a time-scale for achievement.

Restructuring

Restructuring occurs where there is a cash crisis in which matters such as staving off creditor actions, arranging for refinance facilities, identifying and selling loss-making activities, and perhaps changing the management are part of the solution. Sometimes this involves the formal insolvency of a group company, which leaves the rest of the group able to carry on trading.

Workout

A bank will not always wish to continue funding a company in the long term – the workout is the period in which alternative sources of finance are sought. This is done in a structured manner.

Insolvency

Unfortunately, there is no magic wand that can be waved which ensures that a good manager can guarantee that the business will not fail.

If all the management skills and planning turn out not to be enough to save the business, then the business should recognise the financial difficulties before trading makes the position absolutely hopeless. Businesses should not be afraid to seek advice at the earliest opportunity from an experienced insolvency practitioner or from their accountant or banker who will point them in the direction of a number of suitably qualified people.

These advisers can often reshape or reorganise the original business and then, later, sell on part or whole of the business to ensure its survival. In this way, they can safeguard the jobs of some or all of your employees, and the core business will continue to operate.

Conclusion

In this chapter we have considered the reasons for business failure. In many instances it results from simply not following good business practice.

We have also highlighted important strategies to adopt during a recessionary period in areas as diverse as cash flow, management information, sales and marketing and key components of the balance sheet such as stock and debtors.

The important message from this chapter is to watch out for the early warning signs of a troubled business, so that an action plan can be put into place at an early stage together with a time frame for implementation. If necessary, take professional advice to help achieve this.

In the next chapter we consider starting a business all over again!

11

Do it all over again

In this final chapter we review the impact that entrepreneurs have on the UK economy and look at the role of the ex-business owner who, having tasted commercial success, finds that he or she is drawn to repeating the experience.

Finally, having embarked on another business venture, we see what lessons can be learned from the past to make the second journey towards the exit a little easier.

Entrepreneurs and the economy

There are a number of common spin-off benefits to the UK economy that become apparent from a study of entrepreneurial business activity. The major contributions which these businesses make and which benefit us all are:

- jobs;
- exports;
- taxation;
- increased economic activity;
- broadening the total market.

Jobs

The theory has long been expounded that most growth in jobs created comes from the SME sector, but it is only when further analysis is made that the real truth emerges and the actual creators can be identified.

Logically, it would seem that it is from rapid growth businesses that high numbers of new jobs are created. These are businesses where annual leaps in turnover of 30 per cent or more is the norm.

It is a myth that the bulk of rapid growth businesses are new start-ups. Many of the businesses are mature. Although it is important for the vitality of the economy that there is a continuous stream of start-ups, and that these ventures do produce valuable new jobs, a major part of the new job market is dependent on major growth entrepreneurial businesses.

Exports

High growth businesses are far more successful than the average SME in trading internationally. This is largely due to the focus of their approach to sales mentioned earlier. Entrepreneurs do not typically attack large developed markets, as they are unlikely to have a unique proposition which permits rapid growth in these markets. Instead, they identify gaps or niches, then sell aggressively into these gaps. In many cases, these gaps are as evident overseas as they are in the domestic market, hence the export potential.

Taxation

Entrepreneurial activity, particularly when carried out by teams, is more likely to survive and prosper compared with a typical owner/ manager start-up. This makes such businesses important contributors to the national wealth by increasing the tax yield, both as a result of employing people who pay income tax on their earnings and by generating business profits (and finally capital gains) which are taxed too.

The enhanced survival rate is down to the quality of research, vision, strategic thinking and risk control which a true entrepreneurial team brings to a new venture.

Increased economic activity

Once an entrepreneur has opened up a sector by identifying an unexploited niche then it is in the nature of normal commercial activity that others will follow and replicate the original initiative. In this way, even though the companies may be less successful, overall employment and profit (and therefore tax contributions) do rise as a result.

Broadening the total market

Once the entrepreneur faces attack from copyists in the newly exploited niche, sales and margins start to fall, and to take the business on to the next level he or she needs a new idea or product. The only solution therefore is to diversify into related niches by further innovative activity, thus generating new sales, employment and profit.

The serial entrepreneur

Having successfully completed an exit and after a brief period of 'retirement' many entrepreneurs become bored with reviewing their investment portfolio each day and start looking for another project or adventure. Hence the term 'serial entrepreneur'.

This phenomenon, naturally, was founded in the USA and that is still the home of most of today's serial entrepreneurs, although their presence is becoming more common here and throughout Europe. In the USA there are already entrepreneurs who have formed and run new businesses on three or more occasions. These people have become known as 'threepeaters'!

The point needs making that these people may have started more than one business, but they may not be consistently successful. Indeed, the chances of achieving success a second time are slim. An entrepreneur who can point to two or more successful exits is an extremely rare commodity. If you consider that venture capitalists are successful in a big way on only one in six or seven deals, then successful repeater entrepreneurs only demonstrate about twice that hit rate.

The motive for 'doing it again' is often not monetary. The primary motivation to look for a new opportunity normally flows from entrepreneurial characteristics like restlessness and an urge to create and innovate.

Often, too, very successful entrepreneurs have this lingering doubt about their own commercial skills and abilities. Was it their talent that grew the first business or were they lucky? Were they just in the right place at the right time with the right product or service? Does it matter?

229

Not perhaps to us, but to them it seems to, and can lead to new entrepreneurial activity based solely on their need to prove to themselves that the first time was no fluke.

It is important to realise that entrepreneurial behaviour and activity is not automatically synonymous with commercial success. This is where the UK and US markets differ. In the USA, if an entrepreneur has a setback in a venture which may ultimately result in failure it is not the end of the world. The market considers that the entrepreneur will have learnt from the past difficult experience and may become a better businessperson as a result. This means that new ventures can still attract funding even after earlier failure.

The UK experience, unfortunately, is very different. A failed business owner with a new venture or idea will often find it difficult, if not impossible, to source the new capital needed.

It is this negativity which needs to be addressed in the UK if the economy is to benefit to the full from the potential serial entrepreneur. A major cultural change is needed, and the work being undertaken by the Department of Trade and Industry to remove the permanent stigma attaching to business failure in the UK could, if new legislation is introduced, have far-reaching implications in the years to come for new growing businesses and for serial entrepreneurs.

The serial entrepreneur will by virtue of having 'done it' before probably be aged 45 or more, and will be a member of an elite which is now set to grow. The large volume of MBO/MBI transactions in the late 1980s and early 1990s is now maturing and entrepreneurs and institutional backers are seeking exits. This movement will provide a pool of tested and talented people with funds (and devoted institutional backers who want to do another deal) who in time get bored and seek to repeat their entrepreneurial experience. This can only have a very positive input to the UK economic performance.

Finally, it is necessary to point out that there are many instances where second time success mysteriously eludes the entrepreneur. If analysed, there will be many different reasons for this, but among them certainly is that the business owner may not be as hungry or energetic, nor may the same innovation and focus be present. Thus, his or her inner fears may be right – perhaps the first time around they were just in the right place at the right time with the right product or service. It was just a fluke for some people!

What can be learned from the first experience?

There are a number of ways a second time entrepreneur can draw on the experience of the first business case history to make the journey into a second business more comfortable.

In the first place, they will probably have the courage to strike a harder, more commercially sensible deal, when it comes to giving away equity or negotiating the cost of banking facilities.

Perhaps one of the most valuable lessons will be learnt from studying the cycles set out in the earlier chapters of this book and comparing them with your own previous experience. You should be able to avoid many (but not all) of the mistakes made previously and identify difficult and transition issues well in advance, and amend your business plan accordingly.

You should be able to handle the management of change issues more proficiently. Amongst these, the more important are recognising when the time is right to delegate, building your team and designing some robust systems to help with a whole range of operational issues.

By drawing on previous experience, you will be able to be proactive in leading change, rather than being forced to react to an urgent need.

The second time entrepreneur will see the importance of drawing in other team members and providing them with meaningful long-term reward structures earlier in the relationship.

The experience of handling an exit will be invaluable a second time, as there can be a more managed and professional pre-sale grooming process, aimed at squeezing out the final part of the sale consideration. By operating the business with a clear strategic exit in mind, it should be possible to optimise the profit stream and hence the price a new owner is prepared to pay.

The whole issue of management information, design, implementation and usage will be far easier by using reference points from past experience.

A great saving is bound to arise from being more adept at utilising scarce management time. Past experience will allow wasted time to be reduced, and you can focus just on really crucial and important issues.

Perhaps most significant is that the first experience may have helped you to develop leadership characteristics which will make you more professional in handling the vast array of human resource issues which will again come your way.

Appendix 1

DIAMOND perspectives

Dominant business perspectives	Dreaming	Initiating	Attacking	Maturing	Overhauling	Networking	Diversifying
Management focus	• Business planning • Seed funding • Market research	• Cash flow • Winning new business • Establishing a presence	• Cash flow • Supply/demand • Establishing stability	• Planning and control • Assimilating new people • Establishing systems	• Improving performance • Business analysis • Establishing corporate objectives	• Improving corporate image • Developing new structures • Establishing strategy	• Improving brand value • Increasing flexibility • Establishing alliances
Investor focus	• Business plan	• Delivery of plan	• Sufficient returns	• Developing finance strategy	• Improving return	• Retaining stability	• Brand equity
Employee focus	—	• Excitement vs job security	• Challenged resource vs frustrations	• Professional focus vs concern about freedom	• Reward for achievement vs fear of change	• Ownership vs career credits	• Acquired prestige vs lost identity
Finance source	• Own equity • Corporate clearing	• Own equity • Corporate clearing • Efficient cash collection	• Short-term debt • Working capital facility	• Structured finance • Specialist schemes	• Structured finance • Venture capital/private equity	• Finance markets • Venture capital/private equity	• Finance markets • Venture capital/private equity

Marketing and sales focus	• Developing contacts • Establishing concept	• Stimulating demand • Simple promotion • Developing distribution channels	• Improving customer value • Improving customer quality • Increasing customer base	• Customer/market research	• Cost per sale • Customer satisfaction	• Strategic planning • Corporate positioning	• Relationship management • Channel management
IT focus	• Planning basic business requirements/technical architecture	• Basic office system/'packaged solutions' to meet business requirements	• Reliable systems • Improve internal and external communications	• Bespoke systems for competitive advantage	• Re-engineer systems to optimise business needs	• Optimise IT connectivity/extranet	• Flexible, knowledge-based, customer-centric
Supply side focus	• Establishing contacts	• Ad hoc, non-negotiated	• Applying customer criteria to purchasing decisions	• Multiple supplier management • Terms negotiation	• Rationalising supply • Power bargaining	• Some joint ventures	• Strategic alliances • Vertical chain strategies
Constitutional elements	• Family and friends • Influenced by contacts	• Limited equity ownership • Influenced by lenders	• Broadening ownership and influence	• Establishing corporate formal structures and governance	• Employee involvement	• Diverse stakeholder interest	• Complex constitution and governance
Community orientation	• Personal	• Local employment	• Random charitable • Local business associations	• Political (local)	• Co-ordinated charitable	• Political (local and central) • Community programmes	• Political (local and central)

Transitional issues						
• Overcoming gaps in knowledge • Establishing business focus • Improving business plan • Securing finance • Company formation • Establishing premises • Establishing customers	• Practical issues: basic systems for income/expenditure; meeting customer/client promises; dealing with admin • Lack of focus • Getting enough cash to pay bills • Dealing with the unforeseen • Customs & Excise • Inland Revenue • Identifying need for and recruiting staff • Ignoring IT • Quality of product/service • Low customer awareness • Competitor reaction	• Need to assess situation – plan with benefit of real business knowledge • Not robust enough to survive changes • No contingency planning • Identify skill deficiencies • Constrained by initial IT selection • Admin overload • Inadequate communication • Over-dependency on founding team	• Management surpassing leadership • Losing entrepreneurial spirit • In a rut – directionless • Losing touch with market • Executives not incentivised or motivated correctly • Lack of organisational flexibility • Innovation dampened • Inappropriate performance indicators • People skills	• Business could run away with its own success • Overpromise – underdeliver • Burn out (people and concept) • Lack of corporate governance legislation • People skills	• Nobody 'owns' the business • Business too rigid to be responsive • Highly bureaucratic • Missed opportunities in marketing • High turnover of high quality staff • Image becomes 'staid' • Internal territories • Efficient financing • European/economic/export issues • Cumbersome hierarchy • Gap between HQ and front-line

Appendix 2

Start-up workbook

The business start-up workbook includes a number of useful checklists for setting up a business. Below we have included a sample of the checklists – you can obtain a complete copy by contacting your local BDO Stoy Hayward Office.

Have you got what it takes?

1. Have you a basic working knowledge of the skills needed to run a business? ☐

   • Finance ☐

   • Marketing ☐

   • Production ☐

   • Personnel ☐

2. Have you identified why your business will have a competitive edge? ☐

3. Have you made a detailed assessment of the risks of starting a new business? ☐

4. Have you worked out how to reduce the risks? ☐

5. Have you prepared a comprehensive business plan? ☐

6. Do you understand your market and do you know where you expect to achieve sales? ☐

7. Are you willing to commit yourself totally to your business? ☐

8. Are you a determined self-starter? ☐

9. Are you self-sufficient? ☐

10. Can you take setbacks and sort them out on your own? ☐

11. Are you energetic and in good health? ☐

12. Do you have the full support of your family? ☐

Legal and insurance

1. Do you need to obtain a licence before you start trading? ☐

2. If so, have you completed the necessary application formalities? ☐

3. Are you intending to keep computer records on individuals? If so, you will need to register under the Data Protection Act. ☐

4. Has your solicitor reviewed your:
   - terms and conditions of trade? ☐
   - contracts of employment? ☐

5. Do your terms and conditions of trade contain comprehensive reservation of title clauses? ☐

6. Before signing any form of lease or legal agreement have you made yourself aware of all your legal rights and obligations? ☐

7. Do you own a trade mark or copyright which needs protecting? ☐

8. Will you want to grant a licence to others so that they may use your invention or idea? ☐

9. Are you aware that you are legally obliged to insure against certain risks to employees and members of the public? ☐

Employment

1. Has every employee been given a written statement of their terms of employment? ☐

2. Have you familiarised yourself with the law relating to:
   - unfair and constructive dismissal? ☐
   - redundancy? ☐
   - racial and sexual discrimination? ☐
   - sick leave? ☐
   - maternity leave? ☐
   - working hours? ☐

3. Are you informed as to the implications of your workforce having trade union representation? ☐

4. Are you aware of your responsibilities under the Health and
   Safety Regulations? ☐

5. Does your business conform to the required minimum
   standards for fire and other safety issues? ☐

6. Have you investigated the assistance that employers can get
   from their local TEC? ☐

7. Are you aware of the pay and conditions of service which your
   competitors give to their employees? ☐

Insurance

1. Have you appointed a good commercial insurance broker? ☐

2. Have you checked that your broker's premium quotations are
   competitive? ☐

3. Have you made satisfactory enquiries that the insurance
   companies promoted by your broker have a good
   administration and claims record? ☐

4. Before trading starts have you obtained:

   • motor insurance for business use? ☐

   • employers' liability insurance? ☐

   • public liability insurance? ☐

5. Have you carefully considered whether you need insurance
   cover for the following risks:

   • business interruption? ☐

   • product liability? ☐

   • property damage? ☐

   • key man? ☐

   • permanent health? ☐

   • professional negligence? ☐

6. Are all business assets adequately insured for replacement
   values? ☐

7. Have you considered insuring your trade debtors against loss? ☐

8. If your business will involve exporting have you insured
   specifically against those debts? ☐

Work planner

Month

J F M A M J J A S O N D J F M A M J

Planned start-up of
business

Put plan into action

Schedule quarterly
partner meetings

Schedule monthly or
quarterly
communication
meetings with bank

File VAT returns

Pre-year-end tax
planning meeting

Start preparing year 2
business plan

Audit/accounts
preparation
commences

Accounts and
computations filed with
Inland Revenue

Deadline for filing
accounts with Registrar
of Companies

File year-end PAYE
returns

File personal income
tax return

Appendix 3

Useful contacts in the early stages of growth

DTI Employers helpline
0345 143143

DTI Small Firms Publications Orderline
ADMAIL 528
London
SW1W 8YT
0171 510 0169

For various titles, including:

- A Guide to Help for Small Firms

- Financing your Business

- Loan Guarantee Scheme

Business Link – England
0345 567765

Business Connect – Wales
0345 969798

Scottish Business Shops
0141 248 6014

Appendix 4

Taxation issues

Pay as you earn (PAYE)

A sole trader with no employees is not affected by PAYE. All other businesses are affected.

As part of the general system of taxation within the UK, the Government collects income tax under PAYE and National Insurance contributions (NICs). Employers are responsible for the collection of income tax using the PAYE system, which is outlined below.

It is essential that the entrepreneur gets to grips with PAYE. If he fails to fulfil his obligations, and this results in income tax or National Insurance underpayments, the business is held responsible for these tax liabilities and can face significant penalties over and above the statutory interest payable on underpaid balances.

It can be tempting for a business in the early stages of growth to neglect this responsibility, or be tempted to use the PAYE system as another source of business finance, for example, by delaying the regular payment of payroll deductions to the Collector of Taxes. Employers who fail to comply with the rules or who delay accounting for monies that they have deducted will very quickly attract the attention of the Inland Revenue and/or the Contributions Agency. The Inland Revenue and Contributions Agency are responsible for the administration of income tax and National Insurance respectively, however, there is a joint working programme that brings them together. These are the tax authorities which primarily police the system.

As soon as the business registers with the Inland Revenue as an employer, the Revenue will provide the business with various publications which explain specific areas of the taxation. These publications are helpful but the sheer volume can be very daunting to the inexperienced reader. Some areas of taxation are complex and will require advice from a suitably qualified professional.

Provided that you are confident that the person responsible for processing your payroll is competent, and you address any questions with the benefit of advice from the tax authorities or your professional adviser, you should not go far wrong.

As an alternative, consider the services of a payroll bureau. The extra cost compared to doing it yourself may well be worth the peace of mind.

What is a payment of earnings?

Generally, all payments of earnings are subject to the deduction of tax under the PAYE system and National Insurance. For this purpose, earnings are widely defined and the tax rules specifically extend the scope of PAYE to cover certain things which the layman would not necessarily regard as earnings, for example, vouchers which can be surrendered for cash. As an employer, your approach should be to apply the PAYE system and deduct income tax unless you have some authority not to. If this leads to an overpayment of tax, then a claim for repayment can be made at a later date, but if you fail to deduct taxes the business will be held liable and it may have no right of recourse to its employees.

Employed or self-employed?

It is a fundamental feature of the PAYE scheme that it only applies to employees and not to the self-employed.

As a matter of convenience, you cannot simply decide to treat somebody as 'self-employed'. As an employer, you are responsible for making the correct decision based on the appropriate facts and circumstances.

In a number of cases it is quite clear whether or not an individual is truly self-employed. Equally, there are instances when this will be a debatable or 'grey' issue.

If an employer wrongly classifies somebody as self-employed, they can be liable for penalties for failing to apply PAYE, for tax and NI which should have been deducted at source and for interest on the amounts paid late. Clearly, this can involve large sums of money if several individuals have been incorrectly classified and/or the payments to 'self-employed' workers have been made over a number of years. This issue affects all types of businesses. Currently, it is extremely topical within the construction industry.

Both the Inland Revenue and the Contributions Agency have specialists who are responsible for ruling whether individuals are employed or self-employed. In cases of doubt, it is recommended that a full and clear statement of the facts is submitted to one of these status inspectors before any payment is made in order to crystallise this issue. It is not necessary to make an application to both the Inland Revenue and the Contributions Agency in each case as they accept each other's rulings. As there is no specific rule which can be applied to each case and the decision will ultimately be based upon an interpretation of facts, it is advisable to take professional advice in all such matters.

How much do I deduct?

Whether you calculate tax deductions manually or by using a computerised payroll, the Inland Revenue should notify you of a code number which they have calculated for each individual. The PAYE coding notice tells the employer how much tax to deduct through the PAYE system. It is essential that the business only operates code numbers which are notified by the Inland Revenue. If there is a disagreement, the Inland Revenue may be prepared to issue an amended code number.

Income tax is administered under the self-assessment system, which gives individuals responsibility for their own personal tax affairs. Clearly, it is important that employees appreciate this extends to checking their PAYE coding notice.

Paying over PAYE and National Insurance

The net tax deducted under the PAYE system, along with National Insurance contributions (NIC), must be paid over to the Collector of Taxes by each employer on a regular basis. Where average monthly remittances to the Inland Revenue are less than $1,000 (in 1999/2000), the tax deducted may be paid over quarterly. Otherwise, PAYE and NIC have to be paid monthly, within 14 days after the end of each tax month.

If the business falls into arrears with payments, it should negotiate an instalment arrangement with the Collector of Taxes which will enable it to settle the arrears. If it fails to comply with this arrangement, the Collector of Taxes may initially seek immediate payment of all arrears and against the employer's assets if payment is not forthcoming. Interest is charged on the late payment of payroll taxes (PAYE and NIC) from 14 days after the tax year to which it relates.

Annual returns

After the end of each tax year an employer is obliged to complete certain returns within specified deadlines.

- **Not later than 19 May:**
    - the employer has to complete a declaration (P35); and
    - provide each employee with a certificate of gross pay and tax deducted (P60), a copy of which is also submitted to the Inland Revenue (P14).
- **Not later than 6 July:**
    - for all employees with earnings, including the value of benefits and reimbursed expenses, at a rate of £8,500 (in 1999/2000) per annum or more, and generally for all directors, a return of benefits and expenses (P11D) has to be submitted to the Inland Revenue;
    - within the same deadline, the employee has to be informed of the details declared on the P11D to the Inland Revenue
    - for other employees not deemed to be 'higher paid' in this way, such rewards in kind are reported on a shorter form of return (P9D).

In practice, the vast majority of employees who receive benefits and expenses are deemed to be 'higher paid' so the P11D is the most common form of return.

Benefits and expenses

It is the employer's responsibility to decide whether a reward provided to an employee requires PAYE to be accounted for through the payroll or whether it should be declared on the return of benefits and expenses at the year end (P11D or P9D). The basic distinction is that a payment of income or earnings is accounted for under PAYE, whereas anything else will normally need to be declared on the return of benefits and expenses. However, this is not always an easy distinction to make, so if there is any doubt about the tax treatment of any item, the business should seek advice from the tax office which deals with its PAYE scheme or from its professional advisers.

It is worth noting that there are a number of exceptions to this general rule as there are specific statutory reliefs and Inland Revenue concessions which provide tax exemption in certain cases, such as:

- pensions;

- job-related accommodation;

- relocation expenses;

- long service awards;

- annual functions, i.e., christmas parties, when the total cost per head does not exceed £75;

- car parking near the place of work.

It is very important that the P11D makes a full declaration not only of taxable benefits, but also of all expense payments regardless of whether you consider that the employee should be taxed on them or not. Once a complete declaration of benefits and expenses has been submitted, the employee can then claim relief for business-related expenditure.

In order to simplify this reporting arrangement, the business can seek agreement from the Inland Revenue to dispense with this requirement, provided that the Inland Revenue are satisfied that expenses are no more than the reimbursement of business expenditure, and the employees have received no element of bounty or profit. As a result of the arrangement, the Inland Revenue may be prepared to issue a written dispensation if certain conditions are satisfied. Broadly, the conditions are that proper records are maintained and adequate control, including the authorisation of expenses, is exercised.

Under self-assessment, employers are obliged to calculate the taxable cash equivalent of all benefits declared in accordance with specific tax legislation. These include:

- cars and fuel available for private use;

- other assets made available for private use;

- private medical insurance;

- beneficial loan arrangements;
- mobile and home telephones;
- staff entertaining;
- accommodation.

Furthermore, the business must keep records supporting the benefits and expenses declared to the Inland Revenue for at least six years following the end of the tax year to which they relate.

Value added tax (VAT)

This is a tax payable to HM Customs & Excise and is collected on business transactions and imports. VAT is normally payable quarterly when the VAT return is submitted. The amount payable is the total of all the output tax charged to customers for the period, less input tax incurred during the period on all business expenses. If the input tax exceeds the output tax the difference is refunded.

Registration

There are three kinds of registration: compulsory, voluntary and intending.

Compulsory registration

Where a person is in business and making taxable supplies, they must register for VAT if, at the end of any month:

(a) taxable turnover exceeds £51,000 (from 1 April 1999); or

(b) there are reasonable grounds for believing that taxable turnover in the next 30 days will exceed £51,000.

Failing to register will result in financial penalties. However, where supplies are only zero-rated, Customs & Excise have discretion to exempt a person from registration.

Voluntary registration

With turnover under £51,000 a year, a person may still apply for VAT registration if they are able to convince Customs & Excise that this is applicable to their business. There are a number of advantages to voluntary registration:

(a) all input VAT can be claimed, which is especially advantageous if supplies of goods and services are zero-rated;

(b) if trading is commenced unregistered but turnover grows to the extent that registration is compulsory, the addition of VAT will increase prices and so may affect unregistered customers.

Pre-registration expenses

A person can claim up to six months' input tax on purchases made before they are registered for VAT, providing various conditions are met. Also, if a person intends to start a business in which taxable supplies will be made, but have not yet started to do so, they can apply for VAT registration beforehand.

De-registration

A person who is registered for VAT ceases to be liable to be registered for VAT and can apply to be de-registered if the taxable turnover in the next 12 months will not exceed £49,000 (from 1 April 1999).

Supplies

At present there are four categories of goods and services.

(a) *exempt*: on which no VAT is payable under any circumstances (for example, doctors' services);

(b) *zero-rated*: on which, in theory, tax is payable but in practice none is paid because the tax rate is zero per cent (for example, goods and food in shops);

(c) *standard-rated*: on which VAT at 17.5 per cent is charged – this applies to the majority of goods and services;

(d) *reduced-rated*: this mainly applies to domestic fuel which is currently charged at 5 per cent.

Imports

VAT is charged and payable on goods imported into the UK from outside EU Member States, unless special relief applies. The VAT charged on imports is reclaimable subject to the normal rules. The rate of VAT is the same as if the goods had been supplied within the UK.

Exports

Goods exported outside the Member States are zero-rated, provided certain conditions are met.

Returns and payment of VAT

Every taxable person must keep a VAT account summarising the output tax and input tax for the VAT return period. The period is normally three months but can be monthly, which is usually the case when VAT refunds are made frequently. Annual returns can also be made as discussed below.

The output and input VAT are recorded on the return together with additional information. The return should be submitted to Customs & Excise, together with a payment if it is due, no later than one month after the prescribed return period.

Records

Every taxable person must keep records of all their transactions. In particular, all tax invoices and credit notes issued and received, accounting records, and any documents relating to imports and exports must be maintained. The records are to be kept for six years, or a lesser period if Customs & Excise permit.

Assessments

Where returns have not been made, or it appears that the returns are either incorrect or incomplete, Customs & Excise have the power to raise an assessment. The assessment must be made within two years from the end of the return period or, if later, within one year of the facts on which the assessment is based coming to their attention.

Interest and penalties

Interest is chargeable by Customs & Excise where VAT has been under-declared or overclaimed. Repayment supplements are due where Customs & Excise fail to make a repayment on time, plus interest is due where a Customs & Excise error leads to a taxpayer overpaying or underclaiming VAT.

There is a large range of criminal and civil penalties.

Cash accounting scheme

Provided taxable turnover (excluding VAT) does not exceed £350,000, the cash accounting scheme may be used. Under this scheme, VAT accounts are rendered, not on the basis of tax invoices, but on the basis of monies actually paid and received. This offers advantages to businesses giving extended credit to customers and provides automatic bad debt relief.

Retail schemes

Customs & Excise provide a number of retail schemes for calculating VAT; these are intended for businesses for whom the system of issuing a tax invoice for each sale would be impracticable.

Annual accounting scheme

This is available to traders who have already been registered for at least one year, and whose annual taxable turnover (excluding VAT) does not exceed £300,000. This scheme allows them to complete one VAT return each year, instead of the four quarterly returns, and lets them know in advance how much they must pay.

The VAT liability is estimated on the basis of the previous year's payments and divided into 10 monthly portions. Nine of these are paid by direct debit. They then have two months to send in their annual return and make the tenth, balancing, payment.

Businesses with a turnover of £100,000 or less have a further option. They are not required to make interim payments if the previous year's net liability was under £2,000. If it exceeds £2,000 they can make three

251

quarterly payments of 20 per cent of the previous year's net liability and then a balancing payment.

The main advantages of this scheme are:

(a) a reduction in the number of VAT returns required;

(b) an extra month to complete the annual return and account for any balance due;

(c) no requirement to make interim payments if the above qualifications are met;

(d) no requirement to make quarterly calculations or annual adjustments where a retail scheme is used or partial exemption applies;

(e) ability to align the VAT accounting period with the financial period.

Corporation tax

Corporation tax is chargeable on the taxable profits of limited companies. (It applies also for unincorporated associations, which are not considered here.)

Corporation tax covers all of a company's profits. There is not the same distinction drawn as for individuals who might pay, for example, both income and capital gains taxes. Despite this, similar criteria apply for determining the taxable profits of companies and those of partnerships or sole traders.

Taxable profits

Taxable profits are based, in the first instance, on the company's accounting profit before tax. In recent years, there has been increasing harmonisation between accounting and taxable profits.

Nevertheless, there remain certain costs and receipts which are treated differently for the two purposes. An example of this is depreciation, which is not allowed as a deduction against taxable profits but is deducted from accounting profit, and is replaced in this tax computation by a system of capital allowances.

A company pays tax on the profits earned in an accounting period. In most cases, this is the same as the period for which a company draws up its accounts.

Recent Budget statements have seen a steady fall in corporation tax rates. At the time of writing (1999/2000), the rate for 'large' companies is 30 per cent. Smaller companies pay corporation tax at lower rates, the lowest of which is presently 20 per cent (1999/2000). In addition, from 1 April 2000 a new starting rate of corporation tax of 10 per cent will be introduced. This applies to taxable profit of £10,000 or less.

A 'large' company is, in broad terms, one whose taxable profits exceed £1.5 million per annum. Where a company is part of a group, this limit is divided equally between the active group members.

Trading losses

Companies making losses from their trading activities are normally able to 'carry back' these losses one year to reduce (or eliminate) profits made in an earlier accounting period. This carry back can result in a repayment of corporation tax.

Losses not used in this way may be set against future profit from the same trade.

There are various restrictions which apply to the use of prior year tax losses where there is a change in the ownership of a company. The major purpose of these is to ensure that losses incurred in one trade are not available to reduce the tax payable on profits earned in another.

Corporation tax self-assessment

The introduction of corporation tax self-assessment (CTSA) will impact on companies during their first accounting period beginning after 1 July 1998.

The principal effect of this will be to place the burden of proof on the company, rather than the Inland Revenue. As a result, companies will be required to be able to justify figures shown in the tax computations, rather than for the Revenue to show they are incorrect.

CTSA may be expected to increase significantly the record-keeping burden for many companies. For example, companies trading with associated companies overseas will be required, under CTSA, to be able to demonstrate that the prices charged (and all other terms and conditions) are comparable to those which would be paid by an unrelated third party. The failure to hold records which could demonstrate this is an offence under CTSA, whether or not the terms are correct!

Payments on account

Another change which affects 'large' companies at the same time is the introduction of the payments on account regime.

Under this, 'large' companies will be required to pay their corporation tax for a year in four quarterly instalments, the first slightly more than six months into the period.

This will necessitate companies' forecasting their annual taxable profits less than halfway through the year and again at three-monthly intervals.

Any amounts subsequently found to be under- (or over-) paid, when the taxable profits are finally calculated, will be subject to interest. This includes any amounts due in respect of items which could not have been foreseen (e.g., capital gain on the sale of part of the business).

Companies may alter the quarterly payments to reflect their revised forecasts.

In the first three years, payments on account are being phased in, with the proportions payable quarterly increasing from 15 per cent in the first year to 22 per cent in the third. The balance in each of these years is due and payable on the normal date, nine months into the next accounting period.

This means that a 'large' company with an accounting period of the year ending 31 December 1999 will be required to make the following payments between 1 July 1999 and 31 October 1999:

(a) 14 July 1999 – 15 per cent of the estimated 1999 tax liability;

(b) 1 October 1999 – 1998 corporation tax liability;

(c) 14 October 1999 – 15 per cent of the *revised* 1999 tax liability, adjusted to take account of any over- or under-payment on 14 July 1999.

Dividends and bonuses

Shareholder-directors of companies may withdraw funds from companies in a number of ways, the most common of which are dividends and remuneration.

The calculation to determine which of these is the more tax-efficient will depend principally upon the taxable profits of the company and the marginal income tax rates of the directors. There are, of course, other factors to consider, among them the possibility of the Inland Revenue seeking to deny tax relief for 'excessive' bonuses. The directors may also consider the effect on the company's trend of profit before tax when evaluating the size of any bonuses.

If shareholders of limited companies withdraw funds from this company on loan account, not only is this illegal under the Companies Acts, there is also a liability to taxation at the rate of 25 per cent on the amount withdrawn.

Advance corporation tax

With effect from 6 April 1999, companies will not be required to pay advance corporation tax (ACT) on dividends. The cash flow benefit of this will, in some cases, offset the cash flow disadvantages of the payments on account regime.

Those companies currently with excess (surplus) ACT will be able, subject to certain restrictions, to set this surplus against their corporation tax charge, in a similar way as is currently the case.

Appendix 5

Business plans

The business planning process – the steps

It is possible to divide the business planning process into a number of discrete steps. Each of these represents an aspect of the final plan. Set out below are the steps and how to undertake them.

Research and evaluation

Preparing the business plan will involve a certain amount of research and an assessment of what the strengths and weaknesses of the potential business really are. It is also necessary to assess its position in its chosen market. This research needs carrying out through both 'external' and 'internal' evaluations. The external evaluation focuses on:

- the position of the business in its competitive environment;
- its share of the market;
- potential market niches that are capable of being exploited;
- substitute or complementary products.

Having completed this evaluation, it will be possible to identify the opportunities and threats facing the venture.

The internal evaluation looks inside the business and examines the current management skills and availability of resources. As a result of the internal evaluation it should be possible to identify the strengths and the weaknesses of the organisation.

Set out below is guidance on how to undertake the evaluations.

The external evaluation explained

The external evaluation concentrates on examining trends in the relevant industry, the market, customers and competitors.

The industry

Research needs to be carried out into the industry and its background in order to gain an understanding of the market in which the business will be operating.

Therefore, firstly, it is necessary to identify the relevant industry. It can be more complex to identify the real industry than might be expected. For example, if the business is to manufacture pottery ornaments, will it be in the pottery industry or the gift industry? The perception of the customer is an important factor in this decision. The way to approach the development of future business operations will be determined by this perception.

Businesses should try to position themselves in an expanding industry where potential for growth and development is more readily available. Therefore, it is important to assess the opportunities open to the industry.

Identify how stable the industry is. The industry might be in a state of flux because of changing technologies. This can influence the cost structure of the potential business if new operating processes are being introduced.

As a starting point to research the industry, the following will be useful:

- trade journals;
- business and trade associations;
- commercial libraries;
- chambers of commerce;
- research institutions, such as colleges;
- recent press articles and comment.

The following factors should be taken into account when carrying out the research:

- economic trends and social changes, e.g., demographic profiles;
- political activity, e.g., the introduction of new legislation can affect operating costs.

The market

It is important to fully understand the market in which the business will operate. This is more specific than a market study and focuses on potential customers. For example, how has the market changed over the last few years? Will the business be in a position to meet its needs? The following should be considered.

(a) The size and rate of growth of the market. The entrepreneur needs to understand the market segments in which the business operates, how the buying process operates and how to make purchasing decisions.

(b) The perspective the business will have on the market. Consider what the business will bring to the market.

(c) How will the market react to the new entry? What hurdles might there be in introducing the product or service and how can these be overcome? What features of the product or service are likely to be popular?

(d) The market will be split into a number of segments. These will have particular product or service requirements:

    (i)   there may be specialist areas, or low priced, value-for-money segments;

    (ii)   adaptations might be made to the product for particular groups of consumers;

    (iii) there could be segments in the market for which the entrepreneur's business expertise will be particularly suited.

For example, a particularly wide-ranging market with a number of segments is the clothing market. Segments include sportswear, hard-wearing clothes for workers, fashionable clothes for teenagers and so on. They are all different markets and hence there will be a requirement for different targeting strategies.

It is costly to produce different ranges and models. Therefore, it is important to target and focus. Identification of the target segments will help to make assumptions for expenditure, forecasts for distribution, packaging, advertising and promotional activities for the new product or service.

Investigation of markets will help to explore the business issues. Market information will help determine future strategies by identifying the direction in which the new business should be moving. It will also identify boundaries to the future activities.

Consideration of fluctuations in the business cycle, such as seasonality of sales will need to be taken into account as this influences the business plan and associated cash flow forecasts. In the retail sector, it is said that up to 25 per cent of annual sales can be made in the six weeks prior to Christmas.

Within any market, there will be a number of ways in which information on new trends and developments is communicated. For some retail markets, trade exhibitions are held on a regular basis. In other markets, such as the chemical market, key information is published in trade journals.

Customer analysis

To whom is the business trying to sell? The business should know its target customers' preferences including, for example:

- what kind of designs, colours, sizes and quality do they prefer?
- where are the customers and how do they normally buy products/ services?
- when do they buy products or services?
- how many do they want?
- what can they afford?
- what will customers pay more for?
- what will stop customers from buying from the business?
- what level of pre- and post-sales service do they want?
- what are their key buying criteria?

Businesses must know what their customers want, both now and in the future. Data collected from customers is useful to choose and to support an appropriate strategy for the new venture.

The start-up survey found that identifying potential customers and obtaining first sales was relatively easy. In fact, 83 per cent found it easy or relatively easy. Likewise, 53 per cent found making the first sales easy and only 3 per cent found it difficult.

Competitor analysis

It is important that there is an understanding of what the business will be competing against. It would be useful to carry out a review of competitors' products, prices and approach to marketing.

Researching the competition can be difficult as information is not always readily available. For a full analysis of the competition you need to obtain as much information as possible on the following:

- products;
- distribution methods;
- promotional activity;
- brand image;
- sales/market share;
- people;
- key accounts;
- supplier relationships;
- cost base;
- price;
- profitability.

Knowing how profitable competitors are will help to identify strengths and weaknesses in the new business.

The internal evaluation

For the internal evaluation consideration should be given to the availability and use of skills and resources, and how operational procedures will support the business.

Core skills in the management team

The assessors of the business plan will want to be confident that the management team is capable of achieving the stated objectives. Identification of weaknesses in the management team or any lack of management skills is important, so that it is possible to tackle them early on. When assessing the skills available within the new business organisation, the focus should be on the experience and abilities of the key people in the team, their qualifications, background and experience.

The main assessors of the business plan should be the business owners – after all they are the ones who are putting their livelihood at risk. All too often, however, it is left to the financier to provide the critical assessment of the business plan and, unfortunately, this assessment is often narrowly based around the financial implications.

As shown in Figure 1, the survey found that sales and marketing skills were the predominant skills held by the start-up management team, followed by accounting and production, legal and then banking skills.

It is worthy of note that the skills more typically lacking can be bought in on a needs basis. There is no need to start with a finance manager if the entrepreneur is not trained in finance – the external accountant should be able to offer the necessary input. All too often, however, the external accountant is simply asked to prepare year-end accounts and tax returns, so a key skill is absent from the business.

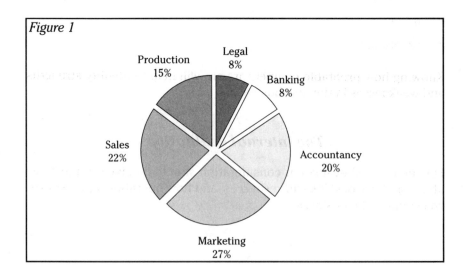

Figure 1

Production 15%
Legal 8%
Banking 8%
Sales 22%
Accountancy 20%
Marketing 27%

Organisational structure and personnel

The availability of skills will not benefit the company unless they are utilised to the best effect. The organisation's structure should be as simple as possible, consistent with providing full control over activities. The ideal structure will show adequate personnel in all departments. None will be over- or under-staffed. Everyone will know what their role is and all responsibilities will have been assigned. Jobs will be challenging but people will not be overworked. Review and assess the intended structure of the business to determine whether the right people are in the right jobs doing the right things.

However, this is not always possible in the early stages of a business. Often, the owner of the business will perform several roles which can eventually lead to problems. It is therefore necessary to consider those roles and to recognise at what stage it may be necessary to take on new employees to fill those roles.

Assets and resources

Good resource management can determine the continuing health of the business and its capacity to tackle new opportunities. Consideration of the costs of maintaining and developing the resource base is an important issue to be addressed in the business plan. This might include the following areas.

Premises
Are the premises to be leased or owned? Money tied up in property can show commitment to the business. If the property is to be leased, it is important to know that the lease is long enough to make the business a success. Are the premises adequate for the business's needs and do they have capacity for planned expansion? If the existing premises will not accommodate the expansion, what are the proposals to increase capacity?

The start-up survey found that 43 per cent thought that finding suitable premises was a straightforward exercise, although with hindsight 17 per cent felt that their initial choice was wrong and would like to move. The reasons given for this are summarised in Figure 2.

Plant and machinery
Assessment will be needed of expenditure required to maintain efficient and effective operations. It will be necessary to establish quickly how

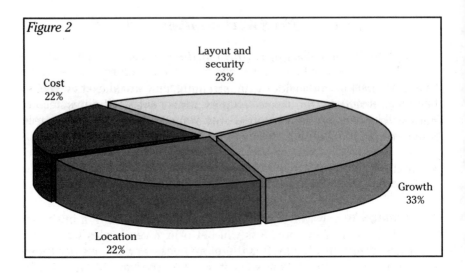

Figure 2

Layout and security 23%

Cost 22%

Growth 33%

Location 22%

much plant will deteriorate as this will determine the level of expected future expenditure on new machinery or maintenance.

Operational procedures

The way the business is to be run and controlled is of paramount importance. Will it be able to manufacture and supply the quantity and quality of new products or services that are projected in the forecast? It is important to understand how the product will be manufactured and what facilities, sub-contractors and equipment will be needed to produce the product.

Operational procedures include all procedures used to run and control the business, including management information and employment policies.

Employment policies

As people are critically important, particularly in a service company, it is important to show that cost-effective employment policies have been developed to attract, retain and motivate employees. This issue is considered in detail in Chapter 5.

The SWOT analysis

Strengths and weaknesses

The next stage is to consider what strengths and weaknesses the business has. Strengths are those features which enable the business to perform better or operate more cheaply or more effectively than others. Strengths might arise from:

- abilities;
- educational background;
- technical knowledge or experience.

Weaknesses are areas capable of improvement, such as a higher cost base or lower productivity relative to the competition. Again, how the business intends to capitalise on those strengths and what actions to take in order to overcome the business's weaknesses should be documented.

Opportunities and threats

Having completed the external and internal evaluations, a number of opportunities for and threats to the business should now be identifiable. These can include:

- market areas;
- potential uses of products and services;
- marketing or promotional techniques.

At the same time, however, threats or risks to the business should also be identified. These include:

- external factors such as inflation, social changes or governmental activity;
- internal factors such as lack of skills that might be required for the future.

Financial forecasts

In the start-up survey, of the 78 per cent of respondents who prepared business plans, detailed financial forecasts were prepared by the vast majority of them and nearly all found them useful (see Figure 3).

It is strongly recommended that the financial forecasts are prepared on a spreadsheet and that thought is given to the key variables as the spreadsheet is set up. This enables a quick and easy examination of the effects of price changes, expenditure levels, credit periods and spending on marketing activities by trying out different alternatives.

It is important to make an estimate of the projected profit or loss. This enables the assessment of the viability, and the sensitivity of the plans for changes in prices, margins and market activities.

Also, a spreadsheet should be flexible in order to test how variations in other key variables, such as sales or interest rates for example, would impact on the forecasts. Any prospective investor would want to be confident that the business can withstand at least minor fluctuations in these variables.

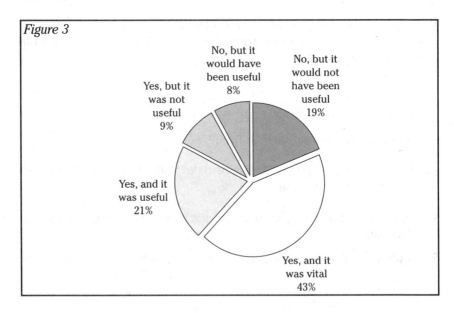

Figure 3

No, but it would have been useful 8%

No, but it would not have been useful 19%

Yes, but it was not useful 9%

Yes, and it was useful 21%

Yes, and it was vital 43%

Writing the business plan

The aim of the plan is to draw together the different elements of the business in a logical way in order to present them as a whole. Forecasts must be realistic and assumptions stated and tested. The business plan might be structured as follows.

Title page – the cover carries the name of the business, address, telephone number, the date of preparation of the plan and the name of a contact at the business so that the reader can ask questions as required.

Contents page – it is important to lay out the contents clearly with each topic and page numbered. This makes locating the information required easier for the reader.

Executive summary – the executive summary should in one or two pages outline:

- a brief description of the business, e.g., products or services, target market;

- its aims and objectives over a stated time period, in particular growth plans (and assumptions underlying this growth);

- finance required;

- the benefits likely to accrue to an external investor (if relevant).

Potential investors in the business will only read on if the summary fully attracts their attention.

Section one: Overview of the business

As an introduction to the proposition, this section is used to briefly describe the background to the new business. This does not normally extend beyond two pages and includes the following topics:

(a) how the idea for the business was first developed;

(b) how the business is to trade, e.g., sole trader, partnership or limited company;

(c) main products or services: a description of products or services proposed. This includes highlighting the particular advantages the products or services have over others in the marketplace. This, for example, includes cost advantages, specialist skills, together with any guarantees and services intended to be offered with the products;

(d) target market: who will buy the products or services;

(e) a summary of financial forecasts giving a picture of the growth and development of the business.

Section two: Sales and marketing analysis

Market

(a) The size of the market in volume and value terms, and what its prospects for future expansion are.

(b) Any barriers to entry. How exposed the business is to major new competitors coming into the market.

(c) Other factors that affect the market, for example, changes in economic climate, trade barriers and government. How these factors affect it.

(d) Any gaps in the market which offer opportunities.

Customers

(a) The likely customer base and the dependency of the business on particular customers.

(b) The seasonality of trade. Whether this presents any particular difficulties in estimating demand for the products or services.

(c) Reasons why the business will appeal to new customers and how the business is to go about converting that appeal into new business (and so take market share from existing suppliers).

(d) Their key buying criteria.

Competition

(a) Details of the major competitors, their market shares and their strengths and weaknesses.

(b) Their marketing strategies and how they compare with the proposed business.

(c) Likely future developments in competition, for example, new competitors and trends.

(d) Vulnerability of the business to any particular competitor.

Section three: Human resources analysis

Management

(a) Who they are and what they have achieved to date.

(b) What their motivations and aspirations are and what their ambitions are for the business.

(c) Why them. How their skills contribute to the whole business.

(d) To what extent they are committed to the success of the business, including financial commitments. What plans there are for aiding their retention, for example, share option schemes, etc.

Organisation structure

It is a good idea to include an organisation chart showing reporting lines and responsibilities for all major areas. In particular:

(a) How responsibilities are distributed. Whether there are any gaps.

(b) How effective succession is to be ensured by the structure.

(c) To what extent the business will be relying on outsiders, for example accountants, bankers, lawyers and non-executive directors.

(d) Looking to the future, how anticipated growth will affect the structure and the skills required.

Personnel requirements

What the present and future employee requirements are and what relevant skills are needed compared to those now present.

Section four: Production and operations

Production process

(a) How the product will be manufactured and what problems are anticipated in the production process.

(b) What the actual and potential capacity of the business is and how sensitive it is to breakdowns, unanticipated short-term demand increases, collective labour practices, etc.

(c) How secure the source of supply for essential raw materials is. Whether there are alternative sources of supply.

Premises and facilities

(a) How suitable the premises are for the business's current and future needs in terms of location, size and type.

(b) Whether the premises are owned or if the business is exposed to increases in rents or termination of a lease.

(c) When machinery will need replacing and what the cost will be.

Section five: SWOT analysis

(a) Outline the opportunities and threats facing the business.

(b) Identify the strengths and weaknesses of the business in pursuing those opportunities or protecting against those threats. Use the 'so what' test when drafting this section. Does that strength really make a difference? What impact does that weakness actually have?

Section six: Objectives

It will not be possible to pursue every opportunity or change every weakness overnight. Focusing efforts is important. Identify:

• short-term tactical objectives;

• long-term strategic objectives.

Objectives should include qualitative and quantitative measures of performance, such as:

- the opportunities intended to be exploited;
- the threats that must be defended against;
- sales volume and value;
- market share;
- profit before tax;
- return on capital employed.

Section seven: Key factors and assumptions

(a) Demonstrate the understanding of the key factors on which the achievement of the objectives depends – for example, that the target market segment continues to expand at a rate of 10 per cent by volume and value each year or that interest rates are static.

(b) State the assumptions in respect of these key factors. A prospective investor will then be able to evaluate whether these assumptions appear reasonable.

(c) The major assumptions should be included in the body of the text, but detailed assumptions included in the appendix. All assumptions should be justified wherever possible by reference to external information, such as industry norms and trends.

Section eight: Strategies

Sales and marketing strategy

(a) How the sales and marketing objectives are going to be achieved through identifying the mix of:

- products/services
- pricing policy
- promotional support
- distribution.

(b) How potential customers will be identified and approached.

(c) How the business will attract customers away from competitors.

(d) How the business will protect its key accounts.

Human resources strategy

(a) What the strategy is for overcoming any weaknesses identified, for protecting against threats and for enabling the growth plans to flourish.

(b) What changes, if any, to the organisational structure will need to be made to realise the strategic objectives.

(c) What the strategy will be for attracting and retaining staff with appropriate skills and of sufficient motivation to grow with the company.

Production and operations strategy

Again, outline plans to overcome weaknesses, to protect against threats and to enable the business to pursue its growth plans.

Section nine: Financial information

As historical information will not be available for most start-up businesses, the financial information will essentially be projections. Projections should cover at least two years ahead and include:

- monthly cash flow forecasts;
- monthly profit and loss forecasts;
- balance sheets at the end of each year.

A summary of the financial projections should be inserted in the main body of the text and the detail contained in an appendix.

Sensitivity analysis should be included showing how the results would be affected by changes in major risk variables, for example, demand, gross margin and any limiting factors.

Appendix 6

Recruiting for a new business

In any small or growing business there is always the dilemma of who within the organisation should deal with staffing matters. If the organisation is, as yet, too small to support a human resources or personnel function, it usually falls to a senior member of management to undertake these tasks. However, bearing in mind the time commitment and skills necessary to fulfil this role, it is very important to make sure that the right person is handling these issues. It will need to be someone who can take the time without feeling under pressure to rush an interview or disciplinary matter. Additionally, the person should possess the temperament and communication skills to deal with everyone from the MD to the tea boy with equal respect.

More and more organisations are choosing to use consultants for this purpose. This way you can have the required expertise without having to resort to the cost of a full-time member of staff to cover your personnel requirements.

Defining the job

The first step must be to define the job for which you are recruiting. Draw up a job specification listing all the major tasks that will be required of the member of staff. This will naturally lead you on to creating a personal profile of the ideal candidate. For instance, if part of the role is to type letters, you will need to know that the person can not only type, but can use the package on your word processor. If they are going to be expected to take telephone calls they will need a clear speaking voice, etc. It is also useful at this stage to extend the personal profile to include personality traits that would be an advantage. For instance, if you are recruiting a salesperson, patience and an outgoing nature are very desirable attributes. If you are looking at a management role then communication, team and leadership skills will be paramount. Lastly, you should look at the environment in which the person will work – are they working with others? If so, you need to think about the type of person who will 'fit' with the existing staff.

Advertising

Having drawn together all this information, you must then decide whether you are going to advertise or use a recruitment agency or, indeed, do both. If you choose to advertise yourself it is important that you get the best vehicle for your advert. For instance, if you are looking for a professional member of staff, it might be more cost-effective to advertise in the appropriate professional journal, rather than the local paper. Equally, if you are looking to recruit a high powered director, for example, a national paper might be more productive than a local one. The style of advertisements differ, from a very cheap 'small ads' advert in the local press, to a large display in a national or journal. But beware – check the costs carefully before making a decision. In most cases you can either write the advert yourself using the information you have put together, or you can pass this information on to a firm who specialise in writing and placing such advertisements. These firms are usually paid commission by the newspaper or journal, and do not therefore charge you any more than going direct to the paper. They will, of course, charge you for any artwork, i.e., logos, etc. that you may wish to include.

If a recruitment agency is your choice then the information you have compiled will help them to narrow down the candidates to those with the appropriate skills and personality. You do not have to restrict yourself to one agency, however much they may tell you that it is the best option. You need the best field of candidates you can get, and this may mean trying several agencies. This method of recruitment will cost you a percentage of the annual starting salary of the person eventually employed. The percentage will differ with the size of the salary. For example, the scale shown in Table 1 applies to several local agencies at the present time.

It must be remembered that these prices can differ from agency to agency and can be changed with the economic climate. These fees are usually subject to a percentage return should the new recruit leave or not perform within a specific period. A typical example of this is shown in Table 2.

There are pros and cons to both of these methods. The recruitment

274

Table 1 Local current recruitment agency charges	
Total annual salary	*Charge*
Up to £9,999	16%
£10,000–£14,999	18%
£15,000–£19,999	20%
£20,000–£29,000	25%
£30,000 +	30%

Table 2 Recruitment agency fee credits	
Period of employment	*Credit*
Up to 2 weeks	85%
Not exceeding 3 weeks	60%
Not exceeding 4 weeks	40%
Not exceeding 5 weeks	30%
Not exceeding 6 weeks	20%
Not exceeding 7 weeks	10%
Not exceeding 8 weeks	5%

agency will take a lot of the work out of the primary process because you will only get information about candidates who fit your criteria, whereas an advert will mean you will get responses from people who are unsuitable and you will have to filter them yourself. However, an advert may attract someone who has not registered with an agency.

A further consideration, depending on the seniority of the position to be filled, would be to employ the services of a 'headhunter', otherwise known as 'search and select' specialists. The service they provide differs from that of a recruitment agency, in that these organisations will source an individual with all the right skills and attributes and then approach them on your behalf. They may well approach someone who has given no thought to a career change prior to contact from the headhunting firm.

As you can see, there is a lot to consider. But make sure you are aware of the financial implications of the route you decide to take. Recruitment agency charges, advertising fees and consultancy costs can all differ from firm to firm, so make sure you know the cost before you set the wheels in motion. At the end of the day, it is for you to decide.

Producing a shortlist

When you are assessing applications, it is important to have your list of criteria to hand so that you do not stray from your original objective, which is to find the candidate whose skills and personality match your requirements. However, to stick to it too rigidly may mean you miss a good candidate on the periphery. For example, if you have decided that you want a certain level of education and you have a CV that has lots of the right experience but does not qualify on the educational front, you would be wise to include that person despite their apparent shortcomings. It is also important to remember that to discriminate against an applicant on the grounds of sex, race, colour, religion, union membership or disability at any stage could result in an employment tribunal case. These are costly and time-consuming for the business and are upsetting for all concerned.

Other selection techniques

If you are recruiting for a high profile position it may be helpful to include a psychometric test or personality survey. There are many computer-driven systems of this sort, but you would be well advised to use a trained analyst to interpret the results. They can normally give a very accurate assessment of the personality traits of an individual, which could be a very helpful tool in recruiting the right person for the job.

Interviews

Having achieved your shortlist you will now have reached the first interview stage. Whether you interview once or twice will depend on the level of the vacancy and the structure of the firm. Interviews should, ideally, be undertaken by two people, one of whom should preferably be knowledgeable on any technical areas involved in the post applied for. You should use a quiet room where you will not be interrupted by telephone calls or visitors. Ideally, you should not put a desk between the interviewers and the candidate. This is instinctively seen as a barrier and can have an adverse effect on free communication. If at all possible, use comfortable chairs around a coffee or occasional table. All of the chairs should be of the same height and should enable the candidate to sit upright but at ease. This is important because you need the candidate to open up to you and to do this they need to feel relaxed and not intimidated.

It is wise to arm yourself with a copy of the job specification, laid out in a form that is easy to read and clear in its interpretation of the tasks involved. A typical example is shown at Figure 1.

Figure 1 Job specification

Title: **Financial Accountant**

Reporting to: Financial Director

Responsible for day-to-day running of the Administration and Finance Department and supervision of the staff performing the following functions:

- purchase ledger

- cash books

- production of statements

- credit control

- time recording

- billing

- petty cash

Specific responsibility for:

- bank reconciliations

- nominal ledger – including postings, balancing, reconciliations

- VAT returns

- private bank accounts, cash books

- HP/finance

- insurance claims

- production of quarterly and annual accounts

It may be necessary from time to time for the holder of this post to undertake other duties of a level commensurate with this position.

A checklist of the questions you need to ask and points you wish to raise is also helpful. Make sure that the questions you ask will elicit the response you require. For example, a good way to find out if the candidate has leadership skills is to ask them to explain a situation in which they have had to work as part of a team. In getting them to explain how they achieved their objective, you can assess whether the candidate led the group, was the ideas person or the facilitator, etc.

Start the interview by putting the candidate at ease. Ask how their journey was, enquire after their family, it will help to get them talking. If the candidate is not familiar with your organisation, give as much detail as you feel is necessary before you give them a thorough description of the tasks involved in the post for which you are interviewing. Give them the opportunity to ask questions as you go along. Ask them open-ended questions so that they cannot give 'yes' or 'no' answers. Get them talking.

However, it is important to have control of the proceedings – some candidates may talk too much if you let them. This is often a nervous reaction to the situation, and does not necessarily mean that they would waste time talking under normal circumstances. Just be aware that you may have to be quite firm in bringing the interview back on course. At the end of the interview give the candidate the opportunity to ask any questions that are still outstanding, and make sure they are aware of the time-scale for hearing the results of the interview. Above all, listen attentively and use positive body language.

Notes

Make sure that you make notes as you go along. If you are interviewing several people, it is difficult by the end of the day to remember each as an individual, and the notes will help to put a personality to each name. It is also important that you keep notes even if you do not appoint a particular candidate. If a discrimination claim is brought against you those notes may constitute evidence.

A useful tool is to give each candidate a rating against particular attributes on a scale of, say, 1 to 5, with 1 being poor and 5 excellent. Areas this should cover would include:

- relevant experience
- relevant skills
- interpersonal skills
- attitude

- adaptability

- body language

These scores will enable you to compare one candidate with another and thus aid the decision-making process.

The 'offer'

The offer letter is the most important document in the employment process. This is actually the 'contract of employment', so be very careful how it is worded. It should be short and concise and should include the title of the post being offered, the salary and any conditions of employment that do not conform to your normal standards. For example, if you would not normally require an employee to complete a trial period, but on this occasion you wish it, you must include it in the offer letter. An example of a basic standard offer letter is shown at Figure 2.

Figure 2 Standard offer letter

Dear . . . . .

Further to your recent interview, I am pleased to be able to offer you the position of . . . . . with this firm at a salary of £. . . . . .

I should be pleased if you would sign one copy of the enclosed Terms and Conditions and return it to me in acceptance of this offer, together with the date on which you intend to join us. If there are any matters which you would like to discuss in further detail, then please feel free to contact me either in writing or by telephone.

I look forward to hearing from you in the near future.

Yours sincerely

Terms and conditions of employment

Under section 1 of the Employment Rights Act 1996 it is a legal requirement that all staff are provided with written particulars of their terms and conditions of employment within two months of the commencement of that employment. The written particulars must include the following:

- the names of the employer and employee;
- the date when employment began;
- the rate of pay;
- the pay intervals (i.e., hourly, weekly, monthly, etc.);
- holiday entitlement (if any);
- job title;
- addresses of the premises at which staff will be required to work;
- the firm's sick pay policy;
- details of any pension scheme;
- length of notice period;
- how to get copies of the firm's disciplinary and grievance procedures.

At the end of this process you will have recruited the best from the field available. All that remains is to keep them happy and motivated!

Managing your employees

You will have spent a great deal of time and money recruiting the best available staff for your business. But to recruit is only the beginning. To get the best from your employees they need to be happy, feel appreciated and valued. It is all too easy to become complacent, and assume that simply because they do not complain then they must be content. This is a universal misconception. Most people need praise to motivate them – indeed, it is a greater motivator than money will ever be. However, praise will only work if it is sincere. To tell someone they have done a good job when they patently have not is ultimately destructive. Most people would rather deal with honest, constructive criticism.

To retain good staff and to keep them loyal you must provide them with a vision of the future of the business to which they can relate. This should include not only the aims and objectives of the business, including its financial potential, but also an idea of where the employee 'fits' into this picture. Some will need to know that they will always have a challenge, others that they have security. All will need to feel that they 'belong'.

The basic building blocks of this relationship must be two-way communication. The tools to achieve this can be many and varied, but can include management open door policies, regular staff meetings and appraisal systems. However, it is imperative that staff believe that what they say will be taken seriously and that the action taken as a result will be explained. They will only believe this if they see results.

The cost of replacing staff means that retaining them makes good economic sense. Training an existing member of staff into a different role is more productive than starting from scratch. They know the firm and its people. They already feel 'ownership' of, and loyalty to, the business. Equally, promoting from within gives other staff a 'safe' feeling. They feel less threatened by someone they already know. These moves build stability into an organisation. However, beware 'carrying' staff who are not productive. Other, better staff will resent it and become demotivated as a result.

Methods of achieving potential

An appraisal system can take many forms but its basic purpose is to encourage staff to achieve their potential for the good of the firm and the individual. Career development is a very positive factor in staff retention and the appraisal should be the vehicle for discussing and promoting this.

Whether it takes the form of an interview or a sophisticated computer package, the appraisal should determine where the employee is now, where they want to be and how they can achieve this. It is then for the employer to give whatever help they can to enable the employees to achieve their objective. Training needs identified through this process should be dealt with promptly. This will benefit both the employee and the firm. It will convey the firm's interest in, and support of, its staff and provide the firm with a better equipped workforce. Money spent on training staff is rarely wasted. You have only to look at organisations such as Marks & Spencer to see the level of loyalty it invokes.

There are conflicting views on whether pay reviews should form part of the appraisal system. Some think that it should cover performance and development, but that salary should be a separate issue. However, it is

281

difficult to see what other mechanism for assessing the employee's value would be better.

Working conditions

Another factor in staff retention is the conditions prevailing within the organisation. This extends beyond giving the employees a comfortable working environment. For instance, it may need to encompass variations in working hours to accommodate outside commitments.

It is wise to listen to your staff and make changes where it is not detrimental to the working of the business. Some simple adjustments can often mean the difference between keeping and losing good staff.

Do make sure that your staff are not working too hard. Some stress can be a good thing and can enhance performance. Too much stress can result in 'burnout'. Encourage them to take the time off to which they are entitled. They will remain fresher and more productive as a result.

Dealing with disciplinary issues

It is essential that problems are dealt with promptly and not allowed to 'fester'. If not nipped in the bud other staff will feel that you are losing control.

Make sure you have a written procedure that all the staff are aware of and stick to it to the letter. Keep file notes of any meetings and copies of all correspondence. A set of example disciplinary procedures is provided at Figure 3.

Figure 3 Disciplinary procedures

Objectives

The purpose of this section is to:

(a) advise employees of the acts and behaviour which will warrant disciplinary action;

(b) give examples of those disciplinary offences of so serious a nature that the employee may be dismissed summarily without having been previously warned;

(c) ensure that equitable and consistent procedures are applied to the investigation of alleged misconduct and also that equitable and consistent action is taken against offenders where necessary.

The procedure

In cases other than those of gross misconduct justifying summary dismissal without notice or payment in lieu of notice, the following procedure will apply. This procedure will also apply in cases of failure to meet the performance standards expected by the Firm from staff members.

(a) Informal warning

Minor lapses of conduct and/or performance will be handled by a manager informally. If there is no subsequent improvement then the formal disciplinary procedures will be invoked.

(b) First formal stage – oral warning

In the first instance the employee will receive an oral warning from a Manager who will explain the nature of the criticism, the level of improvement necessary and the consequences of repetition. A record of the date and the reason for the oral warning will be entered on the employee's personnel file.

(c) Second formal stage – written warning

If the conduct or performance remains unsatisfactory or if the first offence is of a serious nature, a written warning will be given by a Manager stating the reason for the warning, the improvement required and the time-scale in which to do so and the consequences of a lack of improvement. The employee will be given a copy of the written warning and a copy will also be placed on the employee's personnel file.

(d) Third formal stage – final written warning

(i) If the conduct or performance still remains unsatisfactory or if the first offence is sufficiently serious as to warrant such action straightaway, the employee will be advised of the nature of the criticism and will be required to attend a disciplinary interview with one or more Managers. The employee may be accompanied by another member of staff if they so wish.

(ii) At the interview all relevant evidence will be heard and the employee will be given every chance to state their case.

(iii) If the criticism is found proved, the final written warning will be given by a Manager stating the reason for the warning, the improvement required, the time-scale in which to do so and will give notice that dismissal will result if there is insufficient improvement.

(e) Final formal stage – dismissal

(i) In the event of any further criticism the employee will be liable to dismissal.

(ii) The employee will be required to attend a disciplinary hearing in the form set out in paragraph (d)(i) and (ii) above.

(iii) If the criticism is found proved the employee will be dismissed either with or without notice depending upon the seriousness of the offence.

Summary dismissal

(a) The following is a non-exhaustive list of examples of misconduct which may render an employee liable to summary dismissal:

(i) Fraud or the deliberate falsification of records, including timesheets.

(ii) Theft or attempted theft of property belonging to the Firm or a fellow employee.

(iii) Dishonesty in dealings with clients or other members of the Firm.

(iv) Serious negligence, incompetence or misconduct which could cause damage to the Firm's relationship with customers or to the Firm's reputation with third parties.

(v) Misuse of confidential information obtained during the course of employment.

(vi) Causing wilful damage to property belonging to the Firm.

(vii) Violent or aggressive behaviour or language towards clients or other members of the Firm.

(viii) Refusal to obey a reasonable instruction.

(ix) Competing with the business of the Firm on the employee's own account or in association with others.

(x) Failure to ensure adequate insurance cover on a private motor vehicle being used by the employee on the Firm's business.

(xi) Possession of, selling or distributing illegal drugs on the Firm's premises.

(xii) Improper use of the Firm's computer hardware or software.

(b) Whilst an investigation is being made into an allegation of gross misconduct the employee may be suspended without pay for a period not exceeding five working days.

(c) The employee will be required to attend a disciplinary hearing in the form set out in paragraph (d)(i) and (ii) above.

(d) If the allegation of gross misconduct is upheld, the employee will be summarily dismissed.

Appeals to Managing Director

An appeal against any disciplinary decision of the Managers is to the Managing Director and must be made in writing within two working days.

At the earliest opportunity the Managing Director will thoroughly re-appraise the circumstances leading to the decision.

During the appeal the member of staff will have the opportunity to put their case and have the right to be accompanied by another member of staff.

At the appeal any disciplinary penalty previously imposed may be confirmed, lifted, or a lesser penalty substituted, but cannot be increased. The member of staff will be advised without delay in writing and, where possible, orally of the outcome of the appeal and the reason.

It is always the hope that you will never need to use this procedure, but it will help you enormously should you ever find yourself the subject of an employment tribunal to have followed such a procedure doggedly.

The bottom line must be that two way communication at all times is imperative. Bad news travels fast – good news sometimes does not get through. Make sure it does!

Remember to give employees an opportunity to voice ideas as well as complaints. Make it known to the staff that you are available at set times to listen to them and address their concerns honestly. Make sure that all employees are included in the dissemination of information. It is easy to forget the cleaner or the messenger, and it can be demoralising to know you have been 'left out'.

Appendix 7

Useful addresses

Advertising Standards Authority (ASA)
Committee of Advertising Practice
Brook House
2 Torrington Place
London WC1E 7HW
Tel: 0171 580 5555
Fax: 0171 631 3051

The Chartered Institute of Marketing
Moor Hall
Cookham
Berks SL6 9QH
Tel: 01628 427 500
Fax: 01628 427 499

Institute of Direct Marketing
1 Park Road
Teddington
Middlesex TW11 0AR
Tel: 0181 977 5705
Fax: 0181 943 2535

Institute of Public Relations
The Old Trading House
15 Northburgh St
London EC1V 0PR
Tel: 0171 253 5151

The Market Research Society
13 Northburgh St
London EClV 0AH
Tel: 0171 490 4911
Fax: 0171 582 1604

Appendix 8

IT rulebook – making effective use of IT

Needs analysis

- Establish business goals, needs and priorities as the IT starting point.

- Do not allow technology and/or suppliers to drive your needs analysis.

- Ensure IT needs are articulated in business language (not technical jargon).

- Do not simply replicate current systems/procedures – investigate potential benefits of change.

- Listen to and involve managers and end-users in all the relevant business functions/units and establish an ongoing involvement.

- Avoid 'big bang' overambitious plans – assess needs in an incremental way but in the context of the longer-term objectives.

- Where possible, think through and test what you need manually before committing to IT.

- Demonstrate the commitment of top management by their subscribing to the IT project.

- Draw on expert and peer advice and guidance in order to learn from the experiences of others.

- Give consideration to the likelihood of possible enhancements for future needs.

- Be prepared to adopt a flexible stance in the way in which the business's needs are met.

- Look at the marketplace and competitors – do not establish your needs based simply on an inward-looking viewpoint.

- Conduct a financial feasibility study in order to justify the investment level required to meet the needs.

System specification

- Be flexible in setting out your needs but specific in stating what you want.

- Be reasonable in defining your expectations – do not look for perfection – the 80/20 rule can work very well.

- Keep the specification at the functional level – not too detailed.

- Base the requirements on the business needs, not on the technological opportunities.

- Take advantage of the enhancements that IT can bring to your work practices.

- Seek guidance and advice from others, even if it is only of an informal nature.

- Make use of help and assistance from prospective suppliers if offered, but retain control of the process.

- Make sure the specification is clearly written and is in English, not 'computerese'.

- Ensure it is comprehensive, consistent and complete.

- Above all, involve the users in the required formulation process.

Supplier selection

- Do not delegate the selection process entirely to specialist staff – ensure continuing management involvement.

- Do not base your selection on choosing hardware first – let software considerations dominate the process.

- Tend towards off-the-shelf solutions which can allow flexibility and which involve less risk.

- Choose demonstrably expandable and flexible systems. If the preferred system can grow with your business and can form an integral part of your future business and IT strategy then you will be able to achieve your objectives.

- Open systems, relational databases, 4th generation languages, etc. may be necessary, but only in specific circumstances, and you should question the true added value of these offerings.

- Choose a solution which delivers modular growth capability. You should never be put in a position where you need to select a system which would require total replacement of its hardware, software and data structures when you reach a certain size.

- Try not to be a pioneer – you are better off following in somebody else's footsteps and taking advantage of tried and tested solutions rather than reinventing the wheel.

- Adopt a rigorous approach to selection – do not just choose the brother-in-law's company or the devil you know!

- Make sure you identify a variety of alternative suppliers, each of whom submit written proposals.

- Look for stability of ownership and proven commitment to sector/ product by suppliers.

- Verify the financial and technical track record of a supplier you are seriously considering. It is of no benefit choosing the ideal system from a supplier who may not be able to support you in the future.

- Liaise with other users in your sector (e.g., through user groups etc.). Take up references to verify that current customers of the potential supplier are satisfied. Find out what problems they have experienced and verify that you are comparing like with like by ensuring that the systems they have installed are comparable to those being implemented by you.

- Make sure you negotiate the terms in the suppliers' standard contracts. They may be prepared to agree fairer terms, rather than adopt standard clauses, but only if you raise the issues with them.

Implementation

- Start planning early – not a week before the computer arrives.

- Face up to the spectrum of issues and costs involved in effective IT implementation.

- If feasible, and without spending less on the overall system, allow liberally for implementation costs – 50 per cent of the cost of the hardware/software investment is a good rule of thumb.

- Incremental approaches work best and ensure you feed the experience and learning you gain into successive phases.

- Ensure the person charged with the implementation:
  - is a good communicator
  - has credibility
  - has the support of management
  - above all is not 'out there' on his/her own.

- Adopt a rigorous and realistic approach to planning but also be flexible to allow for inevitable delays, etc.

- Work to a realistic yet tough timetable and address head-on any problems that cause delays.

- Do not let your IT supplier dictate your implementation planning and resourcing levels.

- Involve users in implementation planning.

- Work alongside the supplier throughout the process and jointly agree actions.

Operation and development

- Ensure that users have access to good support which they feel is approachable and accessible.

- Ensure that future releases of suppliers' packages can be introduced, regardless of modifications made to previous versions.

- Look for opportunities to develop, enhance, modify and/or rationalise the systems. Installing a new computer system is not the end of the process but the start of an ongoing, dynamic evolution of the use of IT in the relevant area of the business.

- Set the objective of integrating discrete uses of technology in order to provide direct access by managers across a variety of relevant databases and information sources.

- Establish an IT steering group tasked with the responsibility of the constant development and planning of systems in line with the business's strategic plan.

- Develop contacts with other users of similar systems in order to identify opportunities for improvements.

- Set increasingly tough targets for the level of corporate data accuracy and time-scales for the production of management and operational reports.

- Plan, plan and plan.

Appendix 9

Financial services and the DIAMOND model

Introduction

There is a role for financial services in every stage of the development of a business with the possible exception of the very first stage – dreaming.

Financial services can be used in two very different, but complementary, ways. Primarily, the purpose must be protection. No matter how well planned the growth of the business, no matter how successful the expansion, all efforts can come to nothing if there is not a proper mechanism to protect those plans should the unthinkable happen.

This need for protection from the effects of death, serious illness, incapacity appears in the late stages of dreaming and the transition to initiating and remains until at least the maturity stage. If it ever does disappear, then, ironically, it reappears in the diversifying stage if the business, or parts of it, are being sold and the owner is looking for an exit route.

Paralleling the need for protection is the much more optimistic side to financial services – reward.

Effective pension planning, for example, can be a major attribute to a business. Not only can it be instrumental in attracting and retaining high quality staff, for the owner/manager it can become a tax planning tool, a shelter for corporate profits and even a vehicle for purchase of the business premises.

On exit from the business, investment products in conjunction with careful planning can minimise potential tax liabilities, so ensuring that the owner retains as much of the sale proceeds as possible, making these funds available to fund future ventures or retirement.

This appendix looks in detail at some of the financial services products appropriate to each stage of the business's development.

Dreaming

The early stage of dreaming is the only stage where there is no clear role for financial services – because at this point there is no business.

Initiating

By the initiating stage, the owner is the driving force behind the business. Without him the business simply will not survive. The clear need is for protection – either for the individual or for the business or, more probably, for both. Protection comes in many different guises but, in the business environment, is usually packaged with the label key man insurance.

There is often an air of mystique surrounding the term key man insurance. However, in its simplest form, key man insurance is merely a life policy *owned by* the business so that, in the event of a claim, the proceeds are payable to the business and not to the person on whom the cover has been taken out ('the life assured').

The simplest and cheapest form of protection is level term assurance. This is a life policy which provides substantial amounts of life assurance cover. Payment is made only in the event of death, and only if death occurs within the period covered by the policy. There is no payment at the end of the period if a claim has not been made. For this reason premiums are relatively cheap.

On top of basic level term assurance, it is possible to add all sorts of bells and whistles. The most useful are the ability to renew the cover at the end of the period without the need to answer any more medical questions and the ability to increase the cover.

EXAMPLE

Suppose Mr A takes out a policy when he first starts the business at age 40. In the event of his death within five years, this policy would pay to the company a lump sum of £50,000. (Such a policy may well be required by a bank as a condition of providing some of the start-up capital.) The business grows well but still requires short-term overdraft facilities. Thanks to an 'increasability' option, Mr A can increase the cover by 20 per cent every year so that, at the end of the five years, the cover is now £100,000. But at the end of the term the bank would still like the comfort of life cover to support its continued lending.

Unfortunately, during the five years Mr A has suffered a serious illness which would normally have meant that, at the end of the five-year term, further life cover would be very expensive, if not impossible, to obtain. However, as the policy was also 'renewable', continued life cover is still available at the rates prevailing for a 45-year-old man *in normal health.*

As might be expected, every refinement to a basic term assurance policy adds further cost. After all, the insurance company will always calculate its premium on a worst case scenario. However, for an unfortunate few, the worst case scenario could become reality, and without this protection, the business could simply fold.

Happily, the incidence of people dying whilst setting up a business is rare. Much greater is the risk of contracting a condition which, though serious, is often survivable – heart attack, cancer, stroke, etc. Suppose that the 'serious illness' suffered by Mr A above had been a mild heart attack.

Even though life cover was still available to Mr A at the end of his five-year term, that would have done nothing to help Mr A when he actually suffered his heart attack, and yet the risk of business failure would, if anything, have been exacerbated. After all, Mr A, whilst trying to run the business from a hospital bed, would probably have been contributing very little, whilst his salary – much needed to pay for a holiday to give him time to recuperate – would have been a significant drain on the business.

The solution in these circumstances would have been a 'critical illness' policy. This type of policy is designed to pay out a lump sum on death *or earlier diagnosis of a critical illness.* Thus, in the case of Mr A's heart attack, if he had taken out a £50,000 critical illness policy, he would have been able to take time to recover without the added pressure of fear that the business would fold for lack of cash

To underline the importance of this type of cover, did you know that you are four times more likely to suffer a critical illness than you are to die before age 65?

Both term assurance and critical illness policies are also available to private individuals and are a sensible, if not essential, part of personal financial planning. In the business context, however, some of the very genuine reasons for effecting such cover are:

(a) to provide a lump sum to combat cash flow problems;

(b) to fend off predatory approaches from competitors;

(c) to reassure lenders/investors/customers;

(d) to meet the costs of employing a temporary or full-time replacement.

Even though we have said that in the initiating stage the owner *is* the business, that situation can continue well into the business life. Arguably, even at the diversifying stage, Jim Henson was effectively still his business.

Jim Henson was the man who originated 'The Muppets', the animated puppets so familiar on television and in film in the 1980s. Despite having built up a veritable empire, employing hundreds of people, around the household-name characters, Jim was still very much the 'key' man in the company. What happened next is set out in the following extract from the *Financial Times*:

DISNEY DROPS MUPPETS DEAL

Walt Disney has abandoned plans to acquire Henson Associates, the company behind the popular Muppet characters.

The talks ended late last week with the two sides unable to agree terms on a deal that analysts estimated would have been worth between $100 million and $150 million. Disney and Henson had been negotiating for almost eighteen months.

The death in May of Mr Jim Henson, founder of Henson Associates and the instigator of the deal, sparked disagreements between Disney and Mr Henson's five children, who took over the business from their father.

It is believed that Disney argued that Henson Associates was worth less after its founder's death, because he had been the creative force behind all its successful characters.

Mr Henson's children were thought to have been demanding a higher price. The deal, announced in August 1989, envisaged Disney acquiring publishing and licensing rights to all Muppets characters, except those created for the 'Sesame Street' television programme.

Source: Patrick Harverson, *Financial Times*.

The sale did eventually go ahead for an undisclosed sum believed to be about $20 million.

The premiums on key man insurance for $150 million would no doubt have been substantial but the result of not effecting the cover was a loss of around 85 per cent business value to Jim's estate.

The price of cover obviously depends upon the age of the individual, his state of health, the type, period and amount of cover required and various other factors.

Attacking

By now, it is to be hoped that the business has in place the basic life assurance mechanisms to cope with a major catastrophe. By now, also, the business is actually starting to become worth something to its owners. There is still a strong need for protection, but the nature of the need is becoming more expansive.

At the attacking stage we also see the business starting to have the potential to reward its investors and employees.

Looking firstly at protection, there may now be a requirement for shareholder protection assurance (or, in a partnership, partnership cover). Once again, the underlying vehicles for this type of cover are term assurance and/or critical illness policies. The policies are turned into shareholder protection policies by the ways in which they are written in trust and option agreements put in place. An example might make matters clearer.

EXAMPLE

Suppose there is a business, A & B Limited, founded by the two directors Mr A and Mr B, each of whom owns 50 per cent of the share capital. Both directors are married and under the terms of their wills their respective wives will inherit their estates.

Mr A dies and Mrs A inherits his shares. However, Mrs A has a young family and desperately needs cash rather than shares. She has no interest in running the business and may be forced to sell the shares to the highest bidder – possibly a competitor – assuming the shares can be sold at all. Even if there is a market for the shares, what is the competitor going to do – rush in as soon as Mr A dies and offer a high price or wait six months until the business has all but collapsed and pick up the shares for a fraction of their original value?

At the same time, Mr B desperately wants to keep control of the business he helped to found but has a moral obligation to offer his friend's widow a fair price for the shares — if only he had the money.

The solution is shareholder protection cover. In its simplest form, this is a policy taken out by Mr A which, in the event of his death, pays a lump sum, via a trust, to Mr B. Mr B takes out an identical policy written in trust for Mr A.

Of course, in some circumstances, Mrs A may not wish to sell the shares and Mr B may not wish to buy them. This is where a cross-option agreement is required. Either party may exercise the option but neither is compelled to do so.

It is vitally important that both the trust and cross-option wording are professionally drafted. One major insurance company specialising in this type of cover has estimated that up to 75 per cent of current shareholder protection arrangements may have a hidden and completely unintentional tax liability.

Naturally, as the business grows, its value should increase. The shareholder protection arrangements should be sufficiently flexible to cater for this and should be reviewed every five years, or more frequently if growth is dynamic.

Another form of protection which may be considered at this stage is permanent health insurance (PHI).

Permanent health insurance is designed to replace at least a part of an individual's salary in the event that he is off work for a prolonged period of time as a result of accident, illness or injury.

The usual percentage is such that, taking into account state benefits, the person 'takes home' 75 per cent of his pre-disability salary. The benefit does not come into force until the end of the 'deferred period', which can be between four weeks and two years. The longer the deferred period, the less the chance of a claim and so the cheaper the premium.

EXAMPLE

For a 40 year old male, the premium on a four-week deferred PHI policy will typically be more than double that of an otherwise identical policy with a six-month deferred period and three times that of a policy with a two-year deferred period.

Once a benefit comes into force, it will be paid until either the claimant returns to work, dies or, if necessary, right up until the selected termination age – which may be age 65.

The policy can be taken out either by the individual or by a company. The structure of the two routes is different, as is the tax treatment, but both policies ultimately serve the same purpose.

Premiums are generally very affordable. The exception is 'key man PHI', where an income is paid to the business to finance the salary of a temporary 'replacement key man'. Here, premiums tend to be very high and benefits paid for limited periods only. Such policies are not usually within the scope of an infant business.

As the business moves from the attacking to the maturing stage, and having put in place the various layers of protection against disaster, the business can now begin to use financial planning techniques as a source of reward.

The first stage in this process has to be to start to provide the founder with an adequate pension, although this can, of course, be undertaken at a much earlier stage in the growth of a business if resources permit.

Pension planning takes many forms and legislation is constantly changing. It is beyond the scope of this book to cover this in detail. However, the types of arrangement suitable for the small but growing business would be as follows:

- personal pension;
- group personal pension;
- self-invested personal pension;
- executive pension plan;
- small self-administered scheme.

A personal pension plan is a pension policy owned by an individual. He or she may pay into it, as may an employer, on condition that the total contributions by the two do not exceed a certain age-related limit laid down by the Inland Revenue.

As there is a limit on contributions *into* the policy, there is no limit on the benefits which may be taken *out*. Up to a quarter of the fund may be taken as a tax-free lump sum and the balance has to be used to provide a pension. This may be in the form of an annuity or may be 'drawn down' directly out of the fund without the necessity to purchase an annuity until age 75.

In either case, the amount of the fund, which determines the amount of pension available, will depend upon a number of factors: amount of contributions, long-term investment return, age at which benefits are drawn, policy charges and long-term interest rates in the economy when benefits are drawn. Of these, the item over which the individual has the least control is the last one, and this is one of the reasons why the concept of 'draw down' was introduced.

We have used the term 'drawing benefits' merely to emphasise that it is not necessary actually to retire in order to draw benefits, and these may be taken at any time between ages 50 and 75. Indeed, it is often good planning to 'cluster' a policy into numerous 'segments' so that it is possible to 'retire' gradually – perhaps by working a decreasing working week and supplementing reduced earnings from the business with an income from part of a pension policy.

EXAMPLE

John formed a company 30 years ago and now, in his mid-fifties is looking to wind down and work a three-day week as his son, Peter, becomes more involved in the day-to-day management of the business. As John has a clustered policy, he can draw benefits from just some of the 'mini-policies' to supplement his reduced earnings as he takes more of a back seat and hands over the business in stages to Peter over the next five years.

With any personal pension, it is always worthwhile considering what is known as 'waiver of premium'. In plain English this is an 'insurance on an insurance'. In much the same way as PHI will pay a 'salary' if need be up until a selected age, so waiver of premium will pay a pensions premium, if necessary, right up until a selected retirement date. For a young person, the monthly cost of such cover can be pence rather than pounds – but the potential cost of not having this simple cover can be catastrophic.

EXAMPLE

A dentist took out a personal pension. Very shortly afterwards, he suffered an accident which did not disable him completely and he was able to carry on work. Unfortunately, as he had partially lost the use of his arms, he could not continue as a dentist. His adviser had not mentioned waiver of premium. The dentist settled a negligence claim out of court for £96,000. It is thought that had the case reached court, the damages against the adviser could have been considerably greater – such was the estimated loss of earnings to the dentist.

The message, as always, has to be to seek independent financial advice from a qualified adviser.

Once the business has started to repay the founder by giving him the security of a pension, consideration may be given to extending the benefit to other employees.

A well thought-out and well-communicated pension can give the growing business a leading edge over competitors in attracting, motivating and retaining good quality staff. In contrast, we have seen cases where a pension scheme capable of delivering high quality benefits is actually demotivating, either because its structure is so complicated that it is not understood or the benefits have not been communicated properly and so are not appreciated.

One case which springs to mind is that of a company where there was a 'targeted money purchase' scheme. (In simple terms, this means that, provided the employer and employee pay the required level of contribution and this is reviewed annually, then the benefits at retirement *should* correspond to a pre-set target – although there can be no guarantee.)

With a small but growing business, the most appropriate pension arrangement from the point of view of both employee and employer will almost certainly be the group personal pension plan. Essentially, this is a collection of personal pension plans. However, as it bears the employer's name, and the employer often adds a contribution to the employee contributions (which are in any event deducted from salary and collected by the employer), there is a feeling of paternalism.

Since it is not a true company pension scheme, the group personal pension plan is straightforward for the employer to administer and free of many of the constraints of the Pensions Act 1995. At the same time, because the result is a policy in the individual employee's own name, the arrangement is easily appreciated and valued by the employee. Research has shown that, particularly since the Maxwell episode, a well thought-out pension scheme is one of the benefits most sought after by a potential employee.

For many businesses a group personal pension plan will always be the most appropriate form of employee pension provision, even when the business grows to plc status. Many small firms operate group personal pension plans, but even companies of the size of WH Smith and Zeneca now offer this type of scheme to their new entrants.

Similarly, for the sole trader or partnership, a personal pension plan is the only form of pension provision available to someone who, in the eyes of the Inland Revenue, is self-employed. For the employer who forms a limited company, however, the choice extends to company pension schemes, which are mentioned in the next section.

Maturing

At this stage in the business's life, there are more managers and the business is less reliant on one or two 'key' individuals. Nevertheless, the loss of one or two people could still deal the business a severe blow and the need for key man insurance may still be present – only now the 'key' people may not necessarily be the founder but rather a skilled engineer or salesman.

The business should also be worth something intrinsically. Thus, the need for shareholder protection assurance is probably at its peak.

At the same time, the limited company business can start to use a pension scheme not just as a means of saving for a pension, but also as a tax-planning tool.

A company could, for example, set up an executive pension plan (EPP) or small self-administered scheme (SSAS). There are a number of differences between these arrangements and personal pension plans. Firstly, as the names suggest, these are formal (occupational) pension schemes subject to a completely different set of rules to those which govern personal pension plans.

As a very broad generalisation, it is possible to put more money into an occupational plan than it is into a personal plan. If, for example, as the company approaches its financial year end, healthy profits are predicted and these would otherwise give rise to a large corporation tax bill, it is possible for the company to pay some of these into an occupational scheme, whilst obtaining full tax relief.

The flexibility of such schemes does not stop there. Both EPPs and

SSASs allow the scheme, subject to Inland Revenue restrictions, to lend money back to the company.

In the case of a SSAS, it is also possible for the scheme itself to borrow money. One of the most common reasons to do so is the purchase of company premises. In this way, the buildings are being bought with funds upon which some tax relief has been given, and once purchased, become an asset of the scheme. This means that they then grow in value free of capital gains tax. The rental which the company must pay is itself a tax-relievable business expense and it is easy to see how this sort of scheme can be a major attraction to any business. A typical example is set out at Figure 1.

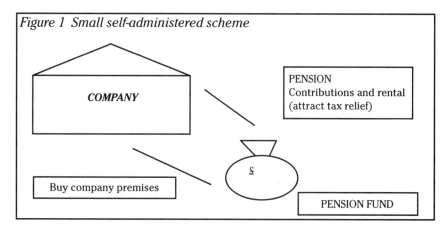

Figure 1 Small self-administered scheme

COMPANY

PENSION
Contributions and rental
(attract tax relief)

Buy company premises

£

PENSION FUND

In view of the potential for abuse of such a scheme, the Inland Revenue quite naturally place particular requirements on the running of both an EPP and a SSAS and this has minor cost implications. Even so, these schemes should both be very strongly considered as planning tools in the development of a limited company.

For the self-employed, it is not possible to be a member of a company pension scheme. However, property purchase is still a viable option via a self-invested personal pension plan (SIPP).

A SIPP is basically an ordinary personal pension plan but, instead of the assets comprising wholly policies with XYZ Insurance Company, part of the assets might be the premises from which the firm trades. A frequent scenario might be that the firm outgrows its present premises and the trader/partners pool their various personal pension policies to form the deposit on new premises. The balance is borrowed from a bank. The trustees of the plan – normally an insurance company – then buy the premises, and the loan is repaid by rental from the firm to the trustees and pension contributions by the partner(s). Both of these are tax-deductible.

(It is important to appreciate that with any purchase of premises through a pension arrangement, it is the trustees of that arrangement and *not* the individual members who own the premises. Since no transaction is allowed between a member of a scheme and the scheme itself, a scheme member cannot sell a property to/nor buy a property from the scheme until at least three years have elapsed during which the property has been owned by a completely unconnected third party.)

Overhauling

By the overhauling stage, most of the financial services products available to an expanding business will have been encountered.

The emphasis is now on incentivisation and there is a natural fit with pension schemes offering high quality benefits and share option schemes.

Employee share incentives

Equity participation schemes have become an increasingly popular element of remuneration both for executives and employees. To some extent this popularity has been stimulated by tax advantages conferred on certain forms of share scheme. However, there are other more fundamental causes for such interest in employee share schemes.

The perceived benefits for the employer of employee share schemes stem mainly from the maxim that employee participation in the ownership of a company aligns more closely the objectives of employees and shareholders, and in so doing motivates and rewards the employee for results which are in the best interests of the company at large.

In addition, employee share purchase schemes, using new issues of shares, result in an inflow of share capital. Any gains that are made by employees upon the disposal of shares are a cost to the marketplace, rather than being a charge against profits, as in the case of cash bonuses. For the employee, share schemes offer the opportunity to realise a significant cash sum in due course.

The advantages of share schemes

Incentive

Employers are finding increasingly that the offer of equity participation in the company is necessary to attract high quality personnel. In some sectors, it is a market requirement to offer share incentives to attract skilled personnel. The provision of share options which are only exercisable after a period of time has the added benefit of encouraging the employee to stay with the company at least until their profits can be realised.

From the employee's point of view, he or she has the added motivation of having performance directly linked with pay. In addition, this may be their only opportunity to realise a large monetary sum from their employment. The downside of employee share ownership, however, is that shares are subject to influences beyond the control of the executives and employees, thus potentially reducing the incentive effect.

Stakeholder

An employee who has a stake in the company is more likely to take an interest in the longer-term growth prospects of the company. Industrial relations are therefore less likely to be strained by the traditional desire to maximise immediate short-term pay at the expense of long-term investment.

Cost to the company

The provision of shares or share options allows companies to increase the employee's remuneration at little or no cost to the company itself. This facet is particularly important for companies that are reinvesting profits for growth, or for companies in a start-up phase. If new shares are issued at the time of the option exercise, then the cost is effectively borne by the existing shareholders, as their holdings are diluted rather than reducing the company's working capital.

Options vs share incentives

There are two distinct types of share schemes. Under a share incentive scheme the employee is issued with shares immediately, often under favourable terms, as a gift or at a discount on the market price. As the employee has immediate beneficial ownership of the shares, he has an immediate interest in share values and yields, and the incentive value of the scheme is apparent to him at the outset.

Under a share option scheme, options are granted to the employee giving him a right to subscribe for a certain number of shares at a specified price, at a specified date in the future. For little or no consideration at the date of grant of the option, an employee has an effectively risk-free interest in the equity of the company. He has no need to invest his own money until he decides to exercise the option, at which stage he may realise a profit on his 'investment' assuming there is a ready market in the shares. If the share price does not rise sufficiently to make the exercise of the option worthwhile, then the employee simply allows the option to lapse.

Unquoted companies

If a company is not quoted there is not a ready market for the shares, and this can reduce the incentive element of shares to employees. This is particularly the case for certain closely held companies in circumstances where there is no prospect of a sale or flotation of the business. In these circumstances, companies may create a market for their shares through either a purchase of own shares or by using an employee trust. The company could also consider the option of using a phantom share option scheme.

Employee trust

An employee trust is a discretionary trust set up for the benefit of employees. Employee trusts can be Inland Revenue approved (providing certain conditions are met) or can be onshore or offshore 'case law' employee trusts. Employee trusts have many uses but in the context of share incentives they provide a means of creating a market for private company shares held by employees. Typically, the employee trust would be funded by the company and would purchase shares from employees. These shares would in due course be passed on to other employees under share incentive schemes.

Phantom schemes

These are bonus schemes that seek to replicate the benefits of share incentives by granting 'phantom' options or shares in the business. The advantage of such schemes are their flexibility, but the downside to the company is that any bonus paid would be a cost to the company rather than a dilution 'cost' to the shareholders.

Reviewing the benefits provided

At the same time, overhauling is a time for review.

The business may wish to review its existing employee benefit provision to ensure that the time and money spent by the employer in putting together a package of employee benefits is appreciated.

Scarce resources can be channelled into creating the most elaborate and comprehensive set of benefits, but if these are not valued and understood, they can actually give rise to feelings of ill will and suspicion. For larger companies, the overhauling stage may be a time to consider 'cafeteria benefits'. Broadly, this means presenting the employee with a 'menu' of possible benefits from which to choose. For example, a younger single person may opt for less holiday and a lower pension contribution in exchange for a more expensive company car and membership of the local gym – or simply a higher salary.

A family man may prefer more time with his family and more death benefits in exchange for a more modest car, whilst a person whose family are grown up and 'off his hands' may place greater emphasis on longer holidays and higher pension contributions.

The range of benefits is at the discretion of the employer. For the employee's own well-being, there should always be a minimum holiday requirement, and minimum amount of death in service cover is a sensible precaution to avoid an awkward moral dilemma in the event of the employee's death.

Similarly, there may be problems for the employer if only a small percentage of the workforce take up, for example, an offer of group permanent health insurance, since the insurer will tend to assume that only those people likely to claim have opted for the cover.

For this reason, full cafeteria benefits work only for very large employers where the numbers opting for any one benefit are substantial, but 'limited range' schemes can work with employers with as few as 100 employees.

Even if the employer does not go to the extent of introducing cafeteria benefits, the simple exercise of asking employees what benefits they most want can pay enormous dividends in terms of appreciation and goodwill. For example, one business with about 50 employees conducted a survey of the benefits which employees did not have and would most like to see introduced. The point which featured more than any other in the responses was some form of death benefit.

It was only then that the employer discovered that, although it had been funding a death in service benefit scheme for employees for over five years, the older employees had forgotten about it and the existence of the cover had been omitted from the pack of information given to new entrants.

By introducing a well written pension scheme booklet incorporating details of the death benefits, the employer was able very quickly and cheaply to capitalise on the goodwill which should have been present all along.

This may be an extreme example, but it is always worth checking to ensure that the benefits being provided are being properly and effectively communicated and, where a benefit is little appreciated, to consider replacing it with one which is more valued – frequently at a lower cost.

Networking

At this stage of its life, the business might be concerned with 'macro' issues. It may well have become acquisitive and will be involved in the possible harmonisation of its own pension and employee arrangements with those of 'target' companies.

This can be an area where considerable care is needed both from an employee relations point of view and legally, so that the employer does not lay itself open to accusations of constructive dismissal.

EXAMPLE

Suppose that a business, which operates a 'money purchase' occupational pension scheme incorporating a death benefit of four times salary and a spouse's pension of two-thirds salary, is acquiring a company which operates a 'final salary' occupational pension scheme with two times salary death benefit and no spouse's pension.

The acquirer has several options:

• it could continue to run the two schemes separately;

• it could try to integrate the target company's employees into its own scheme;

• it could try to integrate both companies' employees into a new combined scheme.

Running the two schemes separately is often an ideal short-term solution, but rarely works in the long term. As and when there is a transferring/secondment of staff between the two companies, the inequalities of the two schemes become more noticed and there is usually a need for harmonisation.

Integration of the target scheme into the existing scheme can be equally problematical. In the example above, the target company employees might feel that, by being transferred to the new company scheme, their death benefits are being improved, but that they are losing out in pension – even though this may not be the case.

The last option, combining the best of both schemes in a new arrangement, is the most expensive in the short term but often the only long-term solution actually to work in terms of employee relations.

With each possible solution, the impact of the changes both in real and emotional cost can be greatly mitigated if the business seeks professional independent advice from a qualified adviser.

Diversifying

For the owner-managed business, this stage can be the culmination of a lifetime's work. At this point, the business has value and is marketable. The entrepreneur is, therefore, probably now looking to a disposal either to retire or to take profits and start the whole process over again with a new venture.

If the disposal is by way of a management buyout, then key man insurance will not usually be an issue for the 'retiring owner'. If, however, a trade sale is being contemplated, the purchaser will often require key man insurance on the vendor, if there is to be a period after the sale when the vendor continues to work for the purchaser, helping the purchaser to become established and to meet the customers and learn the workings of the new business. This process, known as an 'earn-out' period is normally between one to five years and during this time the purchaser will often require key man insurance on the vendor in order to protect his 'investment'.

As far as the vendor is concerned, the sale is likely to generate substantial quantities of cash. Owing to tax mitigation measures, this may not be received in one payment, but, nevertheless, the vendor will eventually have the pleasant problem of deciding how these monies should be invested.

A detailed analysis of investment methods is beyond the scope of this book but suffice it to say that investment should be spread across a mixture of low-risk easy-access investments such as bank/building society/National Savings, low-to-medium-risk investments such as investment bonds and a proportion in higher risk investments such as unit trusts and direct holdings in equities. Naturally, tax-efficient investments such as Individual Savings Accounts and, for the adventurous investor, venture capital trusts and Enterprise Zone investments should not be overlooked.

If, on the sale of the business, the owner-manager decides that he or she would like to retire, his options will depend upon whether his pension provision has been by way of a SSAS or a personal pension plan – although in recent years there has been a blurring of the edges in that many features now apply to both and, at the time of writing, there are tentative plans to extend the provisions to other occupational schemes.

EXAMPLE

With both a SSAS and a personal pension plan it is no longer necessary to use an accumulated fund to buy an annuity and it is possible to 'draw down' an income directly out of the pension arrangement. The annuity does not have to be bought until age 75 but it is possible to do so at any time before then if it is deemed beneficial.

In the case of a personal pension plan, there are three key advantages to this route:

(a) the member is not locking into low annuity rates which might prevail at the time of his retirement;

(b) death benefits available under drawdown can be significantly higher than those under an annuity where, in an extreme case, a person could hand over a large cheque to an insurance company one day and die the next, losing all of the fund;

(c) the arrangement can be used as a means of minimising inheritance tax.

It is important, however, to realise that drawdown is not a universal panacea. For example, there is no guarantee that annuity rates will improve and monies left in the pension fund will generally have to be invested in equities – implying a degree of risk – if the purchasing power of the fund is not to deteriorate.

In the case of a SSAS, the advantages are similar but there is the added feature of particular importance to the owner-manager that, provided he has not started to draw benefits, then in the event of his death, his share of the fund can be 'reallocated' for the use of another scheme member. This is a process which requires particular care and professional advice should always be sought. Where the fund comprises mainly the company premises, however, this feature can be an invaluable tax planning tool.

Conclusion

This appendix has represented just a snapshot of the way in which financial services can impact on the development of a growing business. From protection to reward, there is a role at just about every stage of the DIAMOND model.

Many of the risks in a growing business are uninsurable – in particular the risk of profit or loss – so it must make sense to take out some form of cover for those which can be quantified and insured. At the same time, every owner-manager should be aware of the opportunities through financial services to reward himself and his employees, to use pension plans in particular within the limits of the law to shelter his business from unnecessary tax, and to promote the healthy expansion of a successful business.

Bibliography

Adizes, I. (1990) *Corporate Lifecycles*, Prentice Hall.

Ansoff, I. (1957) 'Strategies for diversification', *Harvard Business Review*, Sept/Oct: 114.

Barclays de Zoete Wedd Research (1993) *The BZW Equity & Gilt Study: Investment in the London Stock Market since 1918.*

BDO Stoy Hayward (1998) *Start-Ups and How to Survive.*

BDO Stoy Hayward (1998, November) *BDO Stoy Hayward Business Trends Report – Quarterly Review.*

Bhide, A. (1996) 'The questions every entrepreneur must ask', *Harvard Business Review*, Nov/Dec: 120.

Birley, S. and Muzyka, D.F. (1997) *Mastering Enterprise*, FT/Pitman.

Drucker, P.F. (1996) *The Executive in Action: Three classic works on management*, HarperBusiness.

Drucker, P.F. (1998) 'HBR Classic: The discipline of innovation', *Harvard Business Review*, Nov/Dec: 149.

Exley, H. (ed.) (1993) *The Best of Business Quotations*, Exley Publications.

Golzen, G. (1998) 'King of hi fi', *Enterprise*, May/June.

Gould, M. and Campbell, A. (1987) *Strategies and Styles*, Blackwell.

Greiner, L.E. (1972) 'Evolution and revolution as organisations grow', *Harvard Business Review,* July/Aug (reprinted in May/June 1998: 55–68).

Grout, J. and Curry, L. (1999) *The Adventure Capitalists*, Kogan Page.

Harverson, P. (1990) 'Disney drops Muppets deal', *Financial Times*, 17 December.

Holmes, G. and Sugden, A. (1997) *Interpreting Company Reports and Accounts* 3rd edn, Woodhead Faulkner.

Johnson, G. and Scholes, K. (1997) *Exploring Corporate Strategy: Tax and cases* 4th edn, Prentice Hall.

Katzenbach, J.R. and Smith, D.K. (1994) *The Wisdom of Teams: Creating the high-performance organisation*, HarperBusiness.

Luthans, F. (1995) *Organizational Behavior*, McGraw-Hill.

McKnight, P.J. and Tomkins, C. (1998) 'The options culture', *Director*, December: 25

Porter, M.E. (1990) *The Competitive Advantage of Nations*, Oxford University Press.

Richer, J. (1996) *The Richer Way*, EMAP Business Communications.

Senge, P. (1995) 'Transforming the practice of management', in F. Luthans, *Organizational Behavior*, McGraw-Hill.

Slack, N. *et al.* (1998) *Operations Management* 2nd edn, Pitman.

Society of Practitioners of Insolvency (1998) *Seventh Annual Survey*.

Strebel, P. (1997) 'Module 17: Managing change' in *Financial Times Mastering Management*, FT/Pitman: 536–556.

Thompson, J.L. and Marshall, C. (1995) *Strategy in Action*, International Thomson Business Press.

Van Osnabrugge, M. *Comparison of Business Angels and Venture Capitalists: Financiers of entrepreneurial firms*, Said Business School, University of Oxford.

Vyakarnam, S., Jacobs, R. and Handelberg, J. (1997) *Formation and Development of Entrepreneurial Teams in Rapid Growth Businesses*, Transitions Consultancy.

Ward, C. (1998) 'World class is aim of new scheme' in The Business, *Derby Evening Telegraph*, 10 November.

Wilson, R., Gilligan, C. and Pearson, D. (1992) *Strategic Marketing Management: Planning implementation and control*, Butterworth Heinemann.

Index

About BDO Stoy Hayward

BDO Stoy Hayward is a leading firm of chartered accountants and the UK member of BDO, the international accounting and consulting group.

BDO Stoy Hayward specialises in providing expert advice to growing businesses of all sizes that are driven by the entrepreneurial spirit. You can get more information from your nearest BDO Stoy Hayward office (see below) or via the BDO Stoy Hayward website: www.bdo.co.uk

Bacup
7–9 Irwell Terrace
Bacup
Lancashire OL13 9AJ
Tel: (01706) 873213
Fax: (01706) 874211
Contact: Peter Healey

Basingstoke
Barclays House
9–10 Victoria Street
Basingstoke
Hampshire RG21 3BT
Tel: (01256) 403700
Fax: (01256) 403777
Contact: Bob Lock

Belfast
Lindsay House
10 Callender Street
Belfast BT1 5BN
Tel: (01232) 439009
Fax: (01232) 439010
Contact: Stephen Prenter

Beverley
Beckside Court
Annie Reed Road
Beverley
East Riding of Yorkshire
HU17 0LF
Tel: (01482) 888000
Fax: (01482) 864975
Contact: Frank Farnill

Birmingham
Beneficial Building
28 Paradise Circus
Queensway
Birmingham B1 2BJ
Tel: (0121) 608 6086
Fax: (0121) 608 6600
Contact: Stephen Craig

Blackpool
263 Church Street
Blackpool FY1 3PB
Tel: (01253) 751515
Fax: (01253) 751160
Contact: Andrew McDonald

Brighton
Nile House, PO Box 1034
Nile Street
Brighton
East Sussex BN1 1JB
Tel: (01273) 324411
Fax: (01273) 779172
Contact: Keith Lickorish

Bristol
Oakfield House
Oakfield Grove
Bristol BS8 2BN
Tel: (0117) 9333311
Fax: (0117) 9333312
Contact: Philip Moody

Bury St Edmonds
87 Guildhall Street
Bury St Edmonds
Suffolk IP33 1PU
Tel: (01284) 763311
Fax: (01284) 704203
Contact: Lyndon Mills

Cardiff
4th Floor
Riverside House
31 Cathedral Road
Cardiff CF1 9HB
Tel: (01222) 225022
Fax: (01222) 224523
Contact: John Davies

Chelmsford
66 Broomfield Road
Chelmsford
Essex CM1 1SW
Tel: (01245) 264644
Fax: (01245) 490682
Contact: Gary Miller

Glasgow
Ballantine House
168 West George Street
Glasgow G2 2PT
Tel: (0141) 248 3761
Fax: (0141) 332 5467
Contact: Neil McNeill

Guildford
Connaught House
Alexandra Terrace
Guildford, Surrey GU1 3DA
Tel: (01483) 565666
Fax: (01483) 531306
Contact: Stuart Bosley

Ipswich
Knapton House
12 Lower Brook Street
Ipswich
Suffolk IP4 1AT
Tel: (01473) 216681
Fax: (01473) 253526
Contact: Martin Beck

Leicester
Eastgate House
Humberstone Road
Leicester LE5 3GJ
Tel: (0116) 222 1101
Fax: (0116) 222 1102
Contact: Chris Darlington

Liverpool
6th Floor
Cunard Building
Pier Head
Liverpool L3 1DS
Tel: (0151) 236 1233
Fax: (0151) 236 5700
Contact: Mark White

London and South East
8 Baker Street
London
W1M 1DA
Tel: (0171) 486 5888
Fax: (0171) 487 3686
Contact: Adrian Martin

Manchester
Peter House
St Peter's Square
Manchester M1 5BH
Tel: (0161) 228 6791
Fax: (0161) 228 1545
Contact: Ian Templeton

Motherwell
84 Hamilton Road
Motherwell ML1 3BY
Tel: (01698) 258178
Fax: (01698) 276138
Contact: David Marshall

Newmarket
Derby House
27 Exeter Road
Newmarket
Suffolk CB8 8LL
Tel: (01638) 565700
Fax: (01638) 565707
Contact: Henry Saltmarsh

Norwich
7 The Close
Norwich
Norfolk NR1 4DP
Tel: (01603) 610181
Fax: (01603) 633618
Contact: David Coventry

Nottingham
Foxhall Lodge
Gregory Boulevard
Nottingham NG7 6LH
Tel: (0115) 955 2000
Fax: (0115) 969 1043
Contact: Alan Baines

Peterborough
Garrick House
76–80 High Street
Old Fletton
Peterborough PE2 8ST
Tel: (01733) 342444
Fax: (01733) 554704
Contact: Adrian Ansdell

Poole
5th Floor, Old Orchard
39–61 High Street
Poole
Dorset BH15 1AE
Tel: (01202) 681221
Fax: (01202) 687211
Contact: Ian Young

Preston
88–96 Market Street West
Preston PR1 2EU
Tel: (01772) 202655
Fax: (01772) 202631
Contact: Robert Rawkins

Rochdale
Lewis House
12 Smith Street
Rochdale
Lancashire OL16 1TX
Tel: (01706) 355505
Fax: (01706) 659486
Contact: David Brierley

Saltcoats
12 Hamilton Street
Saltcoats
Ayrshire KA21 5DS
Tel: (01294) 602491
Fax: (01294) 604901
Contact: Findlay Turner

Sheffield
The Manor House
Ecclesall Road South
Sheffield S11 0AT
Tel: (0114) 236 1888
Fax: (0114) 236 2888
Contact: Martin Venning

Southampton
Park House
102–108 Above Bar
Southampton
Hampshire SO14 7NH
Tel: (01703) 356000
Fax: (01703) 356111
Contact: Tim Bentall

Stranraer
29 Hanover Street
Stranraer DG9 7HZ
Tel: (01776) 703536
Fax: (01776) 705750
Contact: Peter McMahon

Walsall
Tameway Tower
PO Box 30, Bridge Street
Walsall
West Midlands WS1 1QX
Tel: (01992) 720100
Fax: (01992) 645775
Contact: Pat Moore

Wolverhampton
Mander House
Mander Centre
Wolverhampton
West Midlands WV1 3NF
Tel: (01902) 714828 / 421496
Fax: (01902) 711475
Contact: Barry Frankling